THE WHITE HEAT
My Autobiography

TOMÁS Ó SÉ ～

Gill & Macmillan

Gill & Macmillan
Hume Avenue
Park West
Dublin 12
www.gillmacmillanbooks.ie

© Tomás Ó Sé 2015

978 0 7171 6934 4

Typography design by Make Communication
Print origination by Carole Lynch
Printed and bound by ScandBook AB, Sweden

This book is typeset in Linotype Minion and
Neue Helvetica.

The paper used in this book comes from the
wood pulp of managed forests. For every tree
felled, at least one tree is planted, thereby
renewing natural resources.

A CIP catalogue record for this book is available
from the British Library.

ACKNOWLEDGEMENTS

There are a lot of people I need to thank, not only for this book but for my life and my career. I hope I don't omit anyone, as this is the only time, really, I can genuinely show my appreciation for those who helped shape me and who helped me develop both as a person and as a footballer.

First, I'd like to thank all the teachers, coaches and trainers who had to put up with me down the years at school and at under-age level, especially Liam Ó Rócháin, who was a constant throughout my under-age years with An Ghaeltacht. What that man has done for me and our club has been amazing.

The managers and backroom staff – physios like Neasa Long, who kept me purring; Vince Linnane, who minded us for years, all the time; the doctors and masseurs; the county board and its officers, who really could not have done more for us – thank you all.

My teammates with An Ghaeltacht for all those years until I packed it in – we had great days. Brilliant memories. Guys like Tommy Beag, who soldiered with me and had the pleasure of sitting with me through most of secondary school. True friends.

The Kerry lads – the pleasure and happiness I got from playing with those guys is something I will never forget. We went through an awful lot together, and I thank them for carrying me on the best rollercoaster ride ever – and for winning me a few cups along the way.

I was so proud to wear the Gaeltacht jersey and the Kerry jersey, and to be honest I still miss doing so; but I was so lucky to have been able to represent both teams for as long as I did. To all associated with those teams, a huge thanks.

I'd like to thank the supporters of both teams and the wider community of the GAA and the GPA. We have the best supporters in the world, and I've got to meet and know so many of them in Ireland and abroad. Kerry people are spread all over the world, with the common denominators of football and Kerry. Buíochas ó chroí libh go léir.

I also thank Seán Mac Gearailt and all the staff and pupils at Gaelscoil de hÍde in Fermoy. Since I started teaching there in 2001 I have received only help and support from everyone there; I love working at the school and have had great years there. Go raibh míle maith agaibh.

Many thanks to Donagh Hickey for all his support down through the years.

To all my friends everywhere – Kerry, Cork, Dublin, America, England – there are too many to thank, but you know who you are. Thanks for everything.

To Michael Moynihan, who put on paper what came out of my head – a pleasure to work with and a true pro. I trusted him, and he was honest with me too. We worked well together, and this book is what it is only for him. Thank you, Michael, and your family.

To Conor Nagle from Gill & Macmillan, a gentleman and a guy who bought into my ideas for the book and supported me and Michael fully from the word go. I'm really glad we made it work, and thanks again for believing.

Don MacMonagle, for all your photographs – you have captured many a famous picture, and thanks so much for contributing to this book as well. Eddie O'Donnell, thanks for your advice and direction along the way.

To my family – my parents, Mícheál and Joan – who raised and supported me through thick and thin, to my brothers and all my close relations, thanks for everything down the years. You can always turn to family when you need support.

To Mícheál, Ailidh, Éabha – thank you for everything. To Orla and all her family, go raibh míle maith agaibh as an tacaíocht ar fad. Orla, you are the best.

Sin sin. If I've left anyone out I'll remember you in the next edition.

CONTENTS

PART III

PART I

Chapter 1

CROKE PARK

Different days. After sixteen years on the Kerry panel I was no stranger to being in Croke Park for an All-Ireland football final.

Last year I wasn't in the number 5 jersey, though. Young Paul Murphy from Rathmore had that on him, and I was sitting in a box in the Cusack Stand. I was wearing a nice three-piece suit instead of being togged out and counting down the seconds in the dressing-room.

Since retiring, I'd stayed involved in the game through punditry and a newspaper column, so the weekend of the final I was fairly busy. I spoke at a gig in Dublin on the Friday night before the All-Ireland, I went to a GPA function on the Saturday, and I was at *Up for the Match* out at RTÉ that night. On the Sunday morning I spoke in the Croke Park Hotel at a function, before going to another function in a corporate box before the game itself.

Hectic stuff, and completely new to me. After all, I'd been going to Croke Park to play matches since 1996, so it was an entirely different perspective.

———

The first time I was in Croke Park was as a footballer. People might be surprised to hear that, until 2014, I'd never actually watched a football match there – that in seventeen years I was never a spectator at a football match in Dublin 3. I hated the idea of watching teams play for the All-Ireland when Kerry were knocked out, though I went to a few hurling matches and rugby games there, all right.

I started there as a minor in 1996. Charlie Nelligan was manager and Mikey Sheehy was a selector, as were Seán Walsh, Junior Murphy and Derry Crowley. We made the minor final and lost by a point to a very good Laois team.

The Cusack Stand was the only part of the new stadium that was built at that time, so as minors we were still in the old Hogan Stand dressing-rooms. It was basic enough – a low ceiling and a pillar in the middle: that's what I remember most.

Mícheál Ó Muircheartaigh walking into our dressing-room before the match was a big deal for me. With his west Kerry connection he came over and had a word with me – a gentleman, and one of the truly great Kerry GAA men. (I've seen the ability of this man to captivate an audience and a room at first hand. Outside of his commentating, the guy has a knowledge of and interest in all things GAA, but particularly in Kerry football. He would frighten you with it, and we should enjoy his company while we're lucky enough to have him in our midst.)

I was on the bench the following year with the seniors. It was 1986 since Kerry had last won the All-Ireland, and Páidí Ó Sé (PO), who had played then, was now manager. That journey to September had re-energised the county: 'Football's coming home' was the chant at the European Championships, and it spread across the Irish Sea.

As the summer went on, Kerry got better. Seeing those players prepare and train to win an All-Ireland for Kerry, I witnessed first hand the hunger and the work it took to do that.

I was nineteen, sitting on the bench in Croker watching Maurice Fitz give a master class like only he could. I never saw game time that day, but Dara Ó Cinnéide was on the bench with me after coming off late in the game, and the match was tight. He was literally praying aloud beside me, and I was going to tell him to shut up, but, looking at how serious he was, I was actually afraid of him. It meant that much for Kerry to win.

Afterwards it was a special feeling, like Man United winning the Premier League after so many years without it. That was some learning curve for me, to watch and learn from my heroes. Celebrations? I failed every exam I did in Limerick that year. Priorities.

Three years after that, in 2000, I was out at wing-back against Galway, my first start in a senior final. It went to a replay and we won. The Hogan was under construction, so we were presented with the cup on the field, and we did the lap of honour, meeting friends and neighbours.

The fact that I was playing meant a lot more to me. I'd won my first All-Ireland with Kerry, and it means a lot me still that Dad was there for that. He passed away in 2002, so at least he saw two All-Ireland medals come into the house on the same day.

He was a big reason we did well playing football, because he never put any pressure on us. If you played great he'd say, 'Well done,' but if you were terrible he'd say the very same.

He was a very quiet man. He didn't even come to the function that night in 2000: that wasn't his form. He landed in later on to meet us but didn't sit down for the official dinner.

––––

When the final whistle blew against Donegal in 2014 it was special – it always is for those few minutes after the whistle blows, because it's just the players and the management, the people who've been through it all together.

No one realises that it's the last time they'll be alone as a group until the team holiday. In South Africa or Vietnam or wherever, nobody will pester them; but the second they step off the pitch it'll be a round of homecomings, banquets, functions, meetings, more games ...

It reminded me of what I was like myself after a game. If we won I enjoyed it, and I liked to enjoy it myself, to slip away and let it sink in before we headed back to the team hotel. I'd throw on the tracksuit, fire the bag into the bus and get some fella to make sure it was looked after. (Every player looks after their All-Ireland gear.) And I was off down the town to meet a buddy or two in some quiet dingy pub where the regulars mightn't even know there'd been an All-Ireland on, just to sit down for an hour or two and take it in. After that, back to the hotel for three or four days of madness.

It was the same when we lost. It's hard to convey how much it hurt to lose with Kerry. I wanted to win every year and to be the main man every year, but when we lost ... I wanted time to hurt alone before putting on the brave face and saying the right things to people back in the hotel. I have PO to thank for that: he stressed how important it was to win and lose graciously. I like to think I did that.

I was glad the lads were able to enjoy themselves after overcoming Donegal. That's what I missed more than anything: the shared sacrifice, the slagging at training, the bad days you think are the lowest of the low – all that builds the bond, and if I'm brutally honest with myself I felt it a bit at the final whistle.

Still, to be there for the arrival, you have to be there for the start of the journey. I won five times and, by God, it was good, but it was all the sweeter because you'd earned it.

———

When we lost to Dublin in 2013 I didn't say an emotional farewell to the dressing-room. No tears. No taking some toilet roll as a souvenir. Tracksuit on, baseball cap down, and away I went. No one copped you with the baseball cap, and if they did you were gone before they got you.

Croke Park holds a lot of memories for me, good and not so good, but I know I was lucky and privileged to get the opportunity to play there.

I love the place. It belongs to the GAA, which means all of us own it. It's part of our culture. Take the great men who have played there down the years, and the great men who still play there. The colours they brought honour and glory to, the enjoyment they've given thousands.

The green-and-gold number 5 jersey was passed on also. Paul Murphy wore it well for Kerry last September: he won man of the match, a well-deserved award.

The game moves on. Kerry move on. That's what makes them both so special.

Chapter 2

FAMILY

Dad, Mícheál, was an agricultural inspector. I know those jobs are gone now, and it's a pity, because if there was ever a job I'd want, that'd be it. He was around home all the time: I'd say he never did a tap.

Obviously as a kid I didn't understand the ins and outs of it, but basically he'd go out to visit farms on behalf of the Department of Agriculture, and if there was a grant to be given for a shed or tank he'd recommend that it be given or not.

I'd say he never turned anyone down. I'd have been at matches down through the years, and random strangers would come over to me and say, 'Fair play to your dad. He sorted me out there that time.' They had great time for him, obviously enough.

He didn't kill himself with work, certainly. When I was thirteen or so I was in the house when Pat Lynch, his boss, rang, and I picked up the phone. 'Hello, Pat, how are you?' I said, and Pat asked if Dad was there. 'He is, yeah,' says I, not noticing the father waving his hands at me, making the universal 'I'm not here' sign. He was supposed to be on the road doing his inspections, but yours truly gave the game away under questioning.

Dad had a designated area he covered – north Kerry, a lot of the time – and because of that he lived in Listowel for sixteen or seventeen years. They were settled there, himself and my mother, they bought a house there, and the two older lads started school there.

But in 1980, when my brother Marc was born, they moved west to Ard an Bhóthair, and the family is there ever since.

My mother is Joan; her maiden name is Kavanagh. Her family are
Lispole people, but when the farms were given out years ago by the
Land Commission her father got a farm back in Dingle parish. Baile
Riach, it's called. She was the eldest. Her mother died young, so Joan
was put in charge of the rest of them when still very young. After that
she went nursing in England. She met Dad then, and they got married.

There's no sport in her family whatsoever. What they did have,
though, was a savage work ethic, wherever that came from. I could
land back at home in the middle of winter and she'd be up a ladder
painting the house. I'd say, 'What in the name of God are you doing?'
but she'd drive on.

She didn't pass that ethic on, anyway: her four sons would be
your classic case of 'If there's work in the bed we'll sleep on the floor.'
As for Dad, he was … 'lazy' wouldn't be the word, but he was spoiled
by his own mother. When my grandmother was in her seventies her
sons would still be going over to her for their dinner as if it were
thirty years earlier. (The geography helps: you have Páidí's house,
with the shop, the pub and the church across the road, our house
and my grandmother's house all within fifty yards of each other, and
Tom's house a hundred yards down the road. There are O'Donoghues
over there as well, but it's basically all of us together.)

I'd be close to Tom, my other uncle, who had the same job as
Dad. He won a minor All-Ireland with Kerry in 1962. Arthur Spring
was on the same team, and they were great buddies. Tom was a
tough corner-back, and tidy enough, but he got big into golf, and
that became his passion. He got involved in the course back in
Ceann Sibéal and became captain there. He's friendly with Paul
McGinley, and he'd travel the world to see golf.

I got into golf as well, so the two of us still play a lot together, though
that's more to my advantage than his: if he has a putter or a driver he
doesn't like, he doesn't mind me picking it up off him, for instance.

Tom and Dad, being close enough in age, were spoiled, but Páidí
was ruined altogether by my grandmother. The two oldest always

had the outlook with him of 'Oh, God, what is he after doing now?' – the baby brother stuff. If I ever told Dad or Tom I was going to Tralee with Páidí, for instance, they'd say, 'Ah, don't.'

They were hugely proud of Páidí and what he achieved, and they were close enough. I suppose they regarded him – correctly – as being full of messing and craic. Not a pillar of sense, more a child who never grew up. Dad would stroll over to Páidí's pub on Friday and Saturday evenings for a couple of pints; before the drink-driving laws came in he liked to go to Dingle for two pints in Paddy Bawn's before coming back out to Páidí's, and Páidí would mention some story or incident, and they'd be laughing their heads off.

Dad never forced us with the football; he didn't go overboard with the praise if you had a good game, and, more importantly, he was the same if you had a stinker. He didn't force himself on people in company, and as a result he was popular with the people of the parish. After Mass on Sunday our house would be a hive of activity, with loads of local people coming in for cups of tea, and people laughing and chatting.

When Dad died that changed. It's something many people will identify with: the house isn't the same without the same people, and the people left behind change too. It was very hard on my mother. She lost a brother and a sister in the few years that followed, so she had a lot of loss to deal with. We'd have all been very tight. Neasa, Siún and Pádraig – Páidí's kids – would be like brothers and sisters to us, really, and we'd think nothing of bunking down in their house, and vice versa, so losing Dad and Páidí left a huge void.

———

Our own crowd were always very supportive of each other too. The likes of Tom would be very good for coming around you if you'd done something wrong, for instance, to encourage you to put it to bed. He'd travel to all our games and support us, whereas my mother never saw me play football: she never went to a match and stayed at home and went walking and praying.

We all worked in the pub, where there were plenty of late nights – both inside the counter and outside it – when we got older. Tom wouldn't be there that much, but he'd be well aware of what was going on inside.

It's tough on him too: he's the middle brother, and he lost his older and younger brother. He was on the committee that got the statue of Páidí up, and there's great credit due to all of them for that work. Ventry is a good parish: there's good people there, and, as many people know, a lot of the time it's through death and loss that you see the best side of people. I love going back to Ventry on a Friday night and heading into Páidí's for a quiet drink: you meet a couple of locals and have the craic picking teams or arguing the toss about sport. I don't get back as often as I'd wish, but when I land back it's like I was never away.

Summer is different there, when the place is mobbed with tourists, but it's a cycle you could compare to the football season: at springtime it's getting busier, like the league games, and then you have the championship and going hard and busy. Páidí had the pub on the Slea Head road, which meant there was a chance that every tourist going back that way would stop there. His hunch was right: a lot of them did, from daytrippers to the most famous people you could imagine.

To answer a question I often face: no, I wasn't in there the night Dolly Parton was in the pub. I crept over and heard her singing, but I was too young to be allowed into the pub itself. Regrets. I did, however, meet Tom Cruise, Martin Sheen and many more.

Dad would have helped my mother around the house as well; we had a big enough house, and during the summer we'd have students. One summer there were twenty-six girls in the house at the one time, for instance, so there was a fair bit of work in cooking and cleaning for a crowd of that size.

We'd have been bunked into the one room while they were there, and it was a hardy billet when the four of us were all getting that bit older. (Fergal is the eldest: he's now 42. Darragh is 40, I'm 37, and Marc is 35, so it's a pretty tight spread of ages.)

There was no pressure on us as kids, playing football in the back garden, no sense of 'You have to play for Kerry.' We enjoyed ourselves and knocked plenty of craic out of it – home from school, get the homework done, out the back kicking ball for hours. Every day.

If we went for a walk to the shop, to the pub or to my gran's for a visit, the ball was always carried. Soloing left and right. Kicking off walls. Passing to Páidí or Tom or anyone you met along the way.

Fergal appeared a lot older to me then. I was still in primary school, and he was playing on the Gaeltacht senior team, which is a fair difference at that age. He was a very, very good player. I can remember him dictating games in Páirc an Aghasaigh in Dingle as a young fella. There was one game in particular, against Lispole, with Gabriel and Gearóid Casey – a dominant team – and Fergal was the star, at eighteen years of age. He was stylish, left or right leg, all the skills. You'd often hear about a bunch of brothers that the one who didn't play county was the most talented, and plenty of people in west Kerry would say that about Fergal, but he got a bad cruciate injury very young.

He played minor and under-21 for Kerry and then came back after the cruciate to make the fringes of the senior panel in 1996, but I think he might have overworked the leg in training, he was so keen to get back. At that time the science of rehabbing a cruciate injury wasn't near the level it's at now. I know Pat Spillane managed to sort himself out without having an operation, but that was on a different scale.

Fergal was fanatical about trying to make it. We all looked up to him, and when he helped An Ghaeltacht win a first West Kerry Championship in years in 1991 – Dara Ó Cinnéide played as a garsún of sixteen, I'd say – he was one of the main men. He never came back fully from the cruciate, which meant that, of all of us, he was the only one unlucky enough to really have suffered a serious, career-curtailing injury.

When we were in primary and secondary school he was away in university, and when he finished he put down a couple of years teaching in Meath. Now he's a vice-principal behind in Feothanach – he teaches Ó Cinnéide's kids – and he works a small bit of land we have behind there with a few sheep. (He looks after those sheep well; they're pedigree animals. My father was the worst farmer I ever saw, but Fergal's a lot better at it.)

Fergal took over An Ghaeltacht as a coach and we won county championships – he came on in a couple of those games – and we made it to the All-Ireland club final in 2004, of course. He's a sound guy, and because he's back there he has his finger on the pulse. If there's anything going on in west Kerry he'd tell you, but I suppose the three of us closer in age would have hung around more and would have kicked a lot of ball out the back garden.

That's one of the biggest memories of our childhood: two channels on the television – no Playstations – just a few Dinky cars, or else out the back, so if it was dry at all it was the back garden with the football. When we were kicking the ball around outside, Fergal would have been that bit too big for me when he was around; Darragh was more manageable. We had some desperate battles out there altogether.

There were pipes up the side of the house: those made up the goal. One of us would go in goal while the other two played one semi-final, then the keeper came outfield and played the second semi-final, and after that there was the final. There were particular rules: Darragh was the eldest, so he could only use his weak leg, for instance.

Even then I had a bit of a temper. Darragh would be laughing at me, to get a rise out of me during the game, and I'd be laying into him. Often enough it ended up in tears (mine) or bad temper (his): he'd lose the head and throw a dunt, and I'd be gone.

It's easy to say, but when I see kids training now I'd wonder if they get as much out of it in organised training sessions with clubs. If I were on my own as a kid I'd be out there with the ball, aiming at the pipes or practising my fielding off the wall, timing my jump or practising my frees.

There was a big patch of ground behind the house, so we had this game where you took three frees from three different angles (right, left and middle) close in, three frees from the same positions further out, and three more from the same positions at long range. You had to get seven out of the nine, or better, to win the tournament.

Marc was probably the most accurate in those free-taking tournaments, though it was there I first saw Darragh's ability to kick-pass over distance: if he wanted to hit you fifty yards away into the chest with the ball, or to bounce it once front of you, he could manage either, no problem. I think long-range kicking will come back into the game more in future years, but that's another story.

Often my Dad or Páidí would fall in for a bit of craic, but more often than not it was the three of us tussling like wild dogs there with the night rolling in from the sea.

———

Darragh has the kind of confidence I've rarely seen – in anyone, let alone in footballers or teammates. I won't say he justifies everything, but things don't get him down. It's as simple as that. If he shot someone outside the door he'd just come in and sit down and say to you, 'Look, life's too short to be worrying about that, so I'm not going to let it get me down.'

And that helped him in dealing with games. The difference with me is that I'd brood and dwell on things that went wrong in a match and keep turning them over in my mind, and I'd end up getting cranky about them in the end of it or going and talking to someone about them.

Darragh's different. For instance, he's very bright, but he didn't care about school. With the Leaving Cert, my father would meet him after an exam and ask how it had gone for him. 'Do you know what?' he'd answer. 'I was worried enough about that exam going into it this morning, but actually I'm delighted: it went very well.' Fast forward to the results, and he got a few Fs, of course. So he failed the Leaving, but he got into the ESB.

He just has this knack of seeing things in a positive light, and of always landing on his feet. Always did, always will.

We followed Darragh when he broke through onto the Kerry senior team. At that time there were no texts: the player got a letter. 'A chara, You have been selected to represent Kerry in a National League match …'

That would have been about 1994. He'd been on a very good minor team in 1993, but they were beaten by Cork. A lot of them – the likes of Dara Ó Cinnéide, John Brennan and himself – broke through to the senior team, even though at that point Kerry were well and truly in the doldrums.

Darragh was playing midfield from the start, and at the peak of his powers he was 15 stone and strong with it. That time, starting off, he might have been 12½ stone, maybe 13 soaking wet. If you saw a photograph of him from those early days you'd say he was dying sick.

The difference between then and now is that the modern player comes in to play senior and he's already fully developed: he's been doing weights since the age of fourteen. Darragh didn't fill out properly until he was twenty-three or twenty-four.

One thing he always had, though, was a phenomenal leap. Páidí was the man who pointed out to me that Darragh is 6′1″ but that the midfielders he was up against were 6′3″, 6′4″, 6′5″. He was always giving a few inches away, but his leap meant he was able to get up over them. His temper helped drive him on as well: if a guy beat him to a ball he'd let him have it across the ear as hard as he could draw.

We went to the home games, myself, Dad and Marc. The away games when Darragh broke through tended to be in Donegal, Derry, Dublin, often in the north of the country, so we didn't tend to see those – and Darragh got some fair pastings. One time he was shifted to wing-forward and had a fair run-in with Paul Curran of Dublin, who would have been a seasoned, experienced player at that time.

For Darragh it was a fair learning curve in the rest of his career, I'd say – getting bullied, getting thrown around, being on a Kerry team that wasn't really respected at the time. It would have taught me a lot as well, in that it was my first real glimpse of Kerry playing regularly. (I would have been too young to follow them when Páidí was playing.) And it was an inspiration, too.

Once Darragh made it, my whole life revolved around making it too, step by step – making the Kerry minors, then the under-21s, then the senior set-up, even though that was a process that would obviously take me years.

But that was the route Darragh had taken, so it had to be followed. He actually played under-21 for Kerry for four years, which meant he was a minor playing four years above his age group. Famously, Páidí brought him on in an All-Ireland under-21 semi-final; the other mentors – Jack O'Connor, Séamus Mac Gearailt, Bernie O'Callaghan and Tom O'Connor – were trying to decide at the dugout what move to make, but Páidí, down the sideline, just decided off his own bat to throw him on.

Darragh got a fair bit of slack when he was starting off – that he wasn't this or that – but the difference is that he got the time to develop. That's not often the case nowadays, when young players are under pressure to produce the goods straight away at senior level. Darragh himself would always give great credit to Ogie Moran, who was the senior manager that time, for bringing him on and for the way he brought him through.

Darragh's always had a good attitude, though to many people it might seem a strange one. He can laugh and joke with the best of them, but he can also focus when it's needed. If you didn't under-stand him you'd be taken aback, because at half time in an All-Ireland final, if you could get into our dressing-room, you might see Darragh laughing his head off, and a few more of us along with him; but even if we were laughing we'd still be zoned in.

There'd be a darkness to the humour at times, one that's hard to convey to people who don't know us. If someone wrapped the car around a pole we'd be slagging him for a week. Seán Potts used to call it 'black magic': we'd laugh at certain things that other people wouldn't find funny, not out of disrespect but just through having that slightly different slant on things. Dark. Laughing at short-comings. It's not the same thing as ignorance – we knew how to behave in company – it was just a different take on things.

––––

When I look back now, if I hadn't made the Kerry minors I don't know how I would have handled it, because it was the only thing I wanted to do. (I was on the thirteenth hole of Ceann Sibéal when I got the call in to the minor set-up; I remember that vividly.) Playing senior for Kerry would have been great, but at that time it was a distant thing. The progression – minor, then under-21, then senior – was clear.

We had a good minor team, with Tommy Griffin and Aodán and Noel Kennelly, though we lost to Laois in the All-Ireland final. We had a very good under-21 team as well and lost one All-Ireland final to Westmeath – I never saw a team work the referee so well as in the dying minutes of that game. We lost another semi-final to Meath another year, and there was mayhem again, with another referee. (See the pattern? There's always an excuse!)

When I fell in with the seniors in 1997 I knew well that I was only going to be a fringe player starting off, but I wasn't going to let it be said that I wasn't pulling my weight. Darragh was good to me: he was always someone you could bounce things off and get good feedback from, because he was so mentally tough himself. Over the years I'd have spoken to Páidí and Marc a good bit about games and that, but mostly to Darragh in that respect. I wouldn't have come out straight and said, 'I have a problem with this' or 'This is an issue for me in the games': we'd chat away and I'd circle around to what I wanted to hit in my own time. But there was always a benefit to the talk. You'd always be the better for it, because of Darragh's attitude. He always talks sense when it's needed, and he's great for putting things into perspective. He'd advise you well and was probably bouncing his own stuff off me at the same time. Was it a help when I started that he was in the dressing-room? It was.

The difference between my start with Kerry and finishing up was that I was far more confident at the end than I was at the beginning. In general terms I was a quiet, shy lad. The first time I went in to Fitzgerald Stadium for training, most of the lads were in one dressing-room, which was fairly noisy. You had the Breens, the Flahertys, Barry O'Shea, John Brennan, Pa Laide – good men for dishing out the banter, and they had no problem picking away at you about the connection to Páidí, say. So I went off and togged out in the other dressing-room. On my own.

It took me a couple of years to get comfortable in the environment, but Darragh was good for advising you on different things. For instance, in 1997 there was a training weekend planned for Killarney, and at that point socialising was still a big part of the scene, so the boys were going to go for a couple of pints in town on the Saturday night. I was only eighteen, just arrived into the camp, so I was wondering if it'd be a good idea if I tagged along, but Darragh said, 'No, don't. You're only just in the gap. Keep your powder dry and your head down.'

Good advice. I stayed out in the hotel for the night.

The next morning I found out who they met in Killarney: only Roy Keane, inside in Tatler's, chatting away to them for an hour or two. Roy in his pomp. The hero of heroes.

I nearly went through Darragh for a short cut when I heard that. Good advice …

The younger lads would have looked up to Darragh when they came in the way I looked up to the likes of Maurice Fitz when I fell in first: a great, great player, but no airs or graces about him and very approachable, and Darragh was the same. That was always a strength of the Kerry dressing-room: there was nobody acting the prima donna, from number 33 to the captain. That's good for the team. It helps players to settle and to realise their potential.

A lot of people see similarities between Darragh and Páidí – the roguery and the personality. He's doing well in the property business in Tralee, and he's like Páidí in that he has contacts and friends everywhere. There's no fear of him, certainly.

––––

Marc would probably be the most naturally talented. He has this dummy he sells when he's on the ball – Gooch himself would be proud of it. We all know it's coming, and when we'd be watching tapes with Páidí years ago we'd all be laughing, because when Marc got the ball we knew the dummy was coming, but he always got away with it. It's a bit like Seán Cavanagh's shimmy: everyone knows it's coming, but they can't help but fall for it.

In football skills Darragh and Marc would have been miles ahead of me. Their touch would be a lot better, to use a soccer term. If we were in training doing keepy-uppies for the craic, say, they'd be laughing at me. I'd need planning permission to trap the ball.

I had enough skill to get me through, but Marc probably had that skill naturally. The funny thing is that you wouldn't necessarily associate skill with a corner-back, but going on the others – Mike McCarthy's skill levels were unbelievable: dummies, handpassing off left and right … People don't realise the skills involved there, by the way. We had a drill one evening in training with Kerry where you soloed through on goal and handpassed the ball over the bar from the 13-metre line, off your weaker hand. Simple, no pressure, no tackling. And on an intercounty team, with plenty of All-Ireland medals in fellas' back pockets, about half of us couldn't do it.

Going back a bit further you had Mike Hassett, a guy Páidí regarded as very classy, in the mould of Paudie Lynch. He, Mike Mac, Marc – you could compare them to traditional or specialised corner-backs in that they could hammer the shite out of you if needed, but they also had the skills to come out with the ball.

As for me, I'd try to run over the top of a fella rather than dummying my way around him – different from Marc. When you think of Mike Mac, Marc and Tom O'Sullivan in the full-back line, and the natural football ability they had, it was frightening; they all had more football than I had.

Marc's colour-blind, like myself. There was very nearly a row in a snooker hall one time over the brown and the red balls – a row that almost came to fisticuffs, because Marc had a ball up to his eye ('That's red! *Red!*'). We're close, though. We once had a trip to San Francisco, and I'd say we didn't stop laughing from the minute we landed: great craic, start to finish.

There'd be some odd similarities between all our careers with Kerry. Darragh took a couple of years to establish himself at senior level, and I had a year of torture in 1998 when I started and got hosed against Cork. I didn't sleep for practically the whole summer after that game.

Marc's career followed the same arc, and I suppose the common thread is that we weren't physically developed, really, when we came in.

Kerry had big men that time, the Donal Dalys and Barry O'Sheas, and Darragh and so on, but in our physical make-up we were weak enough at nineteen or twenty years of age. And Marc was probably the lightest of us. Breaking in, he struggled the way I did and Darragh did, but he was breaking onto a team that was winning All-Irelands, and expected to continue winning them. There's a different dynamic there immediately, very different from when Darragh was breaking onto a Kerry team in the doldrums, or from when I came onto a team that had just won a first All-Ireland in years. There was pressure on us, but it was a different pressure for Marc.

And coming in as a corner-back was difficult too. That time there were no blanket defences, so you were stuck in the corner, one on one against a top, top forward every day you went out, with nobody sweeping or screening in front of you.

What stood to Marc – and still does – is that he's an athlete. There's not a pick on him still, just whipcord, and that natural skill I've mentioned; but in 2002, when he started, he was like myself and Darragh in our debut seasons: scrawny.

That wasn't a great physique to carry into a game against Armagh, who had the likes of Diarmuid Marsden, who Marc was marking. Physicality was an advantage for that Armagh team, and Marc learnt some tough lessons that day.

But that's part of it. You learn from the hurt and you pick out the lessons and the pitfalls, and Marc certainly drove back harder after that. In his pomp he always marked the opposition's danger man, and while you wouldn't be saying it out loud in the dressing-room before a game, you'd certainly be thinking, That's mo dhuine taken care of anyway. That was just the mark of the confidence we had in Marc as a man-marker.

I certainly couldn't have done that job. If I'd been focused on man-marking there's no way I could have been ranging up and down and across the field, but it was no bother to him. He had quick feet, quick hands – a great man for getting in a block-down, the quickest I ever saw for getting down on your toe. What helped him a lot was the runs with the club from 2003 to 2005. He was our full-back, but he was also our firefighter: no matter who we were up against, he went to the opposition danger man to close him down. That run developed him as a player hugely.

Marc went to university in Maynooth and went teaching in Tralee after, so I wouldn't have been travelling to games with him. But as a teacher he'd have summers off, so I'd see a lot more of him then. Like Darragh, he'd know how to lift you, or to listen to you.

They're a couple of guys who'd do well in management. Darragh's had a run with the Kerry under-21s, though they didn't get out of Munster; they had three games in three years. That happens, because that's a grade where you get cycles: in my time we beat Cork three years in a row, but the reverse can happen easily enough. There's no back door, so you lose and you're out. Compare that with the intercounty minor scene, where one year the Kerry minors lost three times.

If the Kerry under-21s lost I wouldn't have been saying to Darragh, 'Why didn't you do *this*? Why didn't you *that*?' I know the time and effort these guys put into the whole thing. That's one of the reasons I have no time for this trolling of people on social media – cheap shots from anonymous heroes.

Now, if you lose, your head is on the block, and that's truer in Kerry than in most other places. When Darragh stepped down I felt he did it in the right way: he bowed out with grace. He didn't blame anyone, and he took it on the chin himself. That's the class way to do it – you'd often see a fella going out the door having a kick as he goes.

I'd have felt that some of the so-called big names on those Kerry under-21 teams didn't perform, but Darragh didn't say that. He might have thought so, but he didn't say it.

Darragh and Marc have the qualities to succeed in management – they spent years listening to and looking at the likes of Páidí, Jack O'Connor, Pat O'Shea, Éamonn Fitzmaurice. All-Ireland winners, all of them, and you're bound to pick things up from spending so much time training under them.

But intercounty management is a hard, hard posting nowadays. You have to make the right choices when it comes to the people you bring in with you; you have to consider the time commitment involved, and the effect on your family of that commitment. I'd say Fitzmaurice sees his wife, Tina, in the morning over the cornflakes and doesn't see her the rest of the day. The time commitment is crazy, and people genuinely don't understand that.

Marc has good ideas about the game, and I'd say they'd be delighted in Kerry if he got involved in coaching. When you're with an intercounty team you'd often fall in with a club to do one session. (I didn't like that: I'd far prefer planning out a year's training schedule for a club to just one session and pull out of the car park.)

Marc's quieter than Darragh, but he's good company as well. On a night out you'd get your money's worth out of him. He has a great knack for taking people off: poor Páidí is gone now, but if you walked into a pub and Marc was taking him off you'd swear it was PO you were listening to. Old friends of Páidí love that. Even the little lisp Páidí had, Marc could reproduce it. Páidí will never be gone while Marc is around.

Marc is still driving on, and he's still flying inside with Kerry. He's a good man for looking after himself. I'd be rushing and racing, but he never does: everything is well planned out – minds himself, loves his style and is careful with his shoes, say. Very good for minding his diet, too.

———

There might be a perception, a lazy notion, that the Ó Sés could enjoy themselves too much, but nobody worked harder than us in training. We had unbelievable fun – all over the world – but that was when the work had been done. We never wanted it to be said that we were on the Kerry panel because of who we were related to. We never wanted it *thought*, never mind said.

Páidí never showed us any favouritism. Ever. No other player could ever have said, 'Oh, look, typical of that crowd, looking after each other.' If anything, the three of us fought harder and prepared better because of Páidí, and because of having brothers on the selection.

I often hopped off Darragh inside in training, by which I mean I went for him. Literally. The intensity of training was at that level, and, brother or not, if he was opposing you in a mixed match or a training drill, he got it.

We had great times with Kerry. It's great to win an All-Ireland; there's no surprise in hearing that. But winning one with your brothers gives it an extra dimension, a deeper meaning.

The fellas I got most craic from over the years were always the lads – in-jokes, impressions, one-liners that nobody else would get. I talk to them nearly every day, and we'd be close still (without any huggy, touchy-feely stuff). There's been plenty of times we were wrong, but we always stuck up for each other.

Well, almost always. One time myself and Darragh were playing for Munster in the Railway Cup against Ulster, and there were some fair hitters on that Ulster team: Dick Clerkin, Enda Gormley and a few more. They started forcing it with us, and we lashed back with more – hard enough going, but myself and Darragh were taking the battle to them.

Of course, as we were going out for the war in the second half I glanced behind me, and there was the bould Darragh perched on the physio's table with a recently discovered hamstring problem. Out I went to get pummelled.

I never minded taking the fight to the opposition with the two of them on the field with me. I always knew I had back-up.

Chapter 3

PÁIDÍ: THE ROLE MODEL

This is the broader family background. My grandfather, Tommy Ó Sé, his family came from Cathair an Treantaigh. As a young man he went to England, where he married my grandmother, Beatrice Lavin, from Sligo. While working there he had a bad accident: he was hit by a bus and could no longer work. Beatrice kept working, and worked very hard, then and always, but they had to come home, because he was so badly hurt. They got some few bob because of the accident, and when they came back they bought a grocer's shop in Ventry. She worked there.

I only remember my grandfather being sick up in bed – a lovely man, but always unwell. They had three kids, Mícheál – my father, who was the eldest – Tom and Páidí.

Tom was seventy this year, and Páidí would have been fifty-nine, so there was a good gap between the two older lads and PO; the older pair were born over in England, but he was born at home in Kerry.

Páidí was named after Paudie Sheehy, the great Kerry footballer from Tralee, and from a very early age football was everything to him. That's what I admire about PO: my father played junior football for Kerry, and Tom won an All-Ireland minor football medal with Kerry, but they would have lost interest, really.

There isn't any footage of them to be found on YouTube, but supposedly Tom was a tidy corner-back and Mícheál was a good footballer. We poked at my dad, though not too often, that he was a fine-day footballer: good some days but not too fond of the rough and tumble on others. Tom Long, a great Kerry footballer, would have been a first cousin of my dad's; but really there wouldn't have been a huge Gaelic football background in the family, at least until PO came along.

Páidí was insane about football – gripped by it, absolutely and utterly, from an early age. He decided very young that he wanted to be a Kerry footballer, and he dedicated everything to it.

Now, to flesh it out a bit, these three boys were fairly spoilt by their mother. For instance, my father went to school in the Sem – or St Brendan's, Killarney – a famous football nursery that was a boarding school at the time; but Tom didn't want to go there, so he went to school in Dingle. Fair enough. But while he was a schoolboy there he had a car of his own to go in there from Ventry, so he was driving his own car at a time when schoolteachers were cycling the roads.

They wanted for nothing, but because Páidí was the baby he was minded. Like God. Darragh told the famous story of Páidí having a nap at home when he was still playing for Kerry – an early version of recovery, if you like – and the vet, who was calling to dose cows, being told to get lost for those few hours. (Páidí, by the way, would have been dozing in the caravan specially got for him so that the Irish students my grandmother kept wouldn't bother him – or his sleeping patterns.)

That was how Páidí was treated. My grandmother idolised him, and in her eyes he could simply do no wrong, even when he was as wrong as he could be. He could have shot the Pope and she'd have come up with some reason that it was all right.

———

I'd often read *Princes of Pigskin* by Joe Ó Muircheartaigh and T. J. Flynn, a great book about the history of Kerry football, and there was obviously a lot of politics involved in the selection and so on. The likes of Batt Garvey and Michael Murphy, both Ventry men (as was Tom Long, Páidí's first cousin) – all big heroes of Páidí's. Batt played in the famous game in 1947 in New York. Michael taught in our school and had played for Kerry, and they were important to Páidí because the history of Kerry football was important to him.

He loved to talk to older players, and he had an unbelievable memory. He could tell you what Kerry players used to travel in which cars to training and matches from back west; he would have yarns and stories from on and off the field, not only of Kerry players back our way but of all Kerry players. He loved talking about them and talking to them, and he also had an encyclopedic memory of all these guys and, for that matter, of older players from every county in the country. He'd have that interest in Thomas Ashe and Bill Dillon – all those guys going back the years. That tradition was always hugely important to him, and that drove him to do well with Kerry.

———

When it was Páidí's turn for secondary school, then, he wanted to go to the Sem, because it would be beneficial to his football, pure and simple. It certainly wasn't the education that carried him there: he used tell me he'd rather eat the books than read them.

In first year he was on the school senior team, which is fair going by any standards; but in fifth year it all went wrong for him, unfortunately. The school authorities came across some contraband in his room, and he was expelled. At that stage my father was working in Listowel for the Department of Agriculture, and my grandmother told my father to take Páidí up there for a while to mind him.

In Listowel, Páidí went in to St Michael's, the local school, but the football was still front and centre. The biggest colleges competition in Kerry – outside the Munster colleges competitions – is the Sullivan Cup, and Listowel had never won the trophy.

They had a good enough team, but having Páidí on board made them a very good one, and they ended up meeting the Sem in the final. Given that they'd fired Páidí out, he was fairly motivated for that game, and Listowel won. Billy Keane was on that team as well, and he has great stories about that time, whether they're true or not, and about playing with Páidí.

From what I've heard, two things seem to have always stood out about Páidí: that he was a rogue, and that he was mad for football. That passion got stronger and stronger the older he got, once he slotted in with that great Kerry team.

For instance, Páidí left the Gardaí because he was desperate to be at home, to be back in west Kerry. Always. Even in later years, if he was up at a gig in Dublin or at a game or doing some bit of business, he'd always want to come away back home rather than stay the night up there. He'd arrange to have a driver with him so that, no matter what time he'd land back in west Kerry, whether it was one in the morning or later, he'd wake up in Ard an Bhóthair. He was a real home bird, and he loved the area.

When he first joined the Gardaí he was living in Limerick, where he was taken under the wing of another Kerry garda, John Costello, a great Kerryman and an absolute gentleman. He took Páidí in, and he did the same for me when I went to university there.

Life in uniform didn't suit Páidí. He had shift work, which meant he couldn't pick his hours: if he was training with Kerry he had to be in the following morning to go to work. He had no ambitions in the Gardaí, so he came home, because all his ambitions were focused on football. At home, with no pressure of work and with his mother minding him, he basically became a professional footballer far ahead of his time.

He took out a lease on Kruger's pub in Dunquin for that reason alone, plain and simple. It facilitated his training hugely, and that was among the great lessons that we – myself, Darragh and Marc – all learnt from him, living over the road: how seriously you had to approach your training, and even your preparation for training; how you had to have your body right, and all the work that entailed; and how, if you want to reach the top, you give yourself every chance.

I was very young at that time and probably didn't appreciate it. I was born in 1978, so it was only Páidí's time with Kerry from, say, 1984 to 1986 that I really noticed. But even then, when he was coming towards the end of his career, he took it hugely seriously, and his commitment was savage, in all honesty.

At that time Kerry made three All-Ireland finals in a row, and they'd have been training hard all those summers in Killarney, obviously; but on his days off from training, Páidí would go for a run. Up the Clasach road, up over the top of Mount Eagle and down the back into Dunquin and the graveyard, all around Slea Head – 13½ miles altogether. Back to the cross and down to the beach, then, where he had hurdles set up in a field; he'd jump ten of them in a row, then jog across the bottom of the field, sprint up the hill full-out, jog across and jump those hurdles again.

He'd do that maybe ten times in a row. Then he'd go down into the tide, loosen himself out in the water, and jog away back to the house.

The grandmother would have a bath laid on for him there and a glass of port and a big steak ready for him. That was his preparation.

And the following night he'd join up with Kerry again. How could he do it? Because he changed his lifestyle to do it.

You'd hear a lot of talk about the so-called era of professional-level preparation in the GAA, and a lot of people stress how important downtime and recovery are after training. Jesus, Páidí was well ahead of his time: he'd often have a snooze in the middle of the day, which is what all the experts recommend now. People have this image of

Páidí as a wild animal, a gregarious character burning the candle at both ends all the time. Wrong, wrong, wrong.

No man I ever met took Kerry football, or his preparation and training, as seriously as he did. And he carried that over into management when he took that on.

I've been coached by a lot of top-quality guys, and he left more of a mark on me than any manager in how to prepare myself for Kerry and in how important Kerry was. As a result I was a better player.

———

Páidí later had his own pub, but he barely worked in it when he was Kerry manager. I know that: I was there for the summers, and I'd have seen him. He was lucky enough in where it was situated, on the Slea Head road: he had enough traffic coming through to keep him going, but he had no interest in the business until very late in his life. It was all football. He could have had a huge business, but it suffered because all his time went into Kerry.

He'd have been on the phone all day when he was manager – constantly clung to his ear. I remember going into his office back in the nineties and there'd be mobile phone bills on the desk: eight hundred, nine hundred pounds per month. I don't know who was picking those up, whether it was the county board or what, but that's massive even now, let alone then.

That time the set-up was less organised. As manager he did everything: arranging fields to train in, sorting out the food – and he did all the training. He also remembered every man or woman who did him a turn; he might leave it a few months, but he would repay them in some way – a west Kerry salmon, or a long letter showing his gratitude. Those letters, in particular, became famous.

———

Páidí was a great man-manager. That was a huge strength of his. If a guy didn't go well in training or in a game he'd know how to come around him – whether to attack him or gee him up. He was always able to come around you, even if he only wanted you to do a shift in the pub to help out. Marc found that out when he was learning how to drive.

At the time Páidí had a sponsored car, a big two-litre, powerful, and Marc – who was so young he could barely see out over the steering wheel – asked him if he could practise his driving with it.

'Park it up outside the house when you're finished with it,' said Páidí, throwing out the keys to him.

So off with Marc down the road, burning rubber, of course. He managed one corner, but at the next turn he and the car ended up in a bog.

Marc panicked. He ran up to the nearest farmhouse and begged the man there to pull the car out for him. He did, but it was mangled.

There was another young lad in the area who was a known maniac in a car, and one of the regulars in the pub blamed him when he landed in for a pint, but Marc came clean to Páidí straight away. And, in fairness to Páidí, he was very good about it: 'Are you okay? That's the main thing. Don't worry about the car.'

But a few days later Páidí dropped in to our house and said to Marc, 'Can you do a few hours in the pub there for me? I'm stuck.'

Marc had no alternative. The parents didn't know what had happened, and if they knew he was zooming around like a Formula One driver he'd have been dead.

For about four months Páidí had him by the balls, and he squeezed hard. 'Marc, you'll have to work. If you don't I'll have to tell …'

At the end of it Marc couldn't sleep over it. He confessed it all to our mother and father. And the next day, when Páidí came over looking for him, he got his answer. 'Páidí, I told them, so fuck off and get lost.'

Páidí could recognise the differences in people. The player who needed a kick in the arse got it, and the fella who needed an arm around the shoulder got that.

He had been unbelievably proud of playing for Kerry, and he was unbelievably proud of being Kerry manager. He took it so seriously: in 1996 Kerry won the Munster title for the first time in years, and it was 'Football's coming home' stuff, the start of the rejuvenation of Kerry football after the barren years.

They celebrated too hard, and the *Kerryman* used a photograph of Páidí with a small egg-cup of a Munster Championship cup on the front page on the Thursday. It looked bad.

Kerry were actually back training early that week, but it didn't matter: the damage was already done with that photo, and if they fell, there were plenty around who would remind him of it. They trained properly, but the wrong signals had gone out, and when they lost to Mayo in the All-Ireland semi-final he was reminded of it.

However, Páidí learnt a lot from the experience. The following year he went off the beer from the beginning of the season to the night they won the All-Ireland in September. His focus was huge all that year: I was in the car with him from west Kerry every evening, and he'd pick up Dara Ó Cinnéide and Jack Ferriter in Dingle along the way, and he'd be so happy, just heading off into training. (Jesus, we had some craic in that car: for an hour solid, over and back, some fella was getting it, and no one ever held back.)

All that day, before the training session, Páidí would have prepared what he wanted to do and say. He'd go out walking and get the message right in his mind. On the way over in the car he might slow down, with no car in front of us, and his lips would be moving: he was preparing the spiff he was going to give, rehearsing it silently. We'd be tempted to say, 'Jesus, PO, will you drive on!' but you didn't want to disturb him.

If the training went well he'd be in great form on the way home.

We'd stop for ice cream, a big 99 for everybody in the car, and the craic would be fantastic all the way home – stories all the way from Killarney to Ventry.

One evening I was in the car with him on my own and a song came on, 'Dance the Night Away' by the Mavericks, and I made a fatal error. I was in the front seat and I turned it up. 'That's a mighty song,' I said, and he fastened onto it.

Every time it came on after that – and it was the biggest hit that summer, constantly on the radio – he'd look around and start off, 'Where's Tomás? That's his song. Where is he?' Messing.

On the way back from training he'd often ring Radio Kerry and ask for a request to be played 'for my great friend …' and make up some name. The car would be heaving and rocking with laughter until you heard it played.

———

One issue with Páidí was that he expected every player to do what he did, to show that level of commitment to Kerry. We knew what was involved, because we'd always had his example to draw on, and we knew that you had to do extra. With your own uncle as manager you'd do that extra bit anyway.

Páidí was doing analysis before that came in. He wasn't a great man for technology, but he'd watch videos for hours on end, both of us and of the opposition. He brought in team meetings to discuss what way to approach the next game – another first. He moved hotels for our meals, because he wanted better food for us.

On the other hand, he kept us travelling in cars to matches, because the old Kerry teams used to do it that way, I'd say. I still prefer that approach: though it's all buses now, cars are quicker, and if you want to stop, the whole busload doesn't have to stop.

With Páidí everything came behind football. Which is bad, in a way. With Kerry most people would put football number one anyway: if I missed a training session I'd get it from Darragh, from Marc – 'Why did you miss that session?' – and if it wasn't life or death you were in trouble.

People's personal lives suffered as a result. Work suffered. If you were living over the road from Páidí you learnt that, but you learnt that football came first.

Once, when Jack O'Connor was manager, Kieran Donaghy came late to training. Donaghy has dogs that he treats almost as if they were people, and he was an hour late because he had to find one of them, which had gone missing inside in Tralee. Now, it was an important session, an A against B training game, and there we were out on the field waiting for your man. When I heard the reason he was late I nearly had a weakness from laughing, and I can still hear Jack saying, 'Whenever Donaghy can come he can sit there on the fucking bench.'

The closest we had to pets were the few animals we kept at home, and if they were being slaughtered down on the beach we wouldn't be leaving for training even five minutes later than usual.

To be fair to Donaghy, he was always, always 100 per cent committed – he wouldn't have lasted with Kerry anyway if he wasn't.

If a training session with Kerry went badly the dark side of Páidí came out. He'd speed home in the car, because he wanted to be back as soon as possible. Cranky. And he'd get that across at the next session.

No ice creams, either.

He directed his energy mostly towards Kerry. In later years he became a strong club man for An Ghaeltacht, but when he was playing for Kerry himself, if he felt he wasn't right, he wouldn't tog out.

At a stage when he'd won a couple of All-Irelands with Kerry, Páidí was started on the bench by the club manager, Mossy Lord (as he was known), for one game, clearly as a statement, to teach him a lesson.

Gaeltacht were winning early on, and the manager obviously felt he was after making a great call, but in the second half the opposition got on top. They started roaring from the crowd to get Páidí on, and when the manager told him to get ready to play, Páidí told him to go fuck himself and walked away into the dressing-room.

I'm not sure now if Mossy would agree with that sequence of events, but it's a funny story all the same, and Páid was always adding to stories to improve them anyway!

That time the club was struggling, and it was an achievement for Páidí to stand out as a minor and to get into the picture for the Kerry team.

For him as a player Kerry football was number one, while in our time we had a very good club team and obviously won county championships. Our club team had so many Kerry players that, if Kerry were going well in the championship, Gaeltacht suffered as a result, because those county players were all missing. Kerry was sacred to Páidí: there's no way he would have let a camera crew in to make a documentary about Kerry the way he did with Westmeath. He didn't like media in the dressing-room: that time reporters would come into the dressing-room after a game, and he'd go quiet.

That documentary, *Marooned* (2004), is good, and some of his speeches are very good, but they weren't a patch on what he'd say in a Kerry dressing-room. Some of his best speeches came in 2002, and we played the best football of any Kerry team I ever played on that year, even though we eventually lost the final to Armagh.

If we'd managed a draw that day I think we'd have won the replay, but we weren't good enough on the day, and they won it.

That was when the dark days would draw in for Páidí, and he'd withdraw away back to Ventry. I wouldn't go so far as to say he was ashamed, but he'd stay among his own people, in his own pub.

If we lost he'd be in a dark place. It'd eat him up. It would eat us all up, but everyone deals with defeat differently.

I'd say 2002 was the worst for him, because my dad died, and Darragh was also captain that year. Darragh and Páid were very close always. I'd say, right to the end, they'd have been on the phone to each other every day, so it was huge to have Darragh as a captain. Given what we'd won you couldn't complain, but it's one regret that we never had that in the house, the captain bringing in the cup.

That year was hard, because the football had carried us since my father had died, and then it was gone. You'd hear people say, 'It's only a game,' but it was more than that to us. It actually helped us cope, and gave us focus.

It was the most important thing in our lives – more important than family, university, jobs. It consumed us.

———

There was nobody like Páidí for speaking at half time. First he'd calm us down. If we were losing, or if fellas were panicking a bit, he'd cool us down. Then he'd go into the middle of the room, and if there was a bollocking to give, he'd give it.

He was great for questioning a team. I never saw him so tuned in as in 2002 – the talks on the way to games, the talks in dressing-rooms. He kept challenging us as a team. That was the key.

He got nervous before games, I knew that. He kept it hidden, but we knew him too well.

The piseogs would come out then: one day we had to sit in a car for half an hour because he hadn't seen a black cat. I was raging, because I could have spent the half hour doing stretches outside the car.

Another time, in the run-up to an All-Ireland, he was caught speeding by a guard, and he just took the ticket, no arguing.

'I could have got out of that with a couple of tickets,' he told me after, 'but they're a couple of tickets I'll need for the game.'

We won the All-Ireland, and the next time we made the final he was caught speeding again by another guard. He was delighted, thrilled altogether, because the first time he got the speeding ticket we'd won that All-Ireland, so this was a great sign for him that we'd win it again.

And he told the guard all about it, so much so that he eventually let him off, no ticket at all.

Páidí was easy to blame when things went wrong for Kerry. Too easy. Often we, the players, were at fault.

In 2003, when we met Tyrone, I don't think we were prepared for what happened. I don't think Tyrone had ever hit a team as hard as they did us that day, but I don't think we were prepared mentally, and that falls back on Páidí, though I would have expected us to react better on the field as a team.

Only since Páidí died would you realise that he lived and breathed football, and I don't know if he was ever able to let it go. It was his everything.

He was a rogue, and you couldn't believe a word out of him at times, particularly after a few pints. When he got the road from Kerry, for instance, he said, 'I'll never manage again. *Never*.' But, sure enough, six days later he was in a helicopter up to Westmeath, proud as punch with a suit and a smile.

I don't think his heart was in the Clare job when he went there, though. It always seemed to me that he was chasing that high he got from managing Kerry, but no other county would be the same. That said, I think he actually was at peace before he died.

———

I suppose it's a case of blood being thicker than water, but I used to hate fellas saying, 'Kerry aren't going well because Páidí is pinting.'

The season after Westmeath won Leinster, one of their players was quoted as saying that Páidí wasn't tuned in. I didn't say it out loud, but I'd have thought Páidí had a lot to do with them winning the Leinster championship the year before. Would they have won it without him? He put a huge energy and belief into them.

I'd have been protective of him even if he was wrong. He was our idol, growing up, and we were so proud of what he achieved playing football; everywhere you went with him people wanted to talk to him. I wouldn't have boasted about him in school or anything, but I was hugely proud of him. His greatest lesson to us was to win with grace and to lose with grace, and not to be blowing your own trumpet.

But Páidí had an ego. Of course he did. During the season, he hated dealing with the media, because he always wanted Kerry coming in under the radar, with as little fanfare as possible. But during the winter, or in retirement, he'd spend plenty of time in the media. Blackguarding.

Adventure followed us. Everywhere. Before one Munster final in Páirc Uí Chaoimh we met up in the Rochestown Park Hotel in Cork for our lunch and team meeting. Spilled out afterwards, ready for the warm-up.

'Where are we warming up, PO?'

Disaster. Nothing booked. The crowd of us looking at each other in a hotel car park.

Fair dues to PO, he improvised. He drove a car through a partition fence and we were liberated, running onto a green space in the middle of a housing estate. Top preparation, the thirty of us flinging handpasses around as people came out of their houses for the Sunday papers, looking over at us.

One of the suburbanites didn't appreciate the skills on show: 'Hey, clear off out of that!'

One of his neighbours was obviously from down our way, and weighed into the debate: 'Fuck off out of that, they can warm up there, and they'll put manners on ye later down the Park too!'

He was on the board of Bord Fáilte as well, and I met one member recently who said there was no craic at the meetings without Páidí; but he added that Páidí's ability to talk to people, and his knowledge of the tourism industry, were huge assets to the board.

Take the time he met Gregory Peck as an example of that ability. Peck was related to Thomas Ashe, the famous republican from Lispole who died on hunger strike in 1917. Fintan Ashe, who was on the Kerry selection in 1997, was another relation, so when the team went to America with the cup, Peck, who was very strong on ancestry and so on, invited them over to the house in Beverly Hills – massive mansion, beautiful furnishings, the whole lot. Darragh and Páidí went along with Fintan at about ten in the morning. Peck made them welcome, showed them around, and asked if they'd like a coffee. Peck had an Academy Award, for *To Kill a Mockingbird,* and plenty of other statuettes with it, Golden Globes and so on. There's a great photograph of Darragh and Fintan holding up awards on either side of Peck. Páidí was asked if he wanted to stand in for the photo, and he said, 'Sure haven't I five All-Stars at home?'

Everywhere he went stories sprouted. The craic just seemed to follow him around.

As kids, after coming home from school we'd often go over to the pub to play a game of pool. During the winter it'd be empty, practically, and Páidí would play against us, or else he'd be just reading the paper by the fire. Not a sinner in the place. One cold, wet winter afternoon a man strolled into the pub. I looked out the window and saw a huge black Mercedes parked outside, an uncommon sight at the time. I recognised the man who came in: Martin Sheen.

Down to Páidí at the end of the bar to tell him. Martin Sheen. Here. In the pub.

'Who's Martin Sheen?' says Páidí.

We told him, 'A big American actor.'

And out with Páidí, 'Martin, how are you? Welcome,' like they were old friends.

The background was that Páidí had had Tom Cruise in the pub when *Home and Away* was being filmed nearby, and he'd kept Cruise's security going with drink while the filming was going on. Ever since then he'd tell people in the pub that he'd been on the phone to Cruise about this and that: 'We keep in contact,' that kind of blackguarding.

So when Sheen came into the pub Páidí – though he'd never heard of him five minutes beforehand – was right at home with yet another movie star.

We got a weakness laughing when he offered Sheen a drink, only for the actor to reply that he was an alcoholic and, you know, didn't drink any more.

'That's all right,' says Páidí. 'You'll have one?'

Comedy.

Sheen was interested in the football, though. He spent about an hour and a half there, chatting away, and he looked at the photographs. Good company.

Eventually he said good luck and headed off out to his car.

For blackguarding we said to Páidí, 'Hey, tell him to say hi to Cruise for you,' as if Hollywood were just one street on which all the actors lived.

Páidí tore out the door and roared, 'Martin! Martin! Martin! Martin!' across the road until Sheen rolled down the window. 'Say hello to Tom for me, will you!'

———

Páidí liked to bring visitors to see my grandmother, something he always did when Charlie Haughey landed in. Charlie is a hero in

Dingle and still is: he did a lot for the area, and even now if you ask about him there wouldn't be a bad word said against him. He developed the harbour and a lot more. Páidí got to know him early on and would visit him out on Inishvickillane, and Charlie would call in to the pub to see him. He had opened the pub in Ventry officially for Páidí.

The evening I remember him calling in was one of my many shifts behind the counter. I was so young working there that the American tourists would take photographs of me lifting pints up over my head onto the counter. I could barely see what I was doing, and I'd hear, 'Aw, take a picture of him.' *Snap!*

Anyway, Charlie came in and bought a round for a few lads but had nothing for himself. He asked Páidí if it would be all right if he brought in his own wine, which was out in the car, and that was fine: in it came. So the wine was poured out and Charlie asked Páidí if he'd join him. The two of them had their glasses of wine, but while Charlie was sniffing his and rolling it around and tasting it, Páidí had already swallowed his. Straight down. Charlie was saying, 'Oh, savour it, this is a lovely wine,' but then he looked over, and Páidí's glass was on the counter, empty. He said nothing, in fairness, though I could only imagine what he was thinking.

That wasn't our only encounter with Charlie. We went to Dublin one time to present medals at a function, and the highlight was Páidí getting on stage to sing his particular version of 'An Poc ar Buile', with names changed to suit the occasion.

After the function we headed into town – myself, Marc, Páidí and a few more – and we were dropped across the road from Renard's, which was *the* nightspot in Dublin at the time. There was a VIP entrance and an ordinary entrance, and I nudged Marc as we headed across the road: would Páidí be able to pull this one off and get in the VIP door?

The bouncers said, 'Howaya, Páidí! How's it going? How many?'

'Seven,' says he.

'No problem. Head in.'

Of course he was preening that he pulled it off, and as we were heading up the stairs he turned to myself and Marc. 'Ye think I'm an awful eejit, don't ye?'

Anyway, the place was all mirrors inside, floor to ceiling – very confusing, particularly after a few drinks. We'd had a long spin into town, so we all wanted the toilets, and Marc led the way. He thought he was leading us into the gents, but he brought us down a dead end because of the mirrors, to a table where there were people staring at this crowd of six or seven big men advancing on them. Marc slammed into the mirror, I slammed into Marc, and Páidí slammed into me.

It looked desperate. The people at the table were laughing, and Páidí didn't like people laughing at him, so he says, 'Marc, get a taxi there, and go away home like a good man. You've had too much.'

The day after, Marc and I were booked on a flight back to Kerry, but Páidí had some business to do in Dublin, so he was down in himself, because he wanted to be on the road home too. We were killing a couple of hours when Páidí suddenly says, 'I know: we'll call out to Kinsealy.'

He made a call and off we went. Charlie Haughey was an old man at this stage. He made us welcome, and so did his wife, Maureen.

What I recall were the pictures, floor to ceiling, everywhere, of Charlie with various people. I'd have liked to have spent some time looking at those, but we went off to the bar in the house, the lot of us.

It was awkward enough. Páidí was in bad form, head in his hands, and he was the only man who knew Charlie, really. Marc and I were making small talk about the weather. After ten minutes Páidí lifted his head and said, 'Charlie, will we have a glass of wine?'

Charlie got out a bottle and they had a glass or two. Saved the visit.

There was huge respect there. I'd say Páidí's insecurities as a manager, fellas giving out about him, might have held him back from entering politics, though he had a huge interest in politics always. It was one of his great loves.

He loved his family. If you were going through a bad time he'd help you out any way he could, and he was always generous, with his own kids and with us. He'd always back you.

He loved music – traditional music, of all kinds – and he loved politics. I often meet politicians who'd say to me they loved to meet him, because they could sit down and talk politics to him, all the cloak-and-dagger stuff.

But football was top of the pile.

———

Another time we were in New York, inside in the middle of Manhattan, a hotel across from Madison Square Garden, on a team trip. Páidí was giving it socks, and fellas were half-avoiding him in going for a pint, because nobody would have the durability he had. He could leave you in a lúbán somewhere.

I was rooming with Éamonn Fitzmaurice, and one morning we were unlucky: just as we were finishing our breakfast Páidí walked past the door, saw us, and came in.

'We're caught,' I said to Fitzmaurice.

'Come on,' Páidí said to us.

Páidí always had a knack of landing on for a trip with thousands in his pocket. He'd be gathering money for ages beforehand, and he had his own way of giving it out to the players on the trip: he was going to carry us for a day's boozing and give us a wad at the end of it.

We got into a taxi and Páidí says, 'Midtown.'

The cabbie says, 'Hey, man, we are in midtown.'

'Go right and go down two blocks,' says Páidí. 'Then go left and go down three blocks, and leave us off there.'

He knew New York like the back of his hand. We spent the day in and out of bars. We'd go in somewhere and Páidí would ask where Mr such and such was. 'Give him a ring and tell him Páidí Ó Sé is in the bar.' And the owner would arrive in and have a drink – stories from the old days.

We hit about five bars like that, and then Páidí said he was going to bring us to a steakhouse. The place he had in mind was very classy – I think Mike Tyson used to hold press conferences there – and Páidí was telling us all about the food, the best steak you could get in New York, but his real reason for going there was that a few Irish lads worked there and his picture was framed and up on the wall.

In fairness, the manager recognised him when we went in. After a couple of drinks Páidí said, 'Show us the picture there,' so we went around the premises – the manager first, followed by Páid, with myself and Fitzmaurice at the rear.

After a while it became obvious that the picture had been removed, or demoted, and Páidí said, 'You took it down, you fucker, didn't you?' He made a joke out of it, but he still made us leave (the pair of us were bent double laughing at this stage), and we went across the street and had our steak over there in Rosie O'Grady's.

Sure enough, we were only fit for bed after that, but he put three hundred dollars in our hands and sent us back to the hotel, after carrying us for the day. The players loved him and would have driven through a wall for him.

———

It all came unstuck against Tyrone in 2003, and Páidí took it worse than anyone.

It's hard to explain how hard that time would have been for him if you're not from Kerry. I've seen other counties come down hard on managers and players; I've lived in Cork long enough to see that happen. But there's nothing like the knives that come out in Kerry. It's vicious.

I'd say there was a drive from a certain crew to get him out, which I certainly didn't like. That saying 'Tadhg an dá thaobh' summed it up. Some former teammates of Páidí's were saying one thing in public about him and another thing altogether behind his back. I'd hate to think I'd be like that myself.

In 2003 we'd met a team that had introduced a new style of football, and we'd been caught – and caught by a great, great team. I think a lot of teams would have been caught by Tyrone that time, but the problem for Páidí was that his team had then lost in 2001, 2002 and 2003 – a team that was perceived as having talent enough to win more.

He wasn't going to go easily, so he was going to have to be pushed, and he was.

_____

One thing I didn't like at about that time was when he was out in South Africa and gave the interview to Marty Morrissey. I work for RTÉ now, but I have no problem saying that I thought it was wrong that suddenly, during Páidí's trip to the other side of the world, a camera crew and a well-known journalist landed, and then went through with that interview. I don't know how Marty ended up out in South Africa in the first place, come to that.

I know Marty and I like him, and I appreciate the fact that he could have been under pressure from other quarters. We asked Páidí not to do that interview, but there was no talking to him – fairly stubborn, our PO was, when he wanted to be.

He loved being recognised – being the main man – which we all loved: we loved watching him and his antics. On the trip to South

Africa, for instance, he was telling me he'd meet Nelson Mandela while we were there.

That never happened. But while we were in in Cape Town he had a bit of a ritual around the pool: he'd put on runners, togs and a T-shirt, and bake away in the sun with a bottle of beer, and when he got too hot he'd walk over to the pool, plop in – runners and all – climb out, come back, dry off and continue. That was the cycle for the day.

The Kilkenny hurlers were in the hotel at the same time, and a few of them were looking over, obviously thinking, What is going on here?

The current Kerry team stayed in South Africa in 2014, and some of the younger lads, who'd have heard that story, actually went down to the hotel to see the pool and the bar, exactly where it all happened.

His way of operating on holiday would be to pick out the manager or the main man in the hotel the first day we'd land, get him and hand him the biggest tip he'd see all year. After that, anything PO wanted, PO got. If he lifted a finger in the lobby they came running from every direction.

And that was no harm sometimes. On the South African trip most of the touring party were out with us for the first part of it; but they went home, and the crowd who were left went hard at it one evening, staying out till the small hours, or the bright hours, of the morning. I had to bail out – I was in company with Ó Cinnéide, who has the constitution of a bull – so I went up to have a sleep in my room.

When I woke up the next morning I got the feeling that something wasn't quite right. I looked at the door, and it was hanging half off the hinges. Someone had burst it in while I was asleep. I checked to make sure my passport and wallet were still there, and then I went downstairs for breakfast and got the story.

While they were drinking away, someone got it into their head that I was after dying up in the room. How they got that notion I don't know, but PO said he'd go up and check on me.

He hammered on the door but got no answer – I was out for the count – so he took a fire extinguisher and broke down the door. He made sure I was breathing and then went back downstairs to join the party.

'Why didn't you just get a key off reception?' I asked him.

'Sure that didn't occur to me. I was panicked outside the door!' he said, with that bullish head on him.

––––

He'd never remember my birthday, but if he needed a favour he'd remind me: 'I'm your godfather.'

'When's my birthday, so?'

Laughing from Páidí. 'Look, I need some tickets.'

Tickets for a man who had tickets from the Westmeath County Board, the Clare County Board, the Kerry County Board and Croke Park, to name just the known sources.

When he was managing us you'd be afraid to pull out a ticket in front of him, because he'd accuse you of not focusing on the game, but when he was no longer manager it was grand to bother us for 'bits of cardboard' the Saturday before a big game.

––––

After a particular final I was going to go straight home to Cork. I had the train sorted, everything ready. I went for a quiet one in Dublin with Darragh after the game and he said, 'You should stay up. You had a great game: you were close to man of the match,' and I said I would.

We had a great night, and the following day we went down to the Boar's Head in Capel Street for a pint, which became a bit of a tradition for us. (It continues to this day, no matter who wins it. Hugh, the owner, and his family are great GAA people.)

Páidí was there and a few more. We had great craic, and then they were all getting ready to go back to the hotel for the trip home to Kerry.

I was regretting then that I wasn't going back with them, but I headed off on my own along the quays, and the last pub I said I'd have a drink in was O'Shea's Merchant near Christ Church, a big Kerry pub. I walked in the door and there were about thirteen fellas gathered around a table in the back, and, in the middle of them all, Páidí holding court. A big cheer from him when he saw me, and I joined them. More craic. Everyone in great spirits, Kerry after winning the All-Ireland, a fantastic sing-song going with James Begley, Luke Kelly's brother. Outstanding stuff.

'Where are you off to now?' Páidí asked me.

When I told him I was heading back to Cork, of course, he exploded.

'Would you ever cop on and come back to your own county after winning an All-Ireland, and don't be going back to Cork.'

The pints were going down, so I said I'd head back to Kerry with them.

We tore off down the road in his car. John L was his driver, with PO in the front and Begley in the back with me.

Cross-country all the way. We dropped in to Séamus Darby's pub for one, and he's in Toomyvara, which goes to show that we weren't taking the shortest route possible. Half an hour after that PO told John L to pull in at the next pub.

The next place we came to had a big car park, and it was jammed – unusual enough for a Monday afternoon. I saw BBC vans and was wondering what was going on. When we went in, there was Shane MacGowan talking away at the back. We crept in, nice and quiet, but MacGowan spotted Begley, who's a great singer and musician (they obviously knew each other), and he jumped up, shouting, 'James! James!'

MacGowan came down to us, and PO's ego came to the surface. I could see it happening, PO straightening the tie and thinking, Oh, I'll have a great chat here with MacGowan. But MacGowan wanted to chat to Begley.

I could see PO waiting to be acknowledged, and saw that it wasn't going to happen, because MacGowan had no idea who he was, so eventually Páidí butted in.

'Páidí Ó Sé, Shane. How are you?'

MacGowan fobbed him off with 'How are things?' or whatever, before going back to talk music with Begley.

I started laughing to myself when I saw the bruised ego. PO finished his pint, and we had to leave.

The night ended in Foley's of Inch, about 1 a.m., with Begley singing old, old songs in company with a cousin of Páidí's, Bridie Long, Tom Long's sister. Begley was fascinated by her repertoire of old songs.

I was begging them to drop me to Killarney for the homecoming, but nothing would do him then only to carry me to Ard an Bhóthair.

Some day. Some craic. Stories from Dublin to west Kerry.

———

He was invited to a golf classic one time, but it was in Meath.

He hummed and hawed until he was told that they'd send a helicopter to get him – this was during the boom – so he said yes, because he was like a child with helicopters: he loved them.

Máire was keeping an eye on him that time, because he was having a pint or two too many, but himself and my brother Fergal were waiting for the helicopter, and they had a pint while they were waiting.

The helicopter landed in a field, and Páidí and Fergal had to climb over a barbed wire fence to get to it. Páidí's putter fell out of the bag, unbeknownst to him, and Fergal said, 'Your putter's here, Páidí.'

Páidí just said, 'Sure what do I need that for? I'm not going for the golf.'

We'd mimic him constantly, taking him and his sayings off in the pub. Only we would get the joke, when he'd used one of his special phrases, and we'd be laughing to ourselves.

Páidí could be rude. If he was getting an ear-bashing off someone for a long time he'd have a gruff enough response. And that would set us off laughing again if we were there as witnesses.

———

When he went from Kerry in 2003 it hurt. I knew Kerry was his life; I knew what he'd lost out on in his commitment. When we won the All-Ireland in 1997 it had been a huge highlight for him, particularly given the way it had gone wrong the previous season. He had put the life and soul back into Kerry football.

At the hotel that night there was the outer function, open to everyone, and the inner room, for the team and family only, and he was in there with his own pals, happy out.

He said to me that evening when I saw him, 'Go up and get your godfather a pint.' His first of that year.

Going as manager hurt him hugely, and the way he found out – from somebody else – was a blow. Seán Walsh was the chairman, a sound man, but they fell out, and there was a coolness between us as well; but, to be fair, they rectified it. Páidí saw that Seán was trying to do the best for Kerry football, and Seán spoke at his grave in the end.

There was a hullabaloo that we wouldn't play for Kerry because Jack O'Connor was coming in, but that was never going to happen. Páidí was the man who instilled in us the belief that there was nothing more important than Kerry in the first place, and it didn't matter who the manager was. Nothing came before Kerry.

I don't think Páidí came to grips with it for years. I thought that it ate at him and that he chased something similar with Westmeath and with Clare. In the last couple of years before he died I thought he had it cracked. He was in a good place with the business, with the kids. I thought he had dealt with it.

——

I'd share a lot of his traits, as would my brothers. There's a wild streak in me, like Páidí's, according to some people, but I don't know if I agree. Páidí would make contact with people and maintain that contact always: he'd come downstairs on summer days in his dressing-gown, and he'd sit at the kitchen table and write ten letters to people. He'd send fellas personal letters, and the number of people who've come to me and said, 'When this happened to me I got a letter from Páidí' … That's why people had such good time for him.

Sure, he'd mess up every now and again, like the rest of us. But he'd mean what he'd write. After Christy O'Connor Jr's son died in a car crash, Páidí would ring him on his son's anniversary.

That's why there were people who'd do anything for Páidí, though there were also people who wouldn't mind seeing him do badly. And that's not necessarily personal: that's the pressure that comes with managing Kerry.

——

I was in Cork when I got a phone call from my mother, and I knew immediately from the way she was talking that something was wrong. She said that Máire was there with her and that Páidí was dead.

I couldn't believe it. He was bullet-proof to us. He was my god-father, after all. When something like that happens the landscape of home changes for you. For us, it's a small place: our house, the shop, my grandmother's house, the pub, the church. That's all it is. My uncle Tom is a hundred yards away. All Ó Sés.

We were all very close, growing up: after Mass on a Sunday we'd be in each other's houses. Our house was theirs and vice versa: Páidí would often have come into our house and thrown himself on the couch to watch the television, and I'd do the same even now and drop into his house.

He was the heartbeat of the whole thing – the constant. He'd always be there behind the bar, and he'd always put you smiling.

Páidí had great interest in my kids, for instance, and when I told them he had died, young as they were, they cried for him. I cried myself. He was like a brother to us more than an uncle. A lot of people are intrigued by him still. There are flags from many different counties around his grave back west. He was a great family man and is missed sorely by Máire, Neasa, Siún and Pádraig. By all of us. Ard an Bhóthair is a different place now …

———

Years before, when he'd finished as Kerry manager, he was at one end of the bar one evening and I was at the other.

That Mavericks came on the radio, 'Dance the Night Away'.

He didn't see me, but I saw him, laughing away to himself. I knew he was thinking of getting a rise out of me.

PART II.

PART II

Chapter 4

AN GHAELTACHT: THE RISE AND FALL

To understand anything about An Ghaeltacht, you have to get a handle on the size of the place – the catchment area. It's a massive constituency. People would probably have a notion of the geography of the area – west of Dingle, you've a few fair mountains, the coastline, going from the lower part up around the corner, and it's all An Ghaeltacht country.

You land in Tralee, come back the coast road and land into Dingle. First, though, you pass through Anascaul. Go the other way, over the Conor Pass, and you'll pass by Castlegregory first, but most people go the coast road. After Anascaul you go through Lispole and then Dingle.

Now, anything west of Dingle, then, is the Gaeltacht. That's us.

I love west Kerry. What we have around our club you wouldn't see anywhere in the world. Behind my own house you have Mount Eagle; right beside it you have Cruach Mhárthain. The road that splits those two mountains is known locally as the Clasach, and that carries you from Ard an Bhóthair, where we come from, straight back into Dunquin, about three miles over the mountain.

On a good day, which is any day, being on top of one of those mountains is special – looking down into Dunquin and out over the Blasket Sound into the islands (Charlie's famous spot among them). Over to the right the Sleeping Giant rests peacefully in the ocean.

Move inland to the right and you have the famous Three Sisters in Ballyferriter; keep moving and you'll see the majestic Mount Brandon; and as you swivel nearly 360° you're looking down on the parish of Ventry and Ventry Harbour.

Home. I love it.

Go back over Ó Cinnéide's side and you're at the foot of Mount Brandon. Dangerous cliffs – places like Cuas an Bhodaigh, Slea Head.

It's a wild, wild place, but there's beauty there as well. To me there is no place like it on earth. So many people come back to see it, but being back there all the time is lovely: the seasons change, the weather changes, but the landscape stays the same.

I definitely appreciate it a lot more since I moved to Cork. I don't get home as often as I'd like, but I love it back there – the layout of the land, the beaches, Cuan Pier, where we spent many the summer's day diving off the pier on the right-hand side of Ventry Harbour as you look out.

We used to use it to soften the muscles after tough training or matches: there's nothing like seawater – the most refreshing feeling in the world, plunging into the ocean. Slea Head, Coumeenoole Beach ...

I don't know if it'll sound strange to people, but that beauty, and that wildness and ruggedness – you could say that's reflected in the football. When you can say there's control there as well, then you're laughing.

—

Here are the directions: coming out of Dingle there are three roads: one will carry you to Ventry, one to An Mhuiríoch or Ballyferriter, and the other one to Feothanach.

To give you an idea of how big our club area is, if I jumped into my car in Ard an Bhóthair and was going to drive over to Ó Cinnéide's in Feothanach, it's half an hour's drive. You're talking twenty-odd miles. For us to go to Ó Cinnéide's house it's shorter for us to go to Dingle and make the turn than to go cross-country or back west. And, because of that, you wouldn't have known lads well. I wouldn't have known Ó Cinnéide or his gang that well. It's not as though we were all going to school together, for instance: the primary schools feeding our club would be Cill Mhic an Domhnaigh, Ventry, Glens, An Fheothanach, An Mhuiríoch and Baile an Fheirtéaraigh. All those contribute to one club, even though Cill Mhic an Domhnaigh and Ventry are only two miles apart. We went to Cill Mhic an Domhnaigh, a school with maybe twenty pupils, and we wouldn't have known the lads in the other schools that well.

Because of that, until such time as you went back training with these lads in An Ghaeltacht, you had no idea who they were. That was a major difference from most clubs, where kids know each other long before they play together in a club situation.

When I was growing up, in pre-football days we used to have an inter-school competition at primary schools called the Corn Mhic Eoin. That was the only time we would cross paths. I haven't got one of those medals, and I still get the odd smart comment over it. Even now.

The second thing to understand is that there's always been a tradition of football in west Kerry. There's nothing else: no hurling, nothing. Football is God, back there.

I say that to people, and I know they don't get it. It's probably the case in many places around the country, but it's certainly true back there. Even now it's ahead of religion. People might think that's an awful thing to say, but there are more people going to football matches and talking about football than there are going to Mass or talking about religion. And even years ago, when religion was supreme, football was up there too.

Names? How many do you want? Batt Garvey, Bill Dillon, Seán Brosnan, Paddy Bawn Brosnan, Bill Casey, Gega Connor, Seán and Séamus Murphy from Camp, Paddy Kennedy from Anascaul, PO and Tommy Doyle and Mícheál Ó Sé over the road from us, Tom Ashe, Liam Higgins – all these fellas paved a way and opened a path for us to follow. All of them, no matter how long ago they played. Paddy Bawn would always be talked about in Dingle, as would the great Dingle teams he played on that won county championships.

That time good Gaeltacht players went in and togged out for Dingle. Before that they were known as the Aghasaigh, but then they were Dingle, and they had an awesome team. Bill Casey from Lispole would have come in and played with them too when they won numerous county championships.

And the folklore keeps them all alive still – stories of Paddy Bawn and Seán Brosnan coming in off a boat and getting into a car to head to a county final in Tralee, maybe having a couple of pints before- hand and then going out to win the county. All blown up, but all part of the legend.

I love listening to that, just as PO did. He had a huge interest in the history of Kerry football and loved talking about it. One time I was chatting about Jack O'Shea or someone to this old lad outside a shop, and he said, 'Paddy Kennedy would beat 'em all. Look, Paddy Kennedy was the man.'

And I was thinking, Who the hell is Paddy Kennedy?

The old lad says to me, 'Paddy Kennedy would pick out any slate on top of that roof. You could name the slate, and he could jump up and pluck it out and pull it down for you.'

And obviously after hearing that you'd be thinking, Who is this guy? because they were all made out to be gods to you. Clearly they were brilliant footballers and won All-Irelands for Kerry; you only have to go into Paddy Bawn's pub below in Dingle to see the history. You can also see the respect he had for the Railway Cup, which has lost all the meas – and the crowds – it had in his day. But that's another story.

I suppose Paddy Bawn above a lot of them had the aura – the fisherman who was out at sea and would come in and, to judge from some of the stories, stand in at full-back in his wellingtons and put manners on the opposition.

Seán Murphy and his brother Séamus were other legends. Seán was a wing-back, and as a wing-back myself I often had it explained to me that Seán was the Rolls-Royce of defenders. I've never met him, but I'd love to, because I have a fierce interest in former players, and I've met a good few of them.

When I was too young I'd have met Bawn; it's very important to stay in touch with that tradition. It was certainly important to us in the Gaeltacht: we had Batt Garvey and Tom Long as heroes, and Tom was a first cousin of my father's and PO's. Eventually Tom went to live in Killarney and fell in with the Crokes, but he was a Gaeltacht man, and you'd hear the stories that he was one of the greatest Kerry footballers of all time. He retired young as well, by all accounts.

Of course, a lot of people nowadays wouldn't know those names – they wouldn't have a clue who Tom Long was, or a lot of those players – but we were always keen to remember them in An Ghaeltacht.

When we got rid of our old clubhouse – a cold, dark enough place – we put up new dressing-rooms with pictures of these old great teams and players – and of the two men who captained the county to the All-Ireland, PO and Ó Cinnéide.

As I've said, that's the biggest regret, that I never saw Darragh lift the Sam Maguire and bring it back to our own house as captain. But that's the beauty of sport: it's cold, ruthless. On the day, we probably didn't deserve it, and he didn't get the chance to collect the cup.

———

The Gaeltacht field, Gallarus, was built back near Muiríoch, more or less in the middle of the area, and fellas would be cycling in to play there from all points. No cars, apart from maybe Liam Ó Rócháin's, but twenty-five bikes in a row. No lifts, and just the six miles from Ard an Bhóthair.

Nowadays if I'm back home and head down around Gallarus I might see thirty cars parked along by the field, and I'd be wondering, What's the event here, what's going on? Is there a senior game being played? But there's not, it's a kid's game: it's just that they're all being carried there.

When I was a kid the jerseys were red and white stripes, but eventually we changed it to white, with the red sash going across it. And there was a big deal about it: the older crowd weren't too keen on the idea.

See, going back the years, caid was the game played all over the country. You'd have parishes playing against each other – or, to be more exact, kicking the shit out of each other – trying to bring a ball over a line that was drawn between the two of them. The ball could be moved around for hours: it was rough and ready, and the play could range around for miles in every direction. Now, to this day, I'd still call a football a caid, as in 'Tabhair dom an chaid' (Give me the caid). Tradition was very important to the older fellas, and rightly so.

But when they finished playing that game and settled on football in west Kerry, they came to Ballyferriter. Eventually, though, they fixed on Gallarus.

I don't know why. It's a wild place. For most of my career with An Ghaeltacht we were in Division 1 in Kerry, which meant that the top teams would come back to Gallarus to play us: the Stacks, Laune Rangers, the Crokes – all of them. I'd say they hated it: an hour from Tralee, an hour from Killarney, and a pitch as hard as rock built on a beach, and nearly constant wind. I could count maybe three or four times we were ever beaten there in my time.

Although the club draws from a huge area, it's very sparsely populated. It was badly affected in the eighties by emigration, and again in the last decade or so. Emigration has always been an issue, and getting numbers for a team has always been a challenge.

My earliest memories would be of PO going strong with Kerry, county-wise, but An Ghaeltacht were struggling. Division 4, Division 5 – that was the horizon for us.

There were great clubmen, always. The likes of John Long, who played for Kerry, was very strong for the club. But Páidí wasn't that focused on An Ghaeltacht: he had tunnel vision for Kerry, getting himself right for intercounty competition, and he wouldn't have put the same time into the club. I have clear memories of coming back to Gallarus when I was a kid, and he'd be standing by the dressing-room in his clothes. Some days he wouldn't tog, other days he would: it all depended on Kerry. Though, to be fair, he did a lot for the club down the years, particularly after he finished with Kerry.

The change for An Ghaeltacht came with a man called Liam Ó Rócháin. He's been mentioned a lot over the years, and deservedly so.

To give you the context, nowadays there are three or four adults with every kids' team in An Ghaeltacht – under-8s, under-10s, under-12s, all the way up to minor. In our time it began with under-12s, so you'd start going to the field when you were eight or so. And Ó Rócháin was in charge of the under-12s team. On his own. It was the same with the under-14s, the under-16s, the minor team. No selectors, no management team: just him.

A brilliant man. I can realise that now, being an adult myself. To put that time into it, to put up with all the messers … He was a schoolteacher, and you'd imagine that after a day standing in front of a class he'd have had enough of children, but he had the patience of a saint.

We all owe him a massive debt – the players he put through his hands for the club, and the skill levels he helped instil.

I'd always maintain that our skills were very good as kids. We always had a ball when we were around home. Ó Rócháin didn't have us doing any running when we went to training – and we never needed it, either. I met a man recently who was talking about getting his club's under-12s to improve their speed, and I asked him if he was insane. When we trained, we concentrated on the basic skills – kicking and catching, a good match among ourselves – and then were up on the bike and home. Why would we need fitness training when we were cycling a round trip of ten miles every evening?

For us going to Gallarus, it was a five-mile trip on the bike. We never got a lift to training. The odd time if it rained we might pile into Ó Rócháin's car, because he lived near us in Ventry, but usually it was the bike, back to Gallarus, train, over to the shop for a few sweets, and back on the bike for the five miles home.

We did that all the time.

Ó Rócháin's very talented young team was the under-age side that had our Darragh and Dara Ó Cinnéide on it. They were very good, and they formed the basis of the senior team that eventually got to Croke Park.

Our team wasn't as good as theirs, but they helped us, because if they won a Division 1 league at under-12s, the club under-12s were in Division 1 the following year as well, no matter how good or bad the following year's team was. So they were making sure we got good competition, at least, and improving, while they were actually winning counties. They beat the Stacks and Laune Rangers – all the big clubs.

We had handy players on our under-age team – Aodán Mac Gearailt and Vincent Callaghan also played for Kerry – but the important thing was that, between our team and Darragh's team, there was the core of a very good adult team on the way up.

Above their team, then, there were older players, seven or eight fellas who were very good too. By the time we got to minor, under-21, we had a very good set-up.

I certainly didn't stand out that time. I wasn't the main man, the player you'd have picked out to do well at adult level; I don't think I had the confidence back then. For one thing, I played as a forward (centre-forward, corner-forward), and I didn't get the same enjoyment out of the game. I was a bit shy and a bit small, too, with it. More than a bit, in fact: I was tiny.

But when I got to secondary school in Dingle I changed my approach and I changed positions. Bosco Ó Conchubhair was our coach there, a Gaeltacht man. He was in charge of us as first years, and I asked if he'd pick me at wing-back in a trial.

'Go on, try it out,' he said.

I played well. I made sure I played well, and that's how playing wing-back started. I was thirteen or fourteen, but I stayed wing-back all through school and with the club after that.

Why? I don't think I was a natural forward, for one thing: I was more of a direct runner. I enjoyed that, driving forward with the ball. In addition, I just had a burning desire to play in the backs.

What helped a little was that a buddy of mine with the club, Chris Casey, was in the backs that time but wanted to try playing as a forward, so we swapped, if you like. And Chris turned out to be a prolific scorer for us with the CBS. We had a good team, including Tommy Griffin, who played for Kerry after, and we won the All-Ireland B competition in school. The fact that we had the great Liam Higgins as our coach helped a lot.

———

In Dingle you have the West Kerry Championship, which involves five teams – An Ghaeltacht, Castlegregory, Anascaul, Dingle and Lispole. In the days when Páidí was playing with An Ghaeltacht, Lispole were the team to beat: they won something like thirteen West Kerry Championships in a row – phenomenal stuff.

That time you had the likes of Liam and Denis Higgins playing for them, great players, and to this day they would stand out as an example of how a club should behave. To do things properly, to have respect for your club, all that. That's important.

I'd have to say I didn't always have respect for the club, particularly when I came onto the scene first with Kerry. I had an 'Ah, I'm too good for this craic' outlook – a bit of a swelled head, or an attitude that I was after training and playing all year with Kerry, and An Ghaeltacht just wasn't as important: I didn't really have to take it too seriously … Completely wrong.

I didn't give them the respect I should have. I wouldn't show up to training the odd time, and there was one game in particular when I went out the night before. Wrong.

It was Páidí, of all people, who had a word with me to straighten that out – someone who, to be honest, I didn't see as a great club man when he was playing himself. Though, to be fair to him, when his Kerry career was over he was a very good Gaeltacht man. But he had a word with me, saying I had to respect the club.

I was young, twenty or twenty-one, and I needed that. And I respected the club after that and got angry myself when others disrespected the club later, precisely because I'd been a great man myself for going out the night before a game. Dingle is a great spot to be around during the summer, and it's an easy habit to fall into.

My attitude would have been that if Kerry were out of the championship I could do what I liked, which was all wrong: it sent a bad signal to the younger players. I regretted that, but I gave the club as much as I could for as long as I could: I played senior for them for fifteen or sixteen years, and when we were having a run to county finals and All-Ireland club finals I was very dedicated to it.

My first senior game would have been in Comórtas Peile na Gaeltachta, which was held that year in Baile Bhuirne. It is a huge deal back our way, because Irish, obviously, is a huge deal back our way. In the old dressing-rooms back in Gallarus all the signs were in Irish. All the team talks would be in Irish. Players talking at meetings would speak in Irish. Out on the field we spoke Irish to each other.

For us it was important, as part of what we are. Speaking Irish addled the opposition as well, of course, who sometimes wouldn't have a clue what we were saying, and that didn't hurt either. There'd be spurts of English the odd time as well, but it was mostly Irish, and it was something we were really proud of.

Spioraid, croí, caid agus teanga was and is emblazoned on our jersey and in our clubhouse: spirit, heart, football and language.

I think Irish is hugely important. It's vital. You go into schools, teaching Irish, and some of the Irish we're teaching kids in fifth and sixth class … Some of the kids back home, when they go into primary school, they have to learn English.

———

When Darragh and Ó Cinnéide came through to the adult teams in the club, we were still in the novice grade, but they helped the club to win novice and junior titles inside a couple of years. It would be remiss of me not to mention all the club players who ploughed for us for years without huge success but who were as important to our club and its future as anyone else was or is.

I wasn't there for those wins, but I was there when we won the intermediate championship twice, and winning it twice meant you had the option to go up senior, which was a big deal.

But we had the quality to handle it. We had Darragh Ó Sé, Dara Ó Cinnéide, Aodán Mac Gearailt, myself. Eventually we had Marc Ó Sé and Rob Mac Gearailt and very good borderline county players as well: JJ Corduff, Mickey Connor, Seán Sheehy, Kevin Walsh, our Fergal, Paul Quinn.

And An Ghaeltacht had families too, like any rural GAA club: we were providing four players out of our house in Ventry; the Connors were providing as many as seven at one stage; and the Walshes had three or four.

We all got on very well too. The socialising was unreal. I mentioned the parishes and schools, but all the parishes had their own pubs as well, and the socialising went hand in hand with the football. You had Kruger's in Dunquin; in Ballyferriter there were four pubs, Brick's outside that; in Muiríoch there were two, Begley's and TP's. And there was Feothanach with two pubs, Ventry with another two ... We'd knock great craic out of celebrating after a game, but together – always together.

Often you'd be carried in to Tralee or Killarney for a game, and even on the journey back after a win there'd be huge satisfaction in it for the supporters, who we were able to mix it with the big boys. I got great satisfaction from that, the enjoyment we brought to the people of the Gaeltacht for those six or seven years.

In 1999, when I was playing senior for the first time, the supporters got behind us in a huge way, for instance. Our first county championship game in Gallarus was against South Kerry – a replay. We drew with them the first day below in their own place, and there were hundreds of Gaeltacht people made the trip.

By car it's three hours from past Dingle down to Cahersiveen and these places, but some people went by boat. Four or five boats went from the Dingle Peninsula, straight across to Cahersiveen, to save time (it's half an hour's trip in a good boat; a lot longer, and queasier, in a bad one).

Gaeltacht people came from further afield too – from Dublin and Cork and Limerick, all of them after leaving the area but wanting to be there to support us, all of them speaking Irish and wearing the colours. We had nothing won, but we were playing senior, against South Kerry – the South Kerry of Mick O'Connell and Mick O'Dwyer ... *that* South Kerry.

The atmosphere was great, and part of that was the Gaeltacht crowd. I don't care what anyone says: the Gaeltacht people are a different breed. There is something about them – I won't describe it as madness; maybe an unpredictability – that I love. When we played South Kerry they had Maurice Fitzgerald, Denis Dwyer, Jamesie Shea – a good team with serious players, but we got a draw out of it and brought them back west. To Gallarus.

That was a big part of the club's success. Gallarus is a beautiful place to be in during the summer, but winter can be fairly bleak – and I'm being kind with that description. Ten yards past the sideline and you're on a beach. There's a big old stand there, but PO always used to say the field was only fit for camels: it was only grass and sand.

I loved playing in Gallarus when I wasn't fit, because it's small and hard, and I loved to see other teams playing there, because they had to contend with the wind. And there's always a wind. Even on a calm day it's breezy, and usually it's a gale. Ó Cinnéide is the only free-taker I ever saw to master the wind there. He'd aim a free twenty yards to one side of the goalposts and bring it in on the wind over the bar. It was a challenge to a visiting free-taker, and they'd often get to grips with it, but usually it'd take them the whole of the game to do that, by which time it was too late.

The night we played South Kerry the place was mobbed. The club had to put a wire fence around the pitch (for a county championship game you have to have the field fenced in), and it was an unbelievable occasion – crowd, atmosphere – and we got the win.

We got beaten by Crokes later that year, but they'd have been a bit ahead of us at that time. We were happy enough with that for our first year.

———

Funnily, any time we didn't go well with Kerry we seemed to have a good year with the club. We won county championships in 2001 and 2003, when Kerry were knocked out early enough and we were all back training early with the club. The club was so strong that we could afford to have five intercounty players gone for most of the season: we'd still stay up in Division 1, year in, year out. That's the quality of player we had.

In 2001 we played our first county final, against Stacks – with their history, their All-Ireland club titles, their All-Ireland medallists. Mickey Connor was our captain. It was a really special day in Killarney for the team and our supporters: we'd never been at those heights, and it had all started back with Liam Ó Rócháin.

When we won the 2001 county championship we went bonkers, basically. Dingle hadn't won it since the days of Paddy Bawn, and they weren't playing senior, so I'd say it galled them to see us win.

Stacks were the arch-enemy in the sense that they were always the big team when we were kids: they had the Geaneys, Fintan Ashe – a very strong team. And there was always this special thing, townie boys against us, the lads from the country. The banter was great between us, but it could be touchy enough if you were a businessman.

Tomás Garvey, for instance, has a huge supermarket in Dingle with a lot of customers from back our way in the Gaeltacht, so he'd be supporting us financially. The pubs the same: there's one pub in Dingle, Páigín's, or Flaherty's, which is the Dingle GAA pub. After a game you'd come down the hill from Páirc an Aghasaigh, heading west, and the pub is right there – can't miss it. That was the meeting-point after every game for anyone playing above (remember, Dingle is the main location for West Kerry games, and for finals in particular), so afterwards – win, lose or draw – you'd go in and have a pint or two; but particularly if you lost. You could head off after a pint if you liked, but our attitude was that you went in and faced the music if you lost: it was easy to go in when you'd won the game.

There'd be a niggle between us in An Ghaeltacht and the Dingle lads. We were on one colleges team with the secondary school, with a lot of Gaeltacht and Dingle players on it, and we had played against each other in minor championship a few days after the All-Ireland final with Dingle CBS. This was about the time of the Kerry minor trials and so on, so there was no love lost at all, even though less than a week earlier we were all in it together trying to win an All-Ireland for the school.

It was always important for us to get one over on them, and vice versa, but I didn't take it outside the game. Some fellas got into trouble around the town, taking it further than they needed to and falling out badly with lads. I never fell out with any of the Dingle lads, and some of them are my best buddies – the likes of Tommy Griffin.

Once I got over the white line, I wanted to beat them, fair enough. We were winning county championships in 2001 and 2003, and by 2003 Dingle were up senior themselves, and we beat them in the championship. That was very important to us: it would have been like an All-Ireland to them to beat us that time, because we were going so well. (As always happens, though, the tide turns, and it looks like Dingle are the up-and-coming team in the county, with some fantastic young players, so it might come to it that we're cheering them on in county finals.)

When we made it to the All-Ireland club final there was a great story went around that, after we lost to Caltra in Croke Park, one of the Dingle lads, watching the game on the telly in a pub, went down on his knees in front of everyone and said, 'Thanks be to God they didn't win.'

I won't go into any more detail, as I still go into Dingle to socialise. At the time I laughed at it, though some fellas would be dark enough. The bulk of the Dingle lads would have been wishing us well, genuinely, but there's a rivalry there. Of course there is.

It's the same all over Ireland, clubs and counties; it's just that the names are different. That's what I love about the GAA.

But I also love the fact that you can then mix afterwards: everywhere in Ireland you have lads looking forward to a certain date, a certain meeting with another club.

Those West Kerry Championships would always have been played on dark evenings – heavy conditions, muck everywhere – because the various local championships would be put back while Kerry were in the hunt for an All-Ireland. So you'd be ploughing through the mud in December on the hill in Dingle after a year with Kerry. But it was important – hugely important – to do well in the West Kerry Championship.

Ó Cinnéide, for instance, would be a huge club man and would always stress that it was never 'only' the West Kerry Championship. He would have stressed how important it was to do well in those championships for the sake of the club's identity, and for the older members in particular – to keep winning.

Some of the people would consider a West Kerry Championship more important than what you'd do with Kerry, because that is their All-Ireland.

––––––

It was a golden era for the club when we were rolling well. Even getting out of Kerry, to play in the Munster Club Championship, was an adventure.

In 2001 we celebrated too much after winning the Kerry title, but that was understandable: it was the first time for all of us. We came home, partied all night and headed to Killarney for the man of the match award the next day. (Darragh won it.)

But hanging over us in the Munster Championship were Nemo Rangers. We went down to play Nemo, and it was all a bit of a joke –

'This is bonus territory, sure' – but the reality was that we rattled a ball off the crossbar in the second half, and if that had gone in it might have given us the belief to really drive at them. We thought they were gods who were going to blow us out of the water in Páirc Uí Chaoimh, but we weren't tuned in enough. If we'd had the experience we would build up by 2003 we'd have rattled them.

That year – 2003 – would be different. We beat Laune Rangers in a replay, and it was the year of PO's departure as Kerry manager. That hurt us as a club, and we used it going in against Laune Rangers: 'If they can do that to us as a club ...', that kind of thing.

That day Mícheál Ó Sé, from the radio, who wasn't part of the management set-up at all, came into the dressing-room in Tralee and gave a speech in Irish. He talked about who we were, where we were from, how we'd struggled for years, how we'd got to the top of the pile and how the county had treated PO, one of our own … Forget taking the door off the hinges: we nearly broke the dressing-room wall down going out. I was never as high heading out to play a game.

That said, just to show that it's not all about shouting and roaring, we were flat enough that day once the ball was thrown in. I certainly was, despite all the roaring and shouting I was doing myself running out onto the field.

It went to a replay, and in the second game I played one of my best games ever. Because it was the second championship we were able to enjoy it that bit more. We appreciated it. We beat St Senan's of Kilkee, and then there was a fund-raiser for the club, which we had down in Killarney, ahead of the All-Ireland semi-final. We were playing St Brigid's of Dublin the following week.

All of us were there at the fund-raiser, obviously, and there was a good crowd of people there, plenty from Cork, and there was a guy there from Nemo Rangers. He said at one stage, 'Ah, it takes a special kind of team to get to Croke Park, and I don't think ye have it. I think Brigid's will beat ye.'

Saying this to our faces! I only laughed at him, but I'd have put it away for motivation at the same time. In my head, that drove me on, even if it nearly drove me insane at the same time: 'How dare he put us down like that!' At that stage we had a third of the Kerry starters – myself, Marc, Darragh, Aodán and Dara, and more on the fringes – and I thought he was putting us down.

Brigid's had the two Gallaghers from Fermanagh that time, but we beat them all the same above in Thurles.

———

An All-Ireland club final. Uncharted territory.

The place went mental. Schools, businesses, people's houses – all of them had the colours up. Crowds at training; crowds after training. Paid Ó Conchúir of the restaurant An Seana-Ché feeding us the best of fish, fresh from the ocean, or the best of steaks. Paddy Mahony of Iasc Uí Mhathúna Teo. was our sponsor, and he was a fantastic support – loads of gear. Brilliant.

We'd been there with Kerry, though not as often as would be the case in later years, but it was a special time. I know it's a cliché, but these were the lads you'd grown up with, the boys you'd cycled miles to training with. An Ghaeltacht was a club that, up to two years previously, had never won a county championship. Yet here we were, daring to dream, and we injected hysteria into the whole area, from young to old, basically.

If I look back now, did we make any mistakes? Possibly. With Kerry we never stayed in a big hotel in the centre of Dublin for a big game: we always stayed out a bit.

That St Patrick's Day morning we were in a hotel in the city, and there were plenty of supporters in and around the place in high spirits. Players don't need that: they need the peace in order to get zoned in properly. Which isn't to say that the supporters knocked some craic out of it. I wasn't there myself, obviously, but I saw the video afterwards: all the club members met somewhere in Dublin, more than three hundred people, and walked to Croke Park from the city centre, with a real currach on their shoulders. Roaring songs, bands playing – the whole lot.

That day the upper tier in Croke Park was supposed to be closed – a club final would never fill the stadium – but that day they had to open it up, the crowd was so big.

That was about the time I started to blossom as a half-back. I was centre-back, a position I loved, though I didn't get a great run at centre-back for Kerry. Jack put me in there for a few games, but I'd have preferred a good cut at it. When you're wing-back you have one avenue of attack, really: down the sideline next to you. At centre-back you can read the game and dictate things. You see a big knot of lads there? Then you can drive the other way.

And with the club I had that freedom. I was told to go if I wanted to, and I loved it. I was flying. I got man of the match in the county final, the Munster club final and the All-Ireland club semi-final.

But that meant Caltra were able to do their homework on me for the final itself. In that game I had two men on me. I was the defender, but the forward marked me instead. I never played in a game like it. My man couldn't have cared less where the ball was or what was happening: all he cared about was stopping me from running. And eventually I got frustrated and threw him out of the way, and I duly got a yellow card for that. I was thinking, This is going to be a long day here.

At half time in that game I said to Darragh that I couldn't get past this fella, and he would have said to me – roared, to be honest – that that's when you had to be mentally tough, to drive it no matter how and get into the game.

I came into it in the second half a bit more, all right, but it was just one of those games … We lost by a point, having played terribly.

It was heartbreaking. Not winning that game is the biggest regret of my career.

I knew straight away after it that, as a rural club, with the small numbers at our disposal, it would be very hard for An Ghaeltacht to get the chance to get back there.

And, funnily enough, Caltra, the club who beat us, were in a similar situation. They didn't make it back, and they haven't been a power in Galway football since that All-Ireland title either. They had the family thing going on, like us; they were a country side, like us; and they died a death like us as well after it.

The day we played them they were good, in fairness. Michael Meehan was class, and Noel Meehan was outstanding at full-forward; he fell in with Galway after that game. Michael kicked everything off the ground for them in frees, while Ó Cinnéide and Aodán had off-days for us with our frees. I can say that because I had an off-day myself. Darragh played away, ploughed it on at midfield – and to think we were so poor and yet came so close … But we didn't deserve it, simple as that. Did Caltra play above themselves? Maybe.

We had a night out in Dublin afterwards, but it was just gut-wrenching, we were so down. And it was the beginning of the end for the team, really. We never won a county title after that, even though we continued to be competitive in Kerry.

We should have won more, I think. I was talking recently enough to Cathal Dowd, another great player we had, and he said, 'I think we were lucky enough to win the two counties.'

'No, man,' I said. 'We should have won one more, at least.'

I think it was within us to do it. The crucial thing, looking back, was simply that we enjoyed it. There was no real pressure. We enjoyed the training, enjoyed the games. The sessions weren't too long, with no specific physical trainer, unlike now.

My attitude would be that these physical trainers … they're not football men: they're university graduates with no background in the GAA, and some (though not all) train you like an Olympic athlete rather than like a footballer. They might as well be training 1,500-metre runners. Now, they do have their purpose. I respect Cian O'Neill: he's from a football background and tailors his physical preparation plan to a GAA background. But I never trusted some of them. I much preferred the hard, hard stuff John O'Keeffe made us do, the older stuff, to what Pat Flanagan did with us, even though he was very good for Kerry and very good for us.

———

It wasn't all fun and games, of course. There was the time when Darragh was sent off playing for the club behind in Gallarus against Austin Stacks, something a lot of people would be familiar with and would be keen on bringing up in conversation.

It was 2002, and Darragh was Kerry captain. Big following there at the game for the Stacks. Big following for us. Townies versus the country boys. Which we loved.

(Just as background: at about that time we played Strand Road inside in Tralee – Kerins O'Rahilly's – and Bomber Liston was in charge of them. Ó Cinnéide had a free on the right wing, so he was taking it off his left. Bomber roars in, 'Who does this guy think he is, Maurice Fitz?' And what I loved was that there was no spoken reply from us. Ó Cinnéide just put it over and ran out. The perfect answer.)

Against the Stacks that night, on a tight field – two physical teams, big, strong men – what happened was exactly what you'd expect. There was plenty of clattering.

We always pushed the boundaries with referees at club level. Whether it was right or wrong, the feeling existed among players that 'He won't put off a county player,' and this game was right before we were supposed to play Cork in the All-Ireland series – a game that was all the bigger because they'd beaten us already in the Munster Championship in the replay in Páirc Uí Chaoimh.

Anyway, in the Stacks match there was a skirmish, and Darragh lamped some young lad, who landed on the ground. Darragh did wrong, and, after the referee consulted the umpire, he came out and gave Darragh a red card.

There was war as a result. What really angered me right then and there was that some of the Stacks players were on the fringe of the county panel themselves and were egging on the ref to send him off. When it happened they cheered him off the field. I couldn't believe that.

I asked the referee if he'd given Darragh a straight red.

He said he had.

I said, 'Are you insane?' My thinking was obviously, We're playing with Kerry in a couple of weeks – what the hell? It was wrong, but that's the way you'd be thinking.

PO was Kerry manager at the time, and he was at the game, but when he saw the red card coming out he just walked out the gate and went home.

I saw red myself. I was marking Billy Sheehan, who plays for Laois now, and I must have cleaved him about three times: I floored him, left the boot in, drew kicks across him, the poor bastard. Everything. I could have hurt him badly, but I knew well I wouldn't be sent off. If he sent two of us off it was the end altogether.

With fourteen men we became possessed, and we beat them. It was madness.

The referee was out in the middle of the field at half time, and the chairman of the county board, Seán Walsh, walked out to talk to him, right there and then. In full view of everybody. Where else would you see it?

To be fair, it was huge news, the Kerry captain and our midfield general sent off and gone for a huge game against Cork in Croker.

I'd say if you asked Seán now if he'd do it he'd say no, he probably wouldn't go out at all; but that's why the players respected him so much: he was a players' man.

It was obvious what was going on: we'd lost our main man, going in against Cork a couple of weeks later. And the craziness wasn't confined to the pitch. Liam Higgins was a commentator with Radio Kerry at the time, and he was a great footballer in his own time – a great football man, and a great fan of ours, and of Darragh in particular. A very clever guy, well read, taught in the CBS – but he lost his head too. Higgins was roaring in commentary for Radio Kerry – 'I can't believe it!' – and when they went to a break at half time he threw the earphones off and tried to scale the wire to get in at the referee. He'd have done it, too.

The red card was overturned afterwards. Darragh made it back in the end, and we beat Cork.

I don't know if that whole controversy would have bothered other counties, but it didn't bother Kerry. It certainly didn't bother Darragh, who carried on with training as though nothing had happened, and it didn't harm our preparations or make us adjust them in any way. We had Cork in our sights all along.

———

Up to 2006, say, An Ghaeltacht were still competitive, still holding our own. But I think our mistake – and it's one a lot of clubs make – was that we weren't looking after what was coming after us.

We had big problems with numbers: we'd always have a Kerry minor player or two on the way, but we'd lose them when they went to university, or for other reasons. They'd drift away from the game. In total I'd say there were thirty or forty lads lost – or allowed to be lost – to the club in that way, and I thought that was very sad.

If you look at Nemo Rangers in Cork, in comparison, it's just a given that the commitment is always there. I know they're a huge club with tradition and success, but you don't need that to learn the ethos of a successful club, which is basically that you keep putting back into the club: you keep nurturing the youth.

Towards the end, when fellas asked me why I retired from the club, I pointed out that I didn't retire from the club: I retired from all football.

I don't know if I didn't have the desire; I didn't feel I had to be playing it.

———

When the club were going well we were going off playing Kerry in challenge games. With lads in Dublin and Cork and Limerick, we often trained in Killarney rather than bring everyone all the way back to Gallarus.

Yet by 2015 we were in Division 3, down in intermediate. Talk about a fall from grace. An Ghaeltacht struggling – when they shouldn't be – and the players go to America rather than give the club the commitment. I wouldn't blame lads for that, because if I didn't play for the county I might have done the same.

Now, though, there are young fellas involved as officers; there are young people involved with teams. It's brilliant to see the interest there, and what I love is that I could walk back to the middle of the under-10s and they wouldn't know me at all.

That's what makes a club, that everyone is working for the same cause. There was a time in An Ghaeltacht when it was just one man, Liam Ó Rócháin. Then we had one group, and we forgot about other things in the running of the club, and that's important: you have to have it off the field as well.

Towards the end with the club I was getting cranky, and that showed that I didn't have the same fitness. When I was going well I was easily able to mark one of the opposition's best forwards and still contribute handsomely up front: by the end of the hour he'd be marking me, rather than the other way around. At the end, though, I might be put out on some twenty-year-old, and I'd be so exhausted from running around with him, buzzing from sideline to sideline, that I wouldn't be able to get up the field. You'd hear the young lad being told from the sideline, 'Take him for a spin! Take him for a run!'

I'd associate it with what Paul Galvin was saying when he packed it in, that he wasn't enjoying the football. Maybe it was a sign that I should have taken a break for a while.

When I packed it in I didn't miss the games or the training, but as Kerry started chugging last year, and won the All-Ireland, that gave me such a lift that it got the juices flowing again.

Then I started thinking about playing football again, but the logistics meant I couldn't commit myself to the level An Ghaeltacht would need, or to the fitness I would need. For me to go back there it's five and a half hours – a match. Then back. If I was going back I just couldn't do half-committed stuff.

—

I'm in Cork since 2001. I remembered the old Nemo clubhouse in towards Turner's Cross, and I wandered in there one day with Aodán for a pint.

We sat down, and Dinny Allen and Jimmy Kerrigan were in the club as well. They came over and introduced themselves, which I thought was a touch of class.

I liked the attitude out there: no airs and graces, no shouting, 'Look what we've done.' I got connected with them in meeting the likes of Stephen O'Brien, Steven Callinan and Billy Morgan – and there was no Cork–Kerry antagonism, no slagging, no bullshit.

If you were in there with a few pints on you, they wouldn't be telling the world about you and what you were up to. I have great time for that club, and it's not based on them being successful.

Over the years, I was approached by numerous clubs in Cork asking me to play for them, given that I was living here. When I retired, two other clubs in Cork offered me money to play for them.

I have nothing against the other clubs in Cork: after this length of time living in the county I have buddies in all those clubs. But my lining out for Nemo had nothing to do with money. My young lad was up there, and I liked their approach, the way they coached kids. And the way they coached adults, too.

At training one night, the likes of Stephen O'Brien and Colin Corkery were training our team on half the field, and there was a minor team training on the other half. I headed away in after training and came out twenty minutes later, and there were Corkery and O'Brien, after falling in with the minors, taking them in groups.

In our club back home, when a lot of fellas left An Ghaeltacht they *left* it. In Nemo I've noticed that they always come back: even some of the current seniors they have would be involved with under-age teams.

Maybe for that reason there have been rumours for the last few years that I was on the verge of joining Nemo; and when those rumours went around, sure enough I'd have a call from another club – 'Just tell us what's involved' – but none of those rumours were true.

As long as I was able to play, I played for An Ghaeltacht. And Nemo never asked me to play for them. They understood I was a clubman at home.

The obvious question, I suppose, is 'Well, if you're such a clubman, how come you joined Nemo?'

I was thirty-six, thirty-seven, the body was in fair shape, but I'd had a severe back injury – a bulging disc – and I knew it would have been counter-productive to go back with An Ghaeltacht.

They're my club. They always will be. I'll never be a Nemo Rangers man, but as long as I'm connected with them I'll give them what I can. I have a bit of pride in me: I want to show what I can do. I probably want to do more than that, which mightn't be a great idea.

After Kerry won the All-Ireland, I played in Tommy Griffin's over-35s tournament in Dingle, and the body wasn't too bad, so I said I'd give B football a lash.

The Tomás Ó Sé that Nemo got, though, isn't the Tomás Ó Sé who was running up and down Croke Park ten years ago. That time I was able to get up the field, pass the ball off and get back to my position – and to do the same three minutes later. My fitness and my running were my strengths.

Would I be able to do that now? I have my doubts. I don't want to be rolling around on the ground with some kid in west Cork either, but I have enough sense to avoid that kind of thing at this stage.

Well, I'd I hope so, anyway.

Chapter 5

CORK

Cork are the old enemy. The constant. You were guaranteed to meet them at least once every year. Be sure that I wanted to beat them every time: once I crossed the line I wanted to get it over on them, absolutely.

But as a kid I had no hatred of Cork. I had, and have, great respect for them and the great teams and players they've always produced: Billy Morgan, Dinny Allen, Ray Cummins, Jimmy Barry-Murphy, Larry Tompkins, Steven O'Brien. Great names.

Páidí had plenty of Cork pals in his time, and I have plenty myself, particularly as I'm living here now almost half my life. I'd have heard all the stories about lads going nuts in the dressing-room before going out to play Cork, PO among them, but I never heard him talk about them without showing huge respect.

Growing up, I never saw any hatred of Cork from PO, certainly. And I never had any hatred of Cork, either. Apart from when I was on the field.

Being brought up in an area with nothing but football, I always heard about the lads in Rathmore or Gneeveguilla, the border areas between the two counties, having the banter with lads from Cork; but the traffic that went through PO's pub all year round was unbelievable. If you went in there on a Saturday afternoon there'd be people from Dublin, from Cork – and the ball-hopping would be savage, particularly if there was a big game coming up, or just gone.

The big ones were always the Munster final and the All-Ireland final, but even without them the football talk just never stopped: comparing players, comparing games, talking about what was going to happen, how this fella would do, how that fella would go in the game. All football, all the time.

And as a Kerry footballer you're tested against Cork. Judged. No disrespect to the likes of Clare or Tipperary – you could play a great game against those counties for Kerry – but if you didn't do it then against Cork there was a question mark over you. You had to do it against them because they were always the best team in Munster for putting it up to Kerry.

In the early stages of the 1996 Munster Championship, for instance, PO was on the phone to one of the other selectors, and they were talking about players. One of the players PO mentioned was Charlie McCarthy, and his words were, 'He's a man for Cork,' by which he meant that if he could play against Cork he could play against anyone. (And Charlie did play, and played well, for Kerry when they beat Cork down in Páirc Uí Chaoimh in 1996.)

The first time I got a glimpse of the depth of the rivalry, though, was early enough in my playing days. That was when I was playing under-16 in north Kerry, in an under-age intercounty tournament, when I was on the Kerry selection.

Liam Ó Rócháin from our way was a selector, and so was Junior Murphy from south Kerry; but they were also Kerry minor selectors, and they brought in Charlie Nelligan, because he was the Kerry minor coach or manager at the time – a legend in our house and in every house in Kerry, obviously.

Charlie was a bit late to our last game, though, which we lost to Cork. After the game he brought us up to the corner of the field and gave us a spiff, and I saw plenty of hate then. His words always stuck with me. 'Look down there at them,' he said. 'They're after beating ye in your first game, that red jersey. They're the boys ye always have to beat to get anywhere.'

He'd have trampled on their jersey if there was one in front of him, I'd say. His passion was a lot deeper than PO's, even, or mine: after a game I'd be quite happy to sit down and a have a pint with a fella.

I always loved the build-up to the Cork games – reading the papers about it, reading accounts of the past games and looking at videos of them … The desire to win was unbelievable. If you lost, it was galling; if you won, the sense of achievement was massive. It certainly was for me that first time, in the Munster minor final in 1996.

A wet day in Páirc Uí Chaoimh, the crowd coming in for the senior game and getting bigger and bigger. I'd say I had one of my best days ever in a Kerry jersey, at any level, that day.

One part of the experience in particular that stuck with me was the dressing-rooms in the old Páirc. Claustrophobic? They were bad enough when you had a full panel in there as well as selectors, coaches, masseurs; but that time we, the minors, were in one dressing-room, and the next one had the senior team, and both of them using the shower area that connected the two rooms. It was cat.

But when we came in with the cup that day, after winning, the seniors were really revving up for their game. I jumped into the shower, but PO thought of me, in fairness. They were playing the senior final – he had enough on his plate – but he came in to where we were, saw me, and reached in and gave me a hug. 'We'll follow that on today,' he said.

I drenched him to the skin, of course, being still in the shower, but he didn't care.

———

Cork was remote enough to us as a place. There were no Christmas shopping trips up there: I never went further for presents than Dingle. I'd say one of my first visits up to Cork was for a sports scholarship interview at UCC. PO made a phone call to the great Dr Con Murphy about it, and I wanted to go there because of the tradition of Gaelic football there. So, off with me for the interview.

I thought I had it had in the bag, Kerry minor and all that, but Aodán Mac Gearailt, a great pal of mine, ended up getting the scholarship instead. Con putting the good word in for me fecked it up for me, or so I keep telling him. I blamed Con for years for it, obviously, but we got past it eventually.

———

The first day I lined out for Kerry against Cork at senior level was in 1998, in Killarney. Larry Tompkins played the same day for Cork. I'd been a sub the previous year, but I was going well, at corner-back, of all places: I wasn't a corner-back in any way, shape or form.

In training I'd been marking Maurice Fitzgerald a lot and doing well. He was the king at the time, but I'd have had the legs on him at that stage, and if he couldn't get the ball he couldn't hurt you. If he did get the ball, of course, you were finished, because he could do anything with it, and you were likely to spend five minutes getting dizzy as he sold you dummies. But I was quicker than him, so I looked good, and I always liked marking a bigger man, anyway. I never liked marking a small, fast, buzzy player.

So in the run-up to that game in 1998 I'd have spent about six weeks marking Maurice Fitzgerald in training, and then in the Cork game I picked up Aidan Dorgan – the exact opposite kind of player: small, quick, mobile. He didn't kick a lot of ball, but he toasted me, absolutely *toasted* me. He twisted me and turned me, and I got booked after pulling him down a couple of times. Desperate.

When we went in at half time, PO came straight over to me. 'You're gone. We're taking you off.' Darragh came over to me and said not to worry about it.

But after it you had to walk from the dressing-rooms in the corner of Killarney down the sideline, down the length of the stand, and back to the dug-out. The stuff that was roared at me – and at PO. 'Throw on the mother altogether' – all that kind of stuff. (PO himself turned around to me as we walked down along, as much as to say, Now would you look at what you're after drawing on us!)

That had an awful effect on me. I learnt more from that one game than I did from any other, I'd say. It taught me a huge amount about preparation, because that time there was no such thing as analysis, or horses for courses, to put it bluntly.

I wasn't ready for it. It was like a club game where you think the head is right but you go out onto the field and you're picking up some head-the-ball you've never heard of who's testing you, because you're not right.

I thought I was right in 1998, going into the game. There was no shortage of nerves, though. For instance, after the game I showed my togs to Liam Flaherty, and he got a fit of laughing when he saw it: a big shit stain down the back of it. 'How did you even play with those nerves?' said Flaherty.

But what I learnt was to prepare myself. In training I should have been picking up quick players in order to get myself ready for the likes of Dorgan. I'd have focused on him as a player – how he played, what he tended to do with the ball, where he'd go – or else I just wouldn't have been put on him in the first place. I'd have been assigned to a player who suited me.

But that was the way the game was played, even then: you were on a player and that was it. You picked him up, full stop.

I also learnt a little that day about what happened to players after the full-time whistle. Myself and Jack Ferriter walked down the town afterwards. Looking back now, even though I had the baseball cap jammed well down over the face, I had the official gear bag over the shoulder, which was a giveaway. This guy from Dingle came out of nowhere and started abusing me: 'You were fucking useless today, absolutely useless!' and if he said it once he said it ten times.

Jack said to me, 'Don't turn around to him,' but it stuck in my head.

I never forgot it. I didn't sleep for weeks after that. I questioned myself, about everything. My confidence was in pieces.

At the end of my career I'd have been tougher. If that had happened later on, being taken off like that, I'd have demanded a second chance if that was how it had gone in the first half; but, in fairness, I was probably only turned nineteen, and it was a different game then.

But the experience, start to finish, taught me a huge amount. I wasn't mentally prepared, not properly, and even though the sports psychologists came in later, that game taught me more than any psychologist ever would about the mental side of preparation.

Towards the end of my career I thought about using psychologists. I'd have spoken to Enda McNulty, a former Armagh footballer who's worked as a sports psychologist with the Irish rugby team. But I'd have spoken to him only briefly, and by phone. I read Brian O'Driscoll's book and saw that he bought into that hugely, and O'Driscoll would be a hero of mine, but I just couldn't buy into it totally.

For me, the way to get myself ready was to talk to the likes of PO and Darragh and Marc. What they hadn't gone through in the games wasn't worth talking about, and they'd always boost you up. I wouldn't be speaking to the likes of Jack O'Connor or Éamonn Fitzmaurice about those kinds of things. I suppose I always felt in some way that, by admitting it to them, you were showing weakness.

Or I wouldn't talk to them about in that way, at least. I would discuss it with them, but I'd go about it a particular way. Rather than having a big heart-to-heart, formal discussion, I'd mention something small, and that would lead on to a wider chat. Clearly a lot of lads get benefits from chatting to sports psychologists, but it just wasn't for me. I always felt I could sort my own head out myself.

We never dealt with managers and their approach. We discussed what other teams were likely to do, obviously. But when you consider the level of analysis that teams can do now, compared with then, it's ridiculous.

If I were still playing for Kerry now, and marking Aidan Dorgan in the morning, the management would make fifty or sixty clips of Dorgan available to me, and I'd focus on everything he did: where he went, how he moved. I'd get angles from the sky, from pitch side – everything.

But back then it was word of mouth, basically. Management tended to concentrate on the main men in the opposing team, the high-profile players, though I often said in the dressing-room before a game that we had to be wary of those unknown lads, that they couldn't be underestimated.

In fairness, that was always a strength of ours: we gave every opponent huge respect. That's why we never had a slip-up against a Waterford or a Clare or any team like that.

———

One key aspect of those early years was Larry Tompkins standing on the sideline for Cork. It was about 1987 when I was old enough to take notice of football, and at about that time Cork and Meath were *the* teams. If we were playing a game among ourselves as kids we'd call over to PO, and he'd pull out a huge box he had that was stuffed with jerseys from every county in Ireland. We'd pull out Cork and Meath jerseys, and off with us to re-enact the All-Ireland.

And Tompkins was a huge figure then. A hero. He and Liam Hayes and Mick Lyons – they were the lads we were imitating that time, rather than Kerry, because Kerry were in a lull.

As Cork manager Tompkins was up against a good Kerry team, and I thought we just had it over them. For instance, we never lost to Cork in Killarney, and that became a factor for us.

Even in 2013, the last year in which I played in Killarney, Kerry were reckoned to be weak, and Cork were the overwhelming favourites for that game. But that was something we put a huge emphasis on in preparing ourselves for the game: we didn't want to lose our record in Killarney, and we didn't, which means I never lost a championship game to Cork in Killarney in my career.

I got on well with Larry, but early enough in my career he wouldn't have known me too well, obviously.

In 2000 we won the All-Ireland, and along the way we beat Cork in Killarney. It was the hottest day I ever played a game of football: the windows were locked in the dressing-room, and, going down the town after, you had to walk only on the footpath, because the tar was literally melting on the road.

That day I hit Philip Clifford with one of the best shoulders I ever dished out. Everything clicked for us after Steven O'Brien, of all people – one of the greats at holding onto possession and not doing anything stupid – gave the ball away, and we went upfield to score. We drove on after that and won the game.

Later that year, after we won the All-Ireland and the lads brought the cup back west, myself, Fitzmaurice and Noel Kennelly decided we'd hit for Cork. We said we'd head into Tompkins's pub, because it was a GAA pub, and because we were fresh and sober at that stage of the evening.

When we walked in, we were asked for ID. I said, 'Leave it off, we'll go,' and Fitzie felt the same. But there was a bit of a spark in Kennelly, and he produced his ID, but we were told we weren't getting drink anyway.

I was surprised, because if it were PO he'd have welcomed in a team even if they'd hammered his own crowd down into the ground.

But I can imagine Larry and his staff were probably thinking, The boys are after winning an All-Ireland, and here they come to rub it into my face. But if Larry felt we had ulterior motives, I can honestly say we didn't. One of the best lessons we were ever taught was how to behave when you win and when you lose. Later on I got to know him on the International Rules, when he was a selector, and you couldn't find a sounder man.

———

I came to live in Cork after university, in 2001. I came down and moved in with Aodán Mac Gearailt while I was working in Fermoy – he was working in Carrigaline – and from the get-go I've enjoyed living here. I was living out in Douglas from the start, and I'd have stayed quiet always. For one thing I'm a schoolteacher, and I don't need any attention. For another, living in Douglas was always perfect in the build-up to big games.

The only people who'd recognise you would be your own pals, and Cork people have enough sporting heroes of their own walking the streets – soccer players, hurlers, footballers – without paying attention to a Kerry footballer. Half the Munster rugby team lived in Douglas – sure why would they have paid attention to me?

Living in Cork suited me. Always has. I've never had a smart comment or an altercation with supporters in my time there. Never had grief. I'd go out the night of a game and mix away, but never a problem.

Mind you, there was one evening …

We beat Cork in the All-Ireland semi-final of 2008, and the day after, the Monday, we had a training session. After that, all the lads based in Cork – myself, Tom O'Sullivan and David Moran, as well as Kieran Donaghy, for some reason, though he was living in Tralee – went back to Cork and had a few pints.

Now, having lost the game the day before, the Cork lads weren't training, and that night, when we walked into Rearden's, the whole Cork panel were inside there after a day of it, and Doug Howlett, the All Black signed by Munster, was with them.

We went to a corner by ourselves, because we didn't want to be raining on anyone's parade. We came across Mick Galwey in there, so we had a bit of craic with him, a couple of pints. Grand.

When Rearden's closes, the range of choices wouldn't be that big in Cork on a Monday evening, so when we came out onto Washington Street yours truly heard some noise coming from the Courthouse Bar over the road. I knew the barman, so I suggested we go there.

But the barman, Mike, said, 'Look, the Cork lads are in here.'

I said, 'Sure there's no problem.'

In we went. I knew straight away it was a mistake, though. I saw the bottle of whiskey up on the counter. Trouble.

Between the jigs and the reels, myself and Derek Kavanagh got into some pulling and dragging. I had a lovely jumper, and that was the major casualty from the evening.

I was sorry, because I'd have got on with Derek's brother Larry and all the Nemo lads, but it was all handbags, really. Nothing major. I got a buzz from Derek the following day, and it was sorted out straight away. No problem. The stories that went around Cork after that were probably far better than the reality, which was that very little happened (it was more funny than anything else).

The funniest thing was that Doug Howlett jumped off the chair and was ready to get stuck in to the ruck, only for Mick Galwey to tell him to sit the fuck back down or he'd have his head taken clear off his shoulders.

———

I'd have never rubbed it into the Cork lads' faces. We beat them often enough, and they beat us, and I never had a problem with them. Any of them I've met or that I know are sound. I roomed with Graham Canty outside in Australia for two weeks, a lovely fella.

My thing was that I didn't like getting to know players from other counties while I was playing. Since retiring I've got to know a load of fellas, but I wanted to keep a distance from them when I was playing, because it was easier to play against them when you didn't know them.

When we played Cork we went to war with them, and when we lost … I remember losing to Cork plenty of times, such as in the 1999 Munster final down the Páirc, a soaking wet day. We would have been complaining that time about Maurice Fitz getting mauled in the corner by Ronan McCarthy, but sure we'd have done the exact same thing ourselves. It's what you do. That's the beauty of rivalry, and our rivalry with Cork was a serious one.

It hurt to lose. It hurt when we heard them going up the steps of the Páirc and singing their songs when they got the cup, and it didn't do much for the humour. We probably wouldn't have surfaced for a week afterwards. But I knew well to leave it on the other side of the white lines. I was living in Cork, and the last thing I'd have ever wanted was to be getting into trouble, doing silly things off the field.

———

I get on well with Billy Morgan too. You hear plenty of stories about him, that he's mad. We're all mad! PO was mad himself. In my eyes, Billy is one of the great managers of the GAA: All-Irelands with Cork and Nemo, Sigerson – a class act who got every ounce out of Cork, and the exact type of man they need right now.

I asked PO about him one time, and he said, 'A gent – an absolute gentleman. A street-fighter on the line, of course.' That was a great description of Billy, and a great compliment from PO. And Billy would tell you the second part of that himself anyway if you were having a cup of coffee with him, that he'd cut you in two if you met him on the field. The respect those fellas have for the great Kerry team – Billy and Dinny Allen and all these guys, and the respect the Kerry lads have for them – that tells you everything. Billy's a passionate man, and I love that.

One of the great things about the GAA for me is the tradition of a manager visiting the other dressing-room, win, lose or draw. Billy would have been a great pal of our doctor, Dave Geaney, going back to their UCC days, and of course that UCC connection is very strong for Kerry, and very important for Kerry.

In 2009 we beat Cork in the All-Ireland, playing very well the same day, and Daveen went out to ask Billy to come in and say a few words, even though the days of managers going into the opposition dressing-room were gone, really.

But Billy came in. He spoke from the heart and was hugely honest. He got emotional. Daveen was emotional himself – he was crying next to Billy – and the next day the lads were still talking about it, about how Billy came in and spoke so well. You would have struggled to connect the guy speaking so emotionally in the dressing-room with the one you saw on the sideline during a match, because the guy on the sideline can be ferocious. (One of the best stories I ever heard from Dr Con was when someone asked if he'd ever saved a man's life on the field. 'I did,' said Con. 'When Tommy Sugrue [the referee] gave the free against us in 1988 I saved his life, because I stopped Billy going out on the field to him after the game.')

One day we were playing Cork – in Cork – and I was marking Noel O'Leary. How he was up wing-forward I have no idea, but I was flying along the sideline at one stage with him when I heard Billy roaring – and I mean *roaring* – at Noel, 'Take him on! Take him on!' Something snapped inside in me when I heard that, of course, and I gave Noel a good rap with the closed fist into the belly as we were going full pelt. Fair play to him, he took it and kept driving on, but I nearly started laughing when I saw how Billy took it: he lost the head altogether and was roaring in at me. I just loved that attitude.

I never saw Ring, obviously, but for me Billy Morgan and Jimmy Barry-Murphy are the two greatest sporting icons in Cork. Sure PO had a shrine of Billy Morgan photographs back behind in the pub. What more can you say?

———

During the rivalry with Cork, when Conor Counihan was managing them, I thought Jack O'Connor was cuter in doing his homework and in his tactics. Sometimes Counihan would change his teams, but we always expected that. We'd know their strengths; we'd know they'd try to get the ball to Michael Cussen, or to get Paul Kerrigan to run with the ball, and that's where the analysis came in: we were ready for every avenue.

The 'horses for courses' attitude helped us too: you always had a man to go to. I might go out on Pearse O'Neill rather than on a smaller, faster player, for instance. That was down to Jack.

One point you'd have to make is the pressure on the likes of Counihan, and on other managers. I'd be filling up with petrol in Cork after a game, and a random guy might come over and cut the living shit out of the Cork players and management. I'd just say, 'Look, I don't agree with that,' and head off. Very unfair. That team of Counihan's very often had the measure of us in Munster, but they could never get on top of us in Croker. Even though they won one All-Ireland, I felt they possibly could have won more.

When we were playing against Cork in Croke Park in 2007, 2008 and 2009 there was a bit of fear involved for us – a fear of losing to Cork. We knew they were capable of beating us, but, by God, they weren't going to beat us up there.

That time we had a team that could play any way you wanted. If you wanted to mix it up physically, fine, we'd do that. If you wanted to play wide open, fine, we could play that way too. But we knew we had Cork's card marked.

As part of that, Darragh was crucial to us in the middle of the field. I loved his attitude: if he was beaten for one ball, for a second ball, then you'd watch his man for the third ball, because he'd cleave him rather than lose the next one.

At that time people were saying that Nicholas Murphy was getting bullied by Darragh, but I can recall a game I played in against Cork where Nicholas was up in the half-forwards against me, and he kicked me hard in the calves. At first I thought he was just being awkward, but then it happened again, and I got stuck into him.

Darragh was retired at that stage, and when I met him after the game, I said, 'Jesus, your man ...'

'Kicked you across the back of the legs, did he?' said Darragh. 'They all thought I was acting the hard case in the middle of the field, but often enough he started it.' (It's easy to have a laugh about it off the field.)

I was only laughing then, because we all knew that Cork found Darragh a very tough nut to crack.

We had time for Cork. We never disrespected them, but we knew where to go at them, to hit them where they were strongest.

Cork thought they were strongest around the middle, so that's where we hit them. You had Galvin powering in, Séamus powering in, Darragh, Brosnan – we had plenty of big men in there too.

Galvin was very good that way. He'd leave his own man and come out into the middle, and he'd hit the hard men they had. Canty, for instance, was a main man for Cork, but we'd always make certain sure that he wouldn't be coming up the field that often against us. We'd be quite happy to have another one of the half-backs coming upfield instead of him, because he'd lift the whole team if he got running upfield. That's where the phrase 'hammer the hammer' comes from – to hit the strongest players the opposition have.

Did that Cork team underachieve? Possibly, but I wouldn't lay the blame on the players there, because that comes from management and players alike. We lost All-Irelands ourselves: we lost in 2011, and you could say we left an All-Ireland after us that year.

Fellas would ask you if you'd transfer anyone from another team in to play with you in Kerry. Cork had very very good players in Anthony Lynch, Graham Canty, Colin Corkery, Derek Kavanagh, Nicholas Murphy; but I wouldn't bring any player in from that Cork team, for this reason: we had players like Darragh, Maurice Fitzgerald, Séamus Moynihan, the Gooch, Declan. Those were players who, to me, were great, great players – guys who were on a different level.

I don't think Cork had anyone at that level. Possibly Lynch and Canty every now and again, but they were put to the sword by us plenty of times as well. They had plenty of excellent players, and have always had good players, but they just didn't have enough of them all over the field. I just wouldn't put any of them in the class of those five players I mentioned.

Those were guys who could dominate games, particularly if you had a few lads who weren't performing.

People would have focused on who we had out around the middle – and we had great players out there – but look back the field and you had Mike McCarthy and Tom O'Sullivan. Over the years they just quashed the best forwards our opponents had. Constantly.

Against Cork you weren't going to face outstandingly dangerous forwards. In training we'd face Declan, Donaghy, Darren, Galvin, Gooch – it was very, very hard to cover all those all the time. I just felt that, against Cork, if you could mark their top three forwards, where else were the scores going to come from? They weren't going to come from the lads they had out around the middle of the field.

When I saw Aidan Walsh come on the scene, I thought, Here's a guy who could be special. One day down in Killarney against us he might have scored 1-3 from midfield. I was thinking, If this guy is minded and looked after the right way, he could become the next Jacko. And I wasn't alone in thinking that.

He never seemed to push on, though, and maybe that was the hurling. With us in Kerry, coming from where we were, where there was only football, that wouldn't have been a factor. Rugby and soccer came in later on, but none of the footballers played those sports, or if they did it was just to keep fit in the winter. Gaelic football was the game.

In Cork you'd have to admire fellas like JBM, Ray Cummins – people who played both sports, who won All-Irelands and All-Stars in both football and hurling. You'd have to admire that, and respect it.

I respect the Cork lads I played against too. I felt we had a better team than them in that period, and we had to believe that if we were to win games. But we got our beatings too down here.

And things go beyond football too. When we played Cork in Killarney in 2002 my father was there, and I'd say it was the only time he saw myself, Darragh and Marc play together for Kerry. Fergal, my other brother, said he was unbelievably nervous watching it, fidgeting and moving around in the stand.

We drew that game, the replay fixed for a couple of weeks later in Páirc Uí Chaoimh. A couple of days after the drawn game I was talking to my father on the phone, a great chat about the game and how it went. Little did I know that it was the last time I'd speak to him.

There was a bit of a deal made about the game going ahead, but that was never an issue for us, honestly. We never said, 'They're putting that game on, then?' or anything like that. Whether it was being played a month later or two days later, it was going to have to be played.

What was an issue, in a good way, was how many of the Cork lads went to the funeral: Anthony Lynch, Mícheál Ó Cróinín, Noel

O'Leary, Graham Canty – all those lads came down. They came in and met us and offered their respects.

That was unreal. Beyond football. That's the strength of the GAA, how fellas row in if there's a big problem. All the older Cork players were there as well. In fairness, it was an unbelievable show of respect.

The day Dad was buried we trained with Kerry. We went down to Killarney and togged off. It was more to show the lads back in Killarney that we were going to be in the right frame of mind than anything else.

We asked our mother if it was okay; the funeral was over, and there were only a few friends and family around. We went over and togged, and the lads appreciated it.

In the replay itself I got a ball early and drove up the middle with it, past a few lads – but after it I was shattered. Darragh was captain, and that was very important to all of us, to do well for him, and he certainly wasn't using what had happened as a shield. He was driving it on, barking at fellas at half time, shouting orders, all that.

It was hard to take the defeat, though. Cork celebrated at full time like they'd won an All-Ireland, which they were entitled to do; but I was emotional enough myself coming off the field. I couldn't even shake hands with Dr Con: I just headed to the dressing-room. We mightn't have had anything to drink the night of the funeral, but we made up for it the few days after that.

There was a lot made of it, but what was significant was that there were three of us playing, Darragh was captain and PO was manager.

To his credit, PO was immense that year as a manager. People had the notion of a mad dog in the dressing-room, but he was a lot more calculated than that – and far cuter. I never heard a manager speak better in getting his team right for a game: we were pumped every time.

We played the best football I ever saw from Kerry that year, but it didn't matter a damn when we lost the All-Ireland. I'd see the odd article or comment to the effect that, for Kerry, it's all about the football. It's not: at that level it's all about winning. That's why I tip my hat to Éamonn Fitzmaurice, because his Kerry team won an All-Ireland after they weighed up their options and realised they wouldn't win playing pretty football.

We had great careers and we couldn't have any complaints, but, as I've said, that's one regret, that Darragh didn't get to bring the cup back into our own house. We saw it in PO's place but not in our own. We achieved everything you could in football, but not that, and the Armagh defeat was the sickest. The Dublin loss in 2011 was pretty bad, but, given everything that happened in 2002, winning the final would have been sweet.

———

I was always worried Cork might catch us, though, always concerned that we might lose to them, particularly in 2007 and 2009, the All-Ireland finals. The three weeks before those games you'd have fellas whispering it: 'Imagine losing to them. Imagine it.' And me, living in Cork ... Any time we'd lose a quarter-final or semi-final I wouldn't watch the subsequent matches – that'd be bad enough – but the prospect of losing to Cork was unthinkable.

I have the utmost regard for a county that can produce the Roy Keanes, the Ronan O'Garas, the Jimmy Barry-Murphys and the Billy Morgans. All the sports. If Kerry were divided up between sports the same way, there's not a hope that we'd have the All-Irelands we do have.

Cork is the greatest sporting county in Ireland, there's no doubt about that, but I think that comes against their Gaelic footballers. If hurling is the number one sport in your particular area in Cork, then that's the sport you'll go with. I see youngsters in my school in

Fermoy and they're brilliant at all sports; they might get picked by rugby or hurling coaches, but by the time they're sixteen or seventeen a lot of them are sick of sports. They're burnt out.

There's a great effort made in Cork at minding youngsters, but that's hard to do when you have rugby, soccer, football and hurling.

One of my strongest ties to Cork is Dr Con Murphy, of course, the Cork team doctor, football and hurling, for the last forty years. Con is Mr UCC, and he got PO down to coach UCC. He could write a great book, he has so many stories, but the only issue is that he'd bury lads in every county if he told half of them.

He's great company, one of the wittiest men I know, though if you're talking to him he's not listening to you at all half the time, because he's gone into his memory bank for a story that'll bury the one you just told yourself. When we were in Australia with the International Rules and he got a phone from the GAA for the trip, I'd say every player on the panel got a rattle off that phone, with him ringing home with it.

He's a great friend to me – and to lots of players in the GAA. The favours he's done for people, the connections he has … When I was playing, if I hurt myself on a Thursday evening I had only to ring him and I'd have a scan or an X-ray the following day.

But he's Cork behind it all. Last year, when the Sam Maguire was up from Kerry, we had a night with it in the South County, and I invited him over for a drink: no piss-taking, just for a pint.

No, he said, not for me.

I liked that. He's a proud Corkman, emotional and passionate about Cork, and the service he's given Cork is phenomenal.

Are my kids Cork kids? Would they play for Cork? That's a good one. I wouldn't be pushed about that kind of thing, because my father wasn't like that himself. He never pushed us about playing, and I always thought it was the best approach.

But I don't think they're Cork kids, for all that. I had Mícheál up with Con one day, and Con had some of the Cork blood sub jerseys, number 30 and that, in the office, and he gave Mícheál one of them. Now, I knew well he wouldn't be wearing it, but after we went home I forgot all about it.

But about a year and a half later we were back up with Con, and he asked Mícheál about the jersey.

'Ah, when we went home my dad threw that in the bin,' says Mícheál.

Sure I'd forgotten I'd done that. But I had.

With teams, I'd be more attracted to individual personalities than to the teams themselves maybe. For instance, I think Jimmy Barry-Murphy is a class act, so I like to see the Cork hurlers do well on his account. He's a legend, and I'd like to have seen them win the All-Ireland against Clare a couple of years ago.

I like the Kilkenny hurlers too – their stance and their attitude, and the way they keep going, keep winning, keep driving on. Same with United: I latched onto them because of Keane; the likes of O'Driscoll put me onto rugby. Personalities.

———

I was in Cork for the player strikes, of course. I couldn't help but compare how the Cork lads felt about their officials with our situation, and one huge advantage we always had was our county board. They were always seeking to do the best for us, to help us. If I was looking for a pair of boots and I couldn't get the kit man or the secretary, I'd just ring the chairman, and he'd make sure the boots were there for me. Not his job at all, but he'd get it done.

There was no ego there. They were there to facilitate us, to help everyone. For me, with the Cork situation, looking in from outside, I just felt that if someone was put in to manage, unless things were

really, really bad you couldn't stand up and say, 'We don't want you.'
Players play, managers manage, and officers officiate.

I felt that was wrong, but obviously if you have thirty or more
players saying they had issues, there was something up. It always seems
to come back to Frank Murphy when people are giving out, and all I
can say is that he's been a gentleman in all my dealings with him.

Now that doesn't mean one side was right, or the other side was
wrong: the players weren't happy, that was clear, but I never really
dug deep into the issue. The fact that I was living there and can
remember the marches and Kieran Mulvey and so on is my only
reason for bringing it it up.

Maybe it's because I'm not from Cork – it's not in me – that I
don't understand it, and I wouldn't want to understand it, but from
our point of view in Kerry, we never had an issue like that, and
because of that I couldn't understand why someone wouldn't want
to play with their county.

Now, to be fair, if there was an appointment to be made in Kerry
the players would be consulted. They'd be asked about candidates.
That doesn't mean we'd be making the appointment, but the board
would put out feelers about it. And Kerry have got the men they
wanted in recent years.

I don't think that kind of trouble would have happened in Kerry.
It did a lot of damage and probably affected a lot of people, particularly the younger lads. But having said all that, I'd be the first to
admit that I wouldn't be *au fait* with everything that happened.

The trouble in Cork … I'm an outsider. I live there, but I wouldn't
pretend that I know the scene inside and out. Cork is my home,
though; the people are class, and far wittier than in Kerry. The city is
like a village, and I enjoy the people, especially their unreal passion
for sport in general.

One great thing about Cork, and living here, is that I loved the
drive from Cork to Killarney for training. Like anybody else, I'd have

plenty going on in my head when I jumped into the car to head to training, about those problems everyone has. But that hour's spin – that was my hour to get zoned in, to get ready for training. I wouldn't answer the phone. I'd be thinking, 'That didn't go for me the last night in training, so I'll focus in on that this evening,' or whatever, and the same, then, on the way home. I might have had a bad night's training and got into the car like a demon, but I'd have the hour's drive to thrash it out in my head on the way home.

Then, back in Cork, the car would be parked and any issues from the night's training left in that when I went in home. I used that time. Leaving at half four, back at half ten in the evening – it was a long night three times a week, but I loved it, and I still miss it.

As a result, I didn't mind travelling on my own. I'd be walking out of Fitzgerald Stadium, and the lads would be calling after me, 'When you're on the Kerry side of the county bounds we'll have the feet up enjoying the tae and biscuits.' I'd be laughing away with them, but the notion that you'd be living in Killarney and that three minutes after getting in your car you'd be at training … That was strange to me.

Cork was good to me that way too: it helped me to prepare for Kerry.

Chapter 6

DUBLIN

Dublin has always been special – not a surprising opinion from a kid who grew up watching the *Kerry's Golden Years* video, or the 'Kerry–Dublin Golden Years', as it might be called more accurately.

The hype is always there with Dublin. Always. In my time playing them they mightn't always have had the best team, but the buzz about them in the build-up was always fascinating. When you played them in the championship there was always a full house, a massive atmosphere – town versus country. And the seventies were always brought up as well. Though, when I look back now, we created a new rivalry of our own in recent years. No wonder: the banter between the supporters, the colour – everything between Kerry and Dublin is special. Two counties with such huge tradition behind them are bound to generate a special rivalry.

It's similar to Cork versus Kerry. Even in the (rare) days when we were going poorly, Kerry would always reckon we had a chance against Cork. Against Dublin we'd be the same. When we started off in the early 2000s against each other, Dublin weren't going that poorly – they were winning Leinster championships – but we'd always have felt that we had their number.

Take the game in Thurles in 2001.

What a game. The crowd, the atmosphere … In Killarney the crowd tends to be more spread out, but in Thurles it's down on top of you – what I'd imagine a Munster hurling championship game is like.

It was a fine day, but the game had to be put back because of the tailbacks: the Dublin supporters wouldn't know their way around the back roads near Horse and Jockey or Littleton the way they'd know the Clonliffe Road, obviously.

That's hard to take, by the way: you're mentally ready, tuned in to go to war in ten minutes, when the ball is thrown in – and the word comes through that the game won't start for another twenty minutes. They're holding you back when you want to cut loose.

At the time, Dublin had a great system going with the impact sub: with the game in the balance they'd send on Vinnie Murphy, and he'd raise the crowd straight away. He'd hop off his man, and the atmosphere would fire up again to spur them on.

Tommy Carr was managing Dublin, a very passionate guy, and a great guy when you'd meet him now; but back then he was the kind of guy you wanted to beat.

But people will remember that game for one reason and one reason only: Maurice's sideline from out on the right wing to draw it.

When we got the sideline I was thinking that, because we needed a point, we might work it in, that we might go short and create an opening for the equaliser from play. But Maurice was well able for the range: in the last few minutes of the 1997 All-Ireland he'd hit a point from out by the sideline as well – a free, but it might as well have been a sideline, it was so far out. It was a phenomenal point, but we were well ahead at the time, so people didn't pay as much attention to it.

That day in Thurles it was different: we weren't ahead, and it wasn't a case where a point or two in the final score didn't matter. We were one down, time was almost up, the atmosphere was rocking. To have the mental toughness to go for it under that amount of pressure … I'm a huge Ronan O'Gara fan, and he'd have that toughness. Mick Galwey told me the Munster players loved O'Gara because he'd always do it under pressure. Maurice was the same.

Tommy Carr was roaring into Maurice's ear, but he nailed it: up yours. I thought about running over and putting Carr up into the stand, but I was too far away. I was on the right wing, after a good battle with Senan Connell, a jinky guy who'd give you trouble, because he'd go here and there. I always preferred a big guy who'd take you on directly, so Senan often caused me bother.

I was down the wing from Maurice when he hit it, not directly in line to see it sail over, but when it curved in and landed it was inspiring. But people couldn't do the things Maurice could do with a ball. He didn't have to do it every day, because he could do it on the day it was needed most.

He's quiet. Shy. Guys like James O'Donoghue would hop a ball with you, but Maurice was never like that. He was an icon already for us, even though he was still playing.

Dublin didn't then have the younger players coming through that they have now. Their strong men were the likes of Dessie Farrell, who was a very clever footballer. He'd know what buttons to press to get a rise out of you – a great man for chatting to you on the field – and with the big bandage on his leg you'd nearly think, We'll have a great time with this fella: he must be half-crocked.

Nearly. Dessie was deceptively fast, very strong. He was someone we always needed marked closely, because he was a leader for them as well.

I got the road in the second game. I cleaved Collie Moran on his way through. I tried to nail him with a shoulder, and my timing was nearly right. But you have to time a shoulder absolutely right, not nearly right, and I didn't. I was a millisecond late, but sure I might as well have been half an hour late: I planted my leg and got him, when I'd have been better off letting him past.

It was the first time I got sent off playing intercounty. People had this idea that I was a dirty so-and-so. I wasn't. I never pulled a really dirty stroke. That was the worst I did, and even then I was genuinely going for the ball: I just mistimed my challenge slightly. Admittedly, I left my leg in, because I knew I'd mistimed the challenge, and there was no way he was going to get through: bang.

I was down on my haunches, but I knew I was in trouble. I looked up and saw the card in the ref's hand. Red.

As they say, I never yet saw a referee change his mind, so I said nothing and walked off, and sat in the dug-out.

Any time and every time I was sent off I was ashamed. I'd feel that I'd let myself down, and that I'd let my teammates down, which was worse. I'd even be half afraid to talk to them. What good are you to them in training when you won't be starting the next game? I missed the Meath game because of a stupid tackle. I should have just taken it when he got a run on me.

That time the journalists could come into the dressing-room after the game, and they were making a bee-line for me, because I'd been put off. Páidí copped it: 'Don't say a word,' he told me.

I said I'd to go to the toilet, and I stayed in there for an hour, I'd say, looking at the cubicle door. When I came out the journalists were gone, and so was everybody else.

There's no worse feeling. In training after that I was put on the B team and was playing wing-forward to make up the numbers, marking Mike Hassett. You feel ostracised, because the manager and the selectors aren't talking to you about the game: you're no good to them, because you're not available. You might as well be injured.

The night before the Meath game I went out in Dublin for a few pints, and while the lads were warming up the next day Páidí was asking me if there was any craic in Dublin: his town.

We always raised it for Dublin. We wouldn't say it out loud, but our reckoning was always that any team you'd play at intercounty level would have at least two very good forwards in their inside line – 'strike forwards', to use the trendy term.

And we always had top man-markers for them. Tom O'Sullivan and Mike McCarthy never got the credit they deserved, and Marc followed on from them when they left. They would really negate the best forwards in the country.

It was a different, more open game then; but that's something that makes me laugh now, when I see the likes of Donegal getting three or four All-Stars for their defenders. If you were playing with ten men behind the ball, as a defender you'd expect to pick up an All-Star every year. Now Karl Lacey won three All-Stars as a defender, a corner-back with plenty of space from him, and my idea of a defender is marking a guy in space, without two lads sweeping in front of you and making it easier – the way Séamus Moynihan, Mike, Tom and Marc did it.

We didn't articulate a feeling of superiority with Dublin. There was never anyone saying, 'We have a better skill-set than these guys.'

We knew what to do. Against Dublin we could go directly to Johnny Crowley that time if we needed to and be confident that he'd either win it or cause havoc when the ball landed.

Still, nobody saw the 2009 defeat coming. We had it won at half time, which is very unusual for an intercounty championship game, but it was certainly true that day.

We were going bad that year – shocking bad. Nobody thinks of that now, but we should have been gone out the gap before we played Dublin at all. Sligo should have beaten us, absolutely, in Tralee. We were flat as anything.

But the build-up, the sight of the blue jersey, the eighty thousand in the stadium, everyone saying, 'Kerry are gone, and this'll be easy for Dublin' …

When I look back, Dublin couldn't have been right for that game mentally, given all that was going on. And they probably learnt a lot more from the experience – the build-up, the game, everything –

than we did. We were fully tuned in and had been working hard in training; but it just wasn't clicking for us, which was why Sligo could have beaten us.

That's why I'd suggest that Dublin should be sent out of Croke Park too: if they'd had to go up to Sligo that time there might have really been a shock.

Alan Brogan's mother is from Listowel, and at one stage in the second half he said to me, 'Fuck this. I'll head down to Listowel and play for the Emmets.' Tongue in cheek, but it shows you how competitive that game was, or wasn't, after half time.

At that point I never felt they could push over the line: they were just a small bit short. One issue Dublin had, and will always have, is dealing with the media. We'd get fits of laughing at it, because it never changed, and it won't change any time soon.

What would happen every year is that they'd hockey a couple of teams in Leinster, and the hype would start building up. All-Irelands. Three in a row. Five in a row. That suited every other county in Ireland, and it wasn't something they could change.

What they could change, though, they changed under Pat Gilroy. I think he learnt a huge amount from that 2009 game. He's a clever guy, a good guy. For instance, we hit them early in that game and put them back on their heels. They didn't start Ciarán Whelan, and by the time they brought him on, Darragh was rightly in the zone.

We were very direct – pummelled them. We were so sharp and so direct that they didn't have the chance to get men back to support their defence. The difference between us and Dublin at that stage was that our experience allowed us to park that game very quickly afterwards. We'd have said among ourselves immediately that Dublin hadn't been fully tuned in and that we'd had it easier than we expected. We would have picked out passages of play and said to each other, 'Look, they didn't put a hand on you there when you had the ball. You're not going to have it that easy the next day out.'

We were brought back down to earth very quickly – by ourselves. We knew the score at that stage, and as a result it was probably the most satisfying All-Ireland we won in my time with Kerry.

Definitely Pat Gilroy learnt from it. Take a step back and look at the team, and they actually had a lot of young talent coming through. When you mixed that with the likes of Alan and Bernard Brogan, Barry Cahill, Ger Brennan and Stephen Cluxton you have a potentially serious outfit on the way.

Gilroy also learnt that they had to be cocooned away from the media in particular. That had to be done, because they're under a different pressure from every other county in Ireland. There's always pressure in Kerry to perform, but the hype isn't the same, and the crucial thing was that we were under that pressure but were winning All-Irelands. We were coping with that. In Dublin at that time they hadn't won any All-Irelands, but they were still under pressure. The hype was all about them winning an All-Ireland when they hadn't managed it.

After they won in 2011 I'd wonder if it got a bit easier for them, because they had an All-Ireland they could point to. In previous years it couldn't have been easy for them to destroy Wicklow in the first round and then hear all and sundry tipping them for the All-Ireland.

In recent years Dublin have led the way, and it's not enough to just say, 'Well, they have the numbers.' They have brilliant leadership in their county board, and they're pumping money into coaching and youth development. Argue all you want, but they're in a battle all the time with rugby, with soccer, more than any other part of the country, and they're still coming out with All-Irelands, with tons of good footballers.

Now, I understand the GAA's viewpoint, that they need the Dubs in Croke Park for big crowds and gate receipts, but I think it's wrong that they play only there. Nobody had an issue with the Dubs playing in Croker until they started winning all the Leinster championships and All-Irelands, but it's still not fair.

For instance, when Kildare were going well the Dubs would have found it hard to go to Newbridge and win a championship game. Same in Navan when Meath were motoring.

I think playing in Croke Park gives them a bit of a comfort zone, which frightens weaker teams. The other thing is that I'd say none of the Dublin team or management – or supporters – would have a problem with playing elsewhere. I actually think they'd enjoy it, and it'd be good for the Leinster Championship. It'd also improve Dublin as a team to face different challenges.

The other point that people forget is that the decision isn't taken by them but by the Leinster Council. It's something I'd really love to see, the Dublin team on the road with their support, having faced them in that kind of scenario back in 2001. I think everyone would win in that case.

———

Jim Gavin … In his dealings with the media I don't know if he's telling the truth or if he's just talking for the sake of it. I used to mark him in challenge games. He was a wing-forward and was tough enough, a solid grafter for the team. An old adversary. I texted him when they won to congratulate him.

I'd get on well with the people I crossed swords with and the people I played with. The odd time someone would say, 'Surely there was some teammate you didn't like, someone who annoyed you.' There wasn't, though.

We had arguments when we were playing, disagreements where you'd bollock someone out of it on the field. Fisticuffs in training, sure, but that's different: forgotten immediately. As for opponents, I just didn't want to get to know them when I was playing, because you didn't want to find out that 'Hey, such and such is a grand guy,' in case it took the edge off when you played them.

I know the Brogans – sound guys. Eoghan O'Gara got in trouble a few years ago, and when I spoke about it on *The Sunday Game* I defended him. I just called it as I saw it: I thought it wasn't as bad as it looked, and Gilroy was on to me saying fair play.

That's an issue for the Dubs, in fairness: if they step out of line in any way at all there's such media attention on them that it's a huge deal. They have to be very careful. Even if they're not in trouble they're still the most analysed, most written about team in Ireland.

In 2014 the hype about them must have affected them, all the talk about five in a row and that nonsense. But they'll learn from that. We were able to compartmentalise our performances after games: the Tuesday evening after a big game we'd have twenty minutes of chat to bring us right back down to earth.

That would have been very easy for us in 2009, convincing ourselves that we were great fellas altogether and that we'd win the All-Ireland at our ease. But the fact that we'd been through the experience, and that we had plenty of leaders to talk us back down afterwards in the dressing-room, made all the difference.

Dublin have advantages, obviously. There are a lot of players there; they have a lot of resources that aren't available to many counties. And their players live in Dublin, so they can train collectively in the mornings. Kerry can't do that.

There are universities in Dublin, so there's plenty of expertise for them to draw on. All those facilities are there, and that isn't the case for the majority of their opponents. I don't begrudge them their success or their sponsors. In Kerry our sponsors were always fantastic. But Dublin has the biggest population in the country, and it's the most marketable team; a lot of their players are very marketable … Several counties have advantages, but they don't exploit them to the fullest. Dublin are doing that, and have done so for years. They have very strong coaching at a very early age, and you won't see the fruits of that for another ten years.

Keeping an eye on the youth is vital for counties – Kerry are doing it now and reaping the benefits – and clubs alike. Dublin are a bit ahead of most counties, and that's not an accident: it's driven by good administrators, by the county chairman and secretary giving good leadership and direction.

It's always a help when the county board is on the same page as the county team. The likes of John Costello are making sure that that's the case in Dublin, and other counties could learn that you don't need a million potential members in your catchment area to appoint the best people you can.

Chapter 7

TYRONE

I can go back to 1986 with Tyrone, which is one of the first All-Irelands I really took notice of. In all honesty they wouldn't generally have registered with us back west as a superpower, as a team with great players; but that year they made it to the All-Ireland. Plunkett Donaghy, Eugene McKenna – that generation.

That final showed you the value of experience, or the problem when you didn't have experience, to be more accurate. They had Kerry on the rack that day, and they were well on top, but they got turned over.

The team we met were totally different. The Tyrone side we came up against were the best side we came up against, absolutely.

Their leader was certainly a man apart. Páidí was over Railway Cup teams for Munster when he was involved with Kerry, and in 1995–6 he was saying to me how good a player Peter Canavan was. That he was able to stick around for ten years in order to help them win All-Irelands a decade later is a measure of the man. When people ask me about players from the outside, about non-Kerry players, he's one man I'd always say would get his place on the Kerry team.

A serious player. He had it all, but one of the traits I really admired was his bravery. Up in Ulster, with football as it is, to be the player he was, and being the size he was … That took balls, and he showed plenty. He would not shy away from anyone or anything.

That and the unbelievable footballing genius and cuteness he had made him one of the greats.

Even when Páidí was telling us that, though, the flip side was that Ulster took the Railway Cup more seriously than the other provinces did – Munster would often have struggled for players, particularly when the club scene kicks in – so you'd take it with a pinch of salt.

They built through under-age success in the late nineties and early 2000s; but, again, you wouldn't be taking that hugely seriously either. We'd have heard of good Tyrone sides, but that's not a guarantee of anything. Take the Limerick under-21 sides, who didn't really come through. We didn't pay that much attention to reports of great minor teams in other counties.

What was crucial for Tyrone was Mickey Harte and the drive of the players they had – two special ingredients that kept them on top for as long as they were.

Our first big clash was 2003, and tactically we were naïve. Complacent? Maybe.

It's a game that remains a blur to me. I don't remember a whole lot about it, because it passed me by. I'd be good enough to remember this and that happening in games, memories that'd stick with me. But 2003? No.

The one thing I do remember is what everyone remembers: those famous images of Tyrone players swarming all over Kerry guys in possession. That was a shock. There's no comparison with Donegal, in that Tyrone didn't play a sweeper, as such: there wasn't a guy who stood between the full-back and half-back lines. Tyrone's trick was that they all got back so quickly; if they lost the ball around the middle of the field, they streamed back in numbers. If you were in any way hesitant in getting the ball away you were wiped. They also had better players than Donegal all over the field. They didn't need to be as defensive.

Ó Cinnéide was a strong, strong man, but in 2003 he was hammered at one stage around the middle of the field. I watched it back on video there recently and what stuck with me was that there were seven or eight Tyrone players around him, so you'd think, Where are the Kerry players who must be free?

When I look back now, we weren't prepared for it; we hadn't our preparation done. And, in fairness, I'd say Tyrone lifted it as well against us.

We played into their barrow and tried to bulldoze through them, tried to carry ball, tried to think we would win, because we were Kerry, and Tyrone should certainly not be stopping us. The reality is that we should have been moving that ball on as quick as we got it, playing with the hunger and fervour they did. It was a new beginning, another step in the development of football.

Afterwards there was a sense of shock in the dressing-room. Total shock. A sense of 'This shouldn't be happening to Kerry,' which was probably part of the problem: a touch of arrogance. Mentally we weren't ready for a battle, and maybe the green-and-gold jersey drove them on even further.

I wouldn't buy into those comments from Pat Spillane about 'puke football'. I don't think so at all. In full flow, Tyrone were a great team to watch – as are Donegal in full flow – and that's because both those teams had, and have, great footballers.

Mickey Harte's ability to drive them was also a huge asset. So was the cause. They always had a cause to drive them on as well, to inspire them. They wanted to do justice to Cormac McAnallen's memory. Another year the goalie's father died the night before a game, and they lifted it for him the following day. I don't mean that in a derogatory way, not for a second: those are desperate tragedies. But they also drove Tyrone on together.

I love visiting Tyrone, and I love the passion they and their supporters have. They treat their footballers like gods, and there's a huge respect there for Kerry. It's a fantastic place to visit because of that, but of course that drives them on out on the field.

There's a lot said – 'They're better than ye', 'Ye're better than them' – but there was always huge respect between the players on both sides.

You'd hear people say that losing an All-Ireland is like a death in the family, and it almost is. It's the hurt of going home afterwards, facing your own people and trying to come up with a plausible excuse for losing.

Of the three days Tyrone and Kerry played, they were better than us in 2003 and 2005. I'd argue that we should have taken them in 2008: we were good enough to take it, but they beat us fair and square.

People ask me if it bothers me. I've seen other Kerry lads say they don't lose any sleep over it, and neither do I, but it does irk me. It pisses me off, and I regret that we didn't beat them, because I felt we were as good as them, or better. But they'll always have that over us, that we never beat them. It's like *Raging Bull*: Jake LaMotta has the head beaten off him, but he's taunting the other guy, 'You never put me down.' We have all the All-Irelands we have, but we never put them down.

The counter-argument is that we always came back, and the hunger from those defeats drove us on. But they still have that over us.

———

The picture you get of a guy out on the field is often very different from the reality. I found that out myself in 2005 after losing the All-Ireland.

There was a Compromise Rules trip to Australia later in the year, and I was given to understand that if I rocked up to one or two training sessions I'd be on the flight out. I said I'd take the trip, so off I went.

On the drive up, though, I was dreading meeting the Tyrone lads. What was I going to say them? In the whole three hours' drive I couldn't come up with a reasonable conversation-starter, whether through embarrassment or shame or whatever.

All with no basis, of course. I met the Tyrone fellas, and you couldn't meet sounder. Before I landed in, the last man I wanted to meet was Ryan McMenamin, and when I got into the hotel lift, who was in there? Of course.

McMenamin is the classic case of a guy who's 100 per cent different off the field from what he's like when he's playing.

We got hammered out in Australia that year. We mightn't have been the best touring party ever – often I think the All-Ireland winners on the trip see it as a bit of holiday – but I'd have socialised a lot with the Tyrone lads out there.

You can always tell, when you're in conversation with players from another county, whether or not they've won an All-Ireland. When they've won one All-Ireland, and certainly a second, that edge isn't there. They don't have to prove themselves, talking about what press-ups they do or what weights they can lift, because they've got the medal in the back pocket.

And the Tyrone lads were the proof of that. They were relaxed, because they had the medals. One night myself and McMenamin had a few pints in the hotel, and we went back upstairs. If memory serves, we had a curfew, and we were keen on observing it.

We ended up getting lost and fetched up in a room with a basket of bottles of red wine. I don't drink red wine, and neither did McMenamin, but we had a go off one bottle, and then another. We were heading out after our fill of the wine when I saw a fridge in the corner. Opened it. Full of beer, after we'd forced down the red wine. Take the man out of the bog …

———

Tyrone's style of play wasn't a shock to us in 2005 or 2008. We knew what to expect, and we had a wrinkle of our own in 2008, with Kieran Donaghy and Tommy Walsh up front. We thought that might swing it for us, but, in fairness, the quality of the ball going in was bad: we were lamping ball into them and expecting them to do magic with bad ball.

What's a great team? A team that wins, first of all. A team that wins against the head, secondly. A team that wins numerous times, thirdly. And, finally, a team that has a mix of great players.

When a game is going away from a team, when time is running out and the result is in the balance, a team that can work out how to win – that's a great team. Look at the players Tyrone had: Stephen O'Neill, Peter Canavan, Brian McGuigan, Brian Dooher, from the forward line alone.

When our Kerry team met other teams our view was, 'We'll take care of A, B and C, and if they can still beat us they've earned it, and earned it well.' But with Tyrone you had A, B, C, X, Y and Z. It was too much for us to cover.

For instance, they were the first team that simply didn't compete with Darragh: they kept every kick-out away from him. In 2003 they were the first team to do that, and that showed other teams how to deal with him. He was dominating games completely, and they found a way around that.

Seán Cavanagh of Tyrone wouldn't have been a traditional midfielder, for instance. He'd drift between half-forward and midfield. I often ended up marking Ryan Mellon, and he was a guy who always caused me bother.

My attitude going into a big game would be, 'I've got to get up the field today to support the forwards' or 'I've got to chip in today with a point or two to help out.' Against a great team like Tyrone I might have been better off minding my own patch. Against other teams I could drive upfield, but I was shown up a couple of times against Tyrone.

At the start of the 2005 final Mellon rattled two points off me early on, for instance. I came into it more as that game wore on, but he had the damage done. In 2008 – based on what had happened in 2005 – there was a late change. In on the field, as we were warming up, I was told that Mellon was going to be pushed up on me, as a thing to get into my head, but it didn't bother me too much.

———

There'll always be a special connection between Tyrone and Kerry, much like that between Kerry and Dublin going back to the seventies. I always enjoy seeing the likes of Bomber Liston with the Dubs of the seventies, and I'd love for us to have the same relationship with the Tyrone guys as time goes on. I wouldn't have any grudges against any of them, certainly. The likes of Owen Mulligan were great craic when you were out, though his party piece got us into a few scrapes: he'd drink a shot and lob the glass back over his shoulder, and it could brain someone. I think Dr Con might have caught one of them. He'd usually chime in with 'Time to leave, Tomás' at about that point.

I certainly wouldn't like anyone to think I'm sour or begrudging towards Tyrone. They won their All-Irelands fair and square. When the final whistle goes, and you've lost, the fight just goes out of you, like the air out of a punctured football. At the final whistle in one of those All-Irelands, McMenamin was roaring at Declan, 'You'll never beat us.' That's the attitude they had, the attitude they brought to those games.

I've no doubt that they lifted it for us, that fellas who were chugging along at 70 per cent lifted their performance for us. One of the best points I ever saw was from Brian Dooher, bombing down the right wing under the Cusack, into the Hill, and hitting the ball with the outside of his right boot over the bar. It was a sucker punch for us, and it lifted them.

The same with Canavan's goal in 2005, another game-changer. Kevin Hughes came outfield after that, and he lamped me on his way. If I'd seen him coming I'd have lamped him myself, but I didn't. Toughness.

Tyrone had a great mix: star forwards, tough men, versatile players, like Enda McGinley, who could play in different positions. Joe McMahon the same. He was pushed into full-back for the All-Ireland in 2008, and what a game he had.

I have huge respect for Mickey Harte as a person and as a coach. I've met him and spoken to him often, and I have the utmost sympathy for what he and his family have been through personally. I think everyone in Kerry does.

His CV is as good as anyone's, and I'd love to know how he prepares his teams for battle. He comes across as a clean-cut guy, but for a religious man he had players who weren't too religious out on the field. Either they didn't listen to him or he didn't mind that side of the game. It's great to guess, isn't it, because no-one in there will say. I couldn't say they were dirty: they were hard and tough, and you need that to win.

———

In 2011 we faced Tyrone in the championship, and it wasn't the same Tyrone team, certainly. They had a jinx over us in All-Ireland finals, but this match was in Killarney. Whatever about losing to them in Croke Park, if we lost to them in Killarney we'd have lost a lot of our standing as a team. We took the game hugely seriously, and this was one game that I – and the other players – had no problem getting up for. You wouldn't have a problem getting yourself up for

Cork, for Dublin, for a game in Croke Park, and this was certainly one of those games.

But I don't think it was the same Tyrone team at all. It wasn't a patch on some of their great teams, but it was still important to us to win at home.

Afterwards I went away home; I didn't even hang around. It wasn't a case of 'Now, we're better than ye after all.' I didn't feel elated that we'd got one back on them or anything. But I was delighted to hear afterwards that the Kerry support waited around for Mickey and the lads to come out of the dressing-room, and that they applauded him in particular. On a human level, that shows huge respect that goes beyond what happens on the field.

But there were incidents. In one of the All-Ireland finals we lost to Tyrone, Ryan McMenamin came up the field in the dying seconds, passing the ball over my head and trying to follow through on me to take me out of the play. I grabbed him and pulled him down onto the ground, and I hit him a couple of pucks while I had the chance. My head was gone at this stage, because he was holding onto me.

Now, if that had happened in the first minute or two, I could have got the road for it, but it was very late in the game. I could hear the crowd, though, getting incensed by my tangling with him, and then the whistle went. Over.

I stood up and was just thinking, Another one gone, another one beaten by Tyrone. It was just sinking in, and then Tyrone supporters were streaming past me, rushing out onto the field, and a couple of them came for me.

Galvin came across and hit one of them a clip to get him out of the way, in fairness. I just wanted to get off the field, so I got over to the tunnel, where the security was.

I was sore after losing, but I don't think it's the right way to behave after a game to go complaining about this or that. Páidí was always strong on that, on behaving properly when you lost, and we had no complaints – not about the referees, not about the supporters, and certainly not about the Tyrone tactics.

Fellas would give out about the 'puke football' and say you couldn't play against it. Nonsense. I hated that. Tyrone played to win, just like Donegal, just like us. Tyrone showed something we hadn't seen before: savage tackling and wing-forwards ending up on their own 20-metre line.

But that style of play influenced us too. Brian Dooher's style showed Galvin, for instance, what he had to do, and he upped his game as a result. The work he did off the ball from then on was huge, so we learnt from their style as well. We learnt that we had to tackle harder, to work harder, that we couldn't be relying on Darragh if a game was in the balance – that we had to become tougher mentally.

Jack took the league games against Tyrone very seriously, and so did I – to an extent. To me, a league win over Tyrone meant little enough: I wanted to beat them in the championship. I'd almost feel half embarrassed winning a league match, because when it mattered we didn't beat them. Imagine if you said something to them after one of those games: all they'd have to say is 'Wait for Croke Park.' And that would stick with me.

As for the argument over who was the better team: I'm not going to get into that. It's for other people to decide that. Or the debate about whether Gooch was better than Canavan. Those are arguments for other people to have.

But I have the utmost respect for that Tyrone team. I think they'll struggle to find a set of players as good as they had, or a man as good to guide them.

———

Mouthing? I found that funny. How could a fella mouthing put you off your game?

McMenamin gave Galvin a dig in the balls up in the North during one of those league games, and if you saw it now on YouTube or whatever you'd only get a fit of laughing at it. Comical stuff.

Now if it was an All-Ireland semi-final I'd take the head clean off him, and he'd do the same, but you'd have to laugh at it. I knew McMenamin's form, though. I saw him at it in Australia, exactly the same thing.

It was on the 2005 Compromise Rules trip, a savage, physical game, and myself and the Gooch were on the bench watching it. I'd say the Gooch was thinking, What have I got myself into here? In two games I'd say he touched the ball three times, tops. (In one of the games he came over to the sideline and told Dr Con his vision was blurred. When a doctor hears that, he can't take any chances – the player has to come off in case he's concussed – so the Gooch landed next to me on the bench. 'You know you've to get a belt in the first place to get concussed, Gooch,' I said to him.)

McMenamin got into an altercation with one of the Aussies, a big powerful lad, and I was thinking, How will he get out of this? If it was toe to toe the Aussie would have hammered him. Cute enough, he looked the Aussie in the eye and snapped him in the balls: the Aussie dropped like a bag of spuds, and McMenamin jogged on, not a care in the world. I got a weakness laughing at it, but the rest of the Australians were roaring that your man was dead, and they were after McMenamin. But, fair play to him, he took the belts and gave them back for the rest of the game.

————

Tyrone changed tackling as well. If a player has the ball and his opponent goes in aggressively with two hands it's a foul. But if five players surround an opponent and each of them sticks in one hand, that's five hands clattering at you, but it's not a foul. My opinion was that if a guy got up in the air over two or three fellas and pulled the ball down, he didn't deserve to be swarmed by other players: there was no benefit to his high fielding, because five fellas were waiting to hammer him.

I don't blame those guys: that's just the way the rules are. And maybe the man getting up in the air is being stupid – maybe he should flick the ball on – but that's my own view.

Seán Cavanagh wouldn't be going up for those balls, for instance. We'd have always been well aware that he'd cheat, if you like, onto our half-back line: he'd be banking on Tyrone winning the ball in the middle of the field, and they'd put the ball in over the top to him and he'd be clear.

We wised up to that eventually. Seán is a serious athlete, and when he had the ball he had this shimmy … We all knew every time what he was going to do, what side he was going to go, but he always managed to sell the dummy.

He was a hugely important player for Tyrone, but I don't think he'd have been as effective without the bulldozers around him. You look at Tyrone nowadays, and without those strong men around him he can manage it only sporadically, and not at the level he was at when they were going strong. No man can do it on his own, to be fair: if Darragh were in midfield with a poor team he'd struggle too.

For me, Kevin Hughes's role for Tyrone was more important than Seán Cavanagh's. He had to make sure that the likes of Darragh and Kirby around the middle didn't dominate; he was their bully in the middle of the field, and I mean that as a compliment. He was able to motor from start to finish, to cover the ground and put in the hits. Conor Gormley was another Tyrone guy who could snuff out an opponent if there was danger.

Mickey Harte made some outstanding moves too. Switching Joe McMahon back to full-back to mark Kieran Donaghy in the All-

Ireland was like us moving Eoin Brosnan to full-back. Unheard of. But Tyrone were able to adapt, and they could do it before big games.

Peter Canavan's goal in 2005 is what a lot of people remember. I was in the neighbourhood: I reckon still that if I'd sprinted harder I could have got down on his boot, though it's easy to say that in hindsight.

We were naïve. Galvin, a half-forward, was the last man back minding the house when Canavan got the goal. Mike McCarthy was up the field somewhere. If we'd approached that game with the tactical awareness teams have now, with that kind of thinking, would the result have been different? Possibly. We played into their barrow a few times, emptying our backs up into the forward line and getting caught on the counter. A sickener.

There were people in Kerry unhappy that Gooch was struck off the ball in 2005. 'One in, all in' would be my attitude always. It didn't happen down our side of the field, because they wouldn't be going at us, at defenders. My attitude was that your man should have been drilled – put on his backside.

If there's a row, start a row. How often have you heard that about a team on the way down, 'They were so bad they didn't even start a row'? Tyrone were well able to do it: they were mentally strong enough to start a row but maintain their focus afterwards, though the other team would have been distracted.

Did that incident have an effect on the Gooch? I don't know. We weren't asking him at half time if he was right; but, as a general rule, if someone comes in to do you, what would you do? If there's a row with five or six involved, is the referee going to send off five or six? As long as you don't raise your fists you'll be fine.

I played in Cork in 2002, my first time in a back-door game in Croke Park, and there was plenty of niggle. Fionán Murray and Tom O'Sullivan were at it, as were Colin Corkery and Séamus Moynihan, and so were plenty more, and there was a skirmish at one stage. I

Back in the seventies and eighties, Sam was a regular visitor to our house. All I ever wanted was to bring it home myself.

The four of us: Darragh, Fergal, Marc and myself. We had a happy childhood. 'School of Knocks'.

Rearing four lads was always difficult. Marc having a sulk on Darragh's communion day.

Christmas Day was always family. Here we are with Páidí and our cousins Neasa, Siún and Pádraig.

My dad and myself in London. The two of us went over on a short break at the end of the summer. Good memories.

Media day before the 2000
All-Ireland final with Darragh
and Páidí. No doubt he is telling
one of his 'good' stories here.
(© *macmonagle.com*)

Ailidh, Mícheál and myself with
Páidí outside Páidí's bar, 2012.
He always had great time for them
and they were so fond of him.
He always had fun with them.
(© *macmonagle.com*)

The day of Páidí's funeral in
Páidí's house, 2012. A tough time.
He was a huge loss to the whole
family. (© *macmonagle.com*)

Two photos with Páidí at Árd a Bhóthair cross, 2005 and 2015. Now that he is gone, the statue will remind us of him. Not the same as having him around though! (© *macmonagle.com*)

The first and last days I played with Kerry, 1998 and 2013. Two teams peppered with great players and great men. (© *INPHO / Donall Farmer*)

My first day out against Cork in 1998. Aidan Dorgan gave me one of the worst roastings of my life. #learningcurve (© *macmonagle.com*)

Heading to Dublin for an All-Ireland was always a long but enjoyable day. Here we are landing at Killarney train station for the train on the Saturday before the 2000 All-Ireland final. (© *macmonagle.com*)

Cork games were brilliant – tough and always on the edge. This is Martin Cronin putting me on my backside in Killarney in 2002. My dad would die two days later. (© *Brendan Moran / SPORTSFILE*)

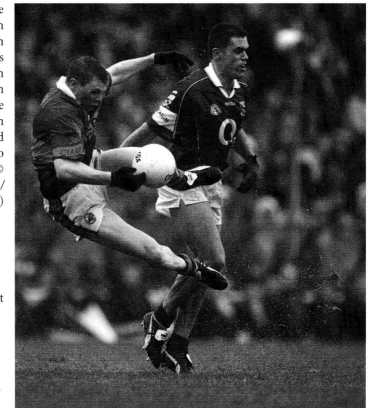

Tyrone had a great team and Peter Canavan was one of the greatest of them all. A nut we didn't crack. (© *David Maher / SPORTSFILE*)

Playing with An Ghaeltacht, 2003. I really loved playing with the club lads. We had a special spirit and bond – and we also had big wins. (© *Brendan Moran /* SPORTSFILE)

Winning with your club is special. With the brothers after winning the county championship in 2003. (© *macmonagle.com*)

Winning an All-Ireland is unbelievable. Friends wishing me well after the 2004 win – Tom Hutch, Billy Mangan and my good friend Seán Breandán Ó Conchúir having a word in my ear. I was minding the match ball for Dara Ó Cinnéide, our captain. (© *Pat Murphy / SPORTSFILE*)

On tour with the Irish International Rules team in 2005 – a great opportunity to get to know fellas. Here with my good friend Dr Con Murphy, the bould Ricey McMenamin, Seán Óg Ó hAilpín and Eoin Brosnan.

Gooch and myself dropped in 2009. I was not a happy camper. We totally deserved what we got but I didn't like the way it was handled. (© *Brendan Moran / SPORTSFILE*)

With the Gooch training before the 2009 All-Ireland final. Tough year for both of us, but we ended it on a high. The Gooch is the greatest footballer I've ever seen. (© *Brendan Moran / SPORTSFILE*)

Coming out of old dressing rooms in Killarney to face the media before the 2008 All-Ireland final. Paul Galvin had been suspended. He was the rightful captain, but I took over as captain while he was suspended. He showed great leadership during a tough time for himself. A great guy. (© *Brendan Moran / SPORTSFILE*)

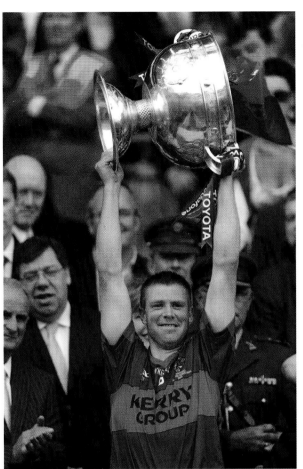

I never got used to this. Made all the hardship worthwhile. 2009. (© *Pat Murphy* / SPORTSFILE)

In Killarney in June 2010 with Jack O'Connor as manager and Éamonn Fitzmaurice as selector. Contrary to what people believe, I got on fine with Jack and thought he was a great manager. (© *Stephen McCarthy* / SPORTSFILE)

Red cards! For a while, they became the norm … No matter how hard I tried to control myself, I kept lashing out. (© *Diarmuid Greene* / sportsfile, © *Stephen McCarthy* / sportsfile, © *macmonagle.com*)

Handing the ball to Stephen Cluxton after the All-Ireland final in 2011. (© *Daire Brennan / SPORTSFILE*)

Mícheál having a bit of craic with Kieran Donaghy and myself after a championship match, 2013. He loves following Kerry, thank God! (© *Diarmuid Greene / SPORTSFILE*)

Game up: the final whistle gone in my last game against the Dubs, 2013. I do miss it. Even now. (© *Brendan Moran / SPORTSFILE*)

Éabha, Orla, Mícheál, myself and Ailidh, 2015.

With Orla on a wild day back west, 2015. I'm very happy living in Cork with Orla. (© *macmonagle.com*)

went in to break it up, believe it or not, but I got an unmerciful lamp into the back. I turned around and Jim O'Donoghue of Cork was there, and whether he did it or not I laid into him. He said, 'Hit me, hit me,' and I did, as hard as I could draw.

After that I heard I'd be in trouble, but it was the time when suspensions were time-related rather than match-related, and by my reckoning if I got only a month I'd be back the night before the final. I'd be fine. From our point of view now it's ridiculous, that you could get suspended but not miss any actual games, but that's how it was.

Fionán Murray is from the Barrs, and Colin Corkery is a Nemo man, and they must have been playing club championship and wanted to get off for it, because they went to Croke Park for a hearing. When I went to Cork Airport to fly up for my own hearing, Murray was in one corner of the airport and Corkery in the other.

Tom O'Sullivan was ahead of me and came over: 'Thank God you're here. What are we going to say to these two?'

'I don't know,' said I, 'but we have to make some kind of an effort.'

Tom was still raw enough about the whole thing and said he was making fuck-all effort, anyway

I found the whole thing comical – grown men behaving like they were seven years old.

I know Colin well, and we had a laugh above in Croke Park before the hearing. Whether it's politically correct or not to say so, it'd be my opinion that there's a lot of 'If you scratch my back …' on those disciplinary committees – that, generally speaking, Kerry would back Cork and vice versa. I think that goes on, and I've no doubt that Cork would have helped me out that evening.

I got grilled for about twenty minutes. I went in with Tony O'Keeffe, our secretary, a sharp guy, and we faced eight or nine guys sitting in judgement.

'You've been brought up on this charge. Do you want to say anything?'

We said we wanted to bring in video evidence, though that mightn't have been the best idea.

Tony was commentating on the piece of video. 'As you can see, Tomás is coming in here …' – film of me running into the mêlée – '… and he's actually breaking up the row …' – me separating two lads, then turning around and lamping Jim O'Donoghue, for all to see – '… and, well, we'll have to take that one on the chin, I suppose.'

I had to explain myself then, and one fella said to me, 'As a man, do you think it's right showing this example to children?'

I wasn't being smart when I answered: 'To be honest, there were a lot of things running through my head, but what other people might think wasn't one of them. There was a lot of argy-bargy, a lot went on before that, and a lot after it. I'm a schoolteacher, and I realise the importance of setting a good example. Have you ever been in that situation in the heat of the moment of an All-Ireland semi-final?'

I knew well he hadn't been.

———

You'd always be curious about how coaches work, how coaching combinations work. I've met Mickey Harte and his family – they're great people, Gaeilgeoirí, great GAA people – and, for what he's achieved at every level, I have huge respect for him. Tony Donnelly was his right-hand man, and I enjoyed a drink with him. Their dynamic was terrific.

The longevity of Harte is something I particularly admire. For years Tyrone have been there or thereabouts, but the problem now for him – and for Tyrone – is that they just don't have the calibre of player, or leader, that they had when they were at their peak. Great teams have a great mix, and timing is everything. They're still competitive, though. And Harte is to Tyrone what Cody is to Kilkenny, or O'Dwyer to Kerry.

Now, Harte had a lot of teams who were well able to come up to the line, and to step over it, so either they weren't listening to him at all or they were listening to him very carefully. Take your pick!

He's able to come up with things like Justin McMahon just shadowing Michael Murphy. Most managers would go blanket defence against a forward like Murphy, but he came up with a different tactic. Aidan O'Mahony did something similar to Murphy in the 2014 All-Ireland, but the difference was that O'Mahony wasn't worried about Murphy once he went outside the 45, beyond the scoring zone. And O'Mahony was on the ball a lot: he must have handled the ball twenty times in that match.

McMahon hardly touched the ball in the game against Donegal.

There are times when a player is told, 'You're up his backside for the day. It doesn't matter if you don't touch the ball: he's not to touch it either.' It doesn't happen often, but it happens. Would I do it as a manager? I would if it meant winning the game. Mike McCarthy got man of the match in a game where he didn't have the ball in his two hands once; but he got his hand in about thirteen times to knock it away from the opposition danger man.

Adapting. Doing what you have to. That's what gets you over the line.

———

You'd think of those great games against Tyrone, and obviously at times you'd think, Feck it, we never beat them. But another side of me would think, Weren't they great games, classic contests? Maybe 2003 wasn't, because we were poor enough on the day, but certainly 2005 and 2008 were great games.

The purists might carp a little, but in intensity, in the level of skill, in the standard of player, those were the best teams I played on and against.

Chapter 8

ARMAGH, MAYO, DONEGAL

When we played Armagh in the 2002 All-Ireland final, we'd lost to Cork and come through the back door. We learnt about ourselves and improved; we'd turned the corner as a team and were going well. But a couple of things are certainly worth remembering.

For instance, the Gooch and Marc were very young at the time. Marc would have got a bit of a hosing in the All-Ireland final off Diarmuid Marsden, very much like the one I got at the start of my career off Aidan Dorgan of Cork. The Gooch was good in 2002, but he wasn't quite the dominant player he'd become later.

At the time that didn't seem to matter, because we were flying it, demolishing teams and playing the best football I ever saw while I was involved with a Kerry team. Steamrolling good teams. This was before blanket defence, mind you.

We played Cork in the semi-final and gave a *tour de force*, for example. Looking back now, I'd say a good rattle would have done us a lot more good: a dour game that you'd have to grind a win out of would have been much better preparation for an All-Ireland final.

That doesn't mean we were cocky. People might like to believe that, but if they do they're forgetting something: we knew exactly how good Armagh were. Don't forget that in 2000 they had pushed us to a replay in the All-Ireland semi-final. They pushed us hard both those days and could have beaten us.

There's a tendency now to lump all the northern teams in together as defensive, but that wasn't really the case with Armagh. They didn't play a blanket defence or anything: what they had were very, very good players.

They had McDonnell, Clarke, Marsden. And of course their two big men, McGeeney and McGrane, were going well that year, not to mention the two McEntees. John hit some unbelievable points off Séamus Moynihan, which was a fair measure of how well he was going, because Séamo was our main man. Me? My own man, Oisín McConville, got man of the match.

We were ahead at half time and there was no panic. We were in a battle, but the atmosphere was calm, it was good. We'd been in control, I felt.

I went up to Páidí to point out that I was doing fine on McConville but that – cute enough out of him – he was drifting in towards our goal. I loved being in the half-back line: I had the chance to attack, but tracking him back towards our goal meant I couldn't do that. McConville was putting me in positions where I wouldn't be as comfortable, in around our full-back line, and I said it to Páidí. But he said, 'Stick with him. Just follow him.'

And that's what McConville kept doing in the second half, drifting in, and eventually they worked the goal out of it.

The other big thing that sticks with me from that game was that we went such a long time in the second half without getting a score. I remember thinking, How long is it since we got a point?

We had plenty of ball – certainly in the last seven or eight minutes we had plenty of possession – but what happened was that we couldn't get past their half-backs. They defended heroically, it must be said, and you certainly couldn't argue with the result. We just couldn't get the ball into our full-forward line.

The fact that we had the ball, but that they blocked us out every which way so that we weren't able to penetrate their defence, made it doubly frustrating. That meant we had to take shots from further out the field, which made it even harder. For a physically strong team they were disciplined enough not to give away silly frees, scoreable frees, and always when you lose by a point you look at this and that. It'd eat at you.

You couldn't say they didn't deserve it: they did. They had six very good forwards, for instance, and they were cute as well. If judged by our second-half performance we probably didn't deserve it, because when they turned the screw on us, that was the difference.

Back in 2000 I saw that up close myself. Cathal O'Rourke was playing wing-forward and had a particular knack … That time things were probably more lax when it came to off-the-ball stuff, but we found it hard to get past them physically, because of the way they focused in on our strengths. Darragh was the main man for us, winning ball after ball in midfield, but we were struggling to get him into the game, because of the way Armagh were countering him. O'Rourke was letting on to go for the ball from kick-outs, but he wasn't: he was aware of where Darragh was on the field, of how he was approaching the ball, so he'd walk across and block his run – 'Oh, sorry about that' – and Darragh couldn't get at the ball.

Darragh told Páidí and the management about it, so for the replay I was shifted over onto O'Rourke and told before the game to keep an eye on that carry-on. The first ball that dropped, away he went – I was thinking, God, he's doing it – so for the second ball I tore into him before it dropped out around the middle of the field, and he ended up on the ground. And that put a stop to it.

Kieran McGeeney was a huge character for them; he was their main man. You'd hear people say it, and they're right: he was a great player. He was one of these fellas who didn't do a pile of talking, but you could tell that the rest of the team all looked up to him. Some centre-backs are inclined to let their men go, to roam upfield or whatever, but McGeeney wasn't like that: he was always there. He understood where our strengths were, and he'd go to one of our fellas if he thought that player was going to rouse the opposition. Tough, hard – but he could back it up. A lot of supposed hard men can't back it up with their play, but he could.

We didn't have the strength in depth either, which isn't an excuse, but it was a fact. Even two years later, in the All-Ireland final of 2004, we had Galvin and O'Mahony. Gooch was then two years more mature, as was Marc, and Declan had landed in at that point as well. There was depth that wasn't there in 2002: that year we had our main men – Séamo, Darragh and the lads – and we'd ploughed that unbelievable furrow with our form. We didn't question ourselves, and Páidí had been amazing on the sideline.

But at half time in that All-Ireland in 2002, when we should have been driving on, we didn't. They didn't let us. And sometimes that happens.

That year, 2002, was the first All-Ireland I lost. That's a tough experience. I enjoyed being asleep after we lost that All-Ireland, because you wouldn't be aware that you'd lost. The morning after you win an All-Ireland, the moment you open your eyes you're thinking, This is going to be a great day. When you lose it's obviously the opposite: you wish you could stay in the bed, but your head is racing anyway – What if we'd done *this*, what if we'd done *that*? – so there's no peace. Downstairs, then, and for the next three days you're facing the same questions with the same answers, over and over.

It's important to learn from that. Losing is where you find the lessons, and they stay with you. It's there where, if you have a talented bunch, and if you actually look at why you lost and where you lost, you can come back better the next time. In that case, then, losing can be the difference. I know that some teams stick it in the back of their heads without confronting it, and that's the mistake that will beat them again.

Certainly in 2006, when we faced Armagh again, there was a strong sense of 'No way will they put one over on us again,' and, though I had a poor year, that was the best game I had. We were after getting stick for losing to northern teams in 2002, 2003 and 2005, so when we faced them … There is this thing in the north where they all row in behind the team from Ulster that's left in the championship longer than the rest, but we were strong that day. Darragh met them head on and drove them this way and that. Physically we imposed ourselves on Armagh, and I don't think they were ready for how we physically drove at them all that day.

Darragh and I had played Compromise Rules with a few of the Armagh lads, and we got on very well – competitors to the last. When they won the All-Ireland in 2002 I felt that they might drive on, that they had the players to do so, but they never did.

Would I call them underachievers? I don't know, because a great Tyrone team emerged just after them. Those two had great battles, and maybe Armagh were a little unlucky, but I certainly felt they might have won more. To give them their due, they dominated the toughest province of them all for a number of years.

You'd also have to point out that Armagh's winning the All-Ireland was the end of an odyssey for a lot of them, for players who'd been playing since the nineties and getting to All-Ireland semi-finals for the previous few years. You can't overestimate the effect of winning an All-Ireland for the first time in your county's history either, not to mention the fact that they led the way for the north as a whole.

Up till then, Kerry, Galway and Meath had been dominating, so Ulster was a bit of a forgotten province to some extent, and they broke through that barrier as well.

I felt that, in part, Armagh believed it was their destiny to get there. Meeting them since we packed it in, you couldn't meet better: McGeeney, McGrane. And you couldn't find a better example, to me, of a GAA man than Joe Kernan. I'd put him on a par with Billy Morgan and Mick O'Dwyer, fellas who played and managed and won in both roles. They're fanatics.

Even the politics got a run in 2002. After we lost that final we were in Jury's, drowning our sorrows, and there were plenty of lads from the north there, all keen to chat to their hero, Martin Ferris. He was a hard-core Kerryman – black, black Kerry – but he was celebrating with them and was going to head up with them, because of the connection he had with them over the years. I thought it was a great sign of him, and of them – though I wouldn't go that far myself with any county.

Losing? … I won a pile. Can I remember much about some of those winning finals? No. Can I remember all those crucial incidents in the ones we lost? Absolutely. Fellas ask about maintaining the hunger: you'd only be bulling to get back, after winning an All-Ireland, to get onto the field in January.

In my whole career they were the three toughest years, 2001, 2002 and 2003. The worst defeat ever was 2001, against Meath. I wasn't on the field (I was suspended), but we were obliterated: towards the end, they were cheering every Meath pass. On the sideline I was thinking, 'This is not Kerry.' That came from nowhere.

The 2002 defeat was another blow, particularly as we'd been playing so well all that year until the final. It's the old argument: would you prefer to win an All-Ireland playing dour football? which to me isn't even an argument. If I had the choice I'd take an All-Ireland any way I could.

———

I've been to Mayo a good few times. I've seen how they operate up there. Willie Joe Padden, for instance, is a huge hero. I've been out and about with Liam McHale, and he's a god in the county, an absolute god. Imagine if these guys had three or four All-Ireland medals: how would they be regarded then? There are fantastic footballers in Kerry with All-Ireland medals, and they'd hardly be known to people.

I love the attitude people in Mayo have. They're positive, hopeful. They don't get sour, and they keep on supporting their team the whole time. You'd hear plenty of nonsense about them supposedly being afraid of Kerry. But when I was a minor in 1996 I saw it up close and personal, and they had no fear of Kerry that day in the All-Ireland senior semi-final. They won well.

I suppose the difference was that Kerry learnt from 1996 and put those lessons into effect in 1997. That's always been one of Kerry's all-time strengths, the ability to learn and adapt. We've always had the footballers, but if styles changed, which they always do, we've adapted. (Winning the All-Ireland against Donegal in 2014 is a case in point.)

That's probably a knock against Mayo, that they don't absorb what they can from previous years. In either 2004 or 2006 I was watching a television report, and the Mayo team were getting a plane up to Dublin for the All-Ireland final, with guys giving interviews … I was thinking, Lads, there's nothing won yet.

Páidí's great saying was that the time to be in the papers was Monday or Tuesday: keep the focus on the game. But there's such an insanity about football up there in Mayo that you can nearly see it start to burn like a forest fire: they win Connacht and the talk starts; they win an All-Ireland semi-final and it's 'This could be it, this could be the year' … It's all played up, and that has to get inside players' minds. (For the other viewpoint, a lot of people in Kerry don't go to any games unless it's an All-Ireland final, which can be a double-edged sword too, of course.)

I think the hype is a far more dangerous issue for Mayo than any supposed fear of Kerry. They've no fear of Dublin, for instance, or of

Donegal. A guy I know in Donegal – someone who's well clued in – suggested to me ahead of the 2014 final that Donegal would have far preferred to play Kerry in it, because they felt Mayo would always make it hard for them.

It's terrible: it's as if they're on the line but, just when they should put the foot down, there's someone hauling them backwards. In 2006 I was marking Billy Joe Padden, and the game was over at half time. That left Jack free to make his moves, to please whoever he wanted to please in whatever parts of Kerry, but it's not often you can say that about an All-Ireland.

Our plan was simple: Johnny Crowley was so powerful that he'd say to us, 'Drive it in to me whatever way ye want. Give me it 60–40 and I'll make something out of it.' And he did: if he didn't win it, the man who did knew all about it. Ó Cinnéide was always able to win ball over his head as well, so we had a great outlet there always.

Talk about a change in the game: I was quizzed after Kerry won the 2014 All-Ireland about James O'Donoghue and how many balls he'd won over his head in the season, and I couldn't think of too many. Nowadays forwards are receiving a postal service (save Kieran Donaghy): the ball's more or less delivered into their hands. Crowley and Donaghy always offered you a different target.

People often point to the start we had in 2006, the early goals that set us on our way. But Mayo got a flying start against us in 2004: Alan Dillon got that goal in the first few minutes. The difference was that a team like Tyrone would make that count against you: they were cuter on the field, cuter on the line, and they'd press home an advantage. They had their enforcers, who wouldn't allow you to get back in the game, and even if you did, well, they had great, great forwards to hunt for more scores. We didn't feel the same about Mayo – or about Cork, after Colm O'Neill got the goal early on in 2009.

The other crucial point in 2006 was that, at the other end of the field, we always had the players who could snuff out Mayo's danger men. If it wasn't Mike McCarthy or Tom O'Sullivan doing it, it was someone like Éamonn Fitzmaurice. Ciarán McDonald had been having a great season for Mayo in 2006, but Fitzmaurice was so well tuned in that McDonald didn't get a sniff of the ball in that final. Aidan O'Mahony won man of the match for his display against McDonald another time.

That's not to disparage McDonald or any of the Mayo lads. McDonald is one of the greatest kickers of a ball I have ever seen. A tough man too, and what a gent off the field. And they had great players – David Heaney, Alan Dillon. I often had a poor game against them myself, to be honest.

David Brady asked me one time at a radio gig about what we would have been saying at half time about Mayo, and he clearly felt we were saying they were chokers or whatever. Not at all. We knew that Mayo had the potential to beat the tar out of anyone, but right now that's just potential. Being known as the best team never to have won an All-Ireland is cold comfort to any side, but the longer the drought goes on, the more of an issue it becomes, and the more pressure it lamps onto the current crop.

I think they'll win an All-Ireland, the current Mayo team. They deserve it. I have huge respect for the likes of the O'Sheas, and Keith Higgins is one of the best defenders around: he got in something like seven blockdowns in the All-Ireland semi-final replay against Kerry in 2014, which is phenomenal, even if Donaghy's goal came as a result of one of them.

To win an All-Ireland you have to have your tight backs, and Mayo have those; you need physicality, which they have; you need good men around the middle of the field, which they have. Are they relying too much on Cillian O'Connor? Possibly. They might be short one top, top forward to go along with him.

They're definitely a tougher proposition than they were, and they're right to be. The one thing about Mayo was that if you knocked on their door it was inclined to open far too easily, and the beatings they took against us were inclined to be fired in their faces – mostly by the media, it has to be said, because their own supporters rowed in behind them quick enough after those losses.

James Horan certainly toughened them up when he came in, and he was right to do so. If Tyrone were losing they'd start a fight or do something to stop the rot; we'd have done the same ourselves. Horan focused in on what Mayo needed, and they probably needed a harder edge, and that does them no harm. They should have beaten Kerry in Croke Park in 2014, and as for the replay in Limerick … That was special.

That's one game I wish I could have played in. When the ball was being fired out to the middle of the field, and big men going for it, clattering with lads piling in for the breaking ball, that's where you'd want to be. That was one time I wanted to be playing for Kerry, certainly. It seemed so physical. Maybe it was the dimensions of the field, or the closeness of the crowd to the action, but you could hear the clattering. You could almost feel it.

In Croke Park you always seem to have space. In another stadium you'll kick a ball and it'll go over the sideline, but that never seems to happen in Croke Park: there always seems to be that extra bit of room.

I gave out that the game was moved to Limerick. It was nothing to do with the atmosphere, which was one of the best I ever experienced; but I thought it was all wrong to move the game out of Croke Park. Are we about money or about spectacles and bringing it back to the people? We had a big ship to pay for up in Dublin, but that's well paid for now. You could have All-Ireland quarter-finals in places around the country and you'd have the kind of atmosphere you get at Munster hurling games in Thurles.

A lot of things went Kerry's way that day, and you need a bit of luck to win any All-Ireland.

Then again, by the time this book is in the shops Mayo could have Sam back west with them. I'd like it if they did. Maybe the new management team will help them, but, as I said, they need a couple of new forwards. You have to pounce when you have the players available to you, because a couple of retirements or injuries and the cupboard can look pretty bare all of a sudden.

———

I first came across Jim McGuinness when he was in Tralee IT. That was when they had half a dozen All-Stars on their Sigerson Cup team, and he was the captain, the main man. Charisma, the long hair, the guy starting parties … One of the lads in Tralee that time told me McGuinness would drive back up to Donegal every single weekend for club games or county games, and that was long before the roads were any good. A driven man now, and a driving man then.

I think McGuinness is a great manager, one of the best we've seen. He came in to take over a talented Donegal team who weren't achieving: we all heard the stories of Donegal in Croke Park, landing on with two bags, one for the game and one for the few days afterwards. That was the attitude that was there.

The way he changed that and got Donegal an All-Ireland within two years, putting a system in place to beat the traditionalists … He's started a revolution, for good or bad, and I'm glad he did what he did.

A lot of people are down on defence, but if you watch Donegal going well they're an unbelievable team. They have terrific footballers all over the field, and it makes me kind of cranky when people say, 'Look at the defence; it's all defence.' That drives me mad. Frank McGlynn, a terrific player. The McGees, Neil and Éamon, hardy boys but talented players. Anthony Thompson. Karl Lacey won three All-Stars as a corner-back when Donegal were playing open football, one-on-one defending: that's quality. And Michael Murphy … They're all fantastic players.

But McGuinness is the man. He laid it on the line and obviously said, 'Ye can go this way, or ye can carry on the way ye've been going.' And now he's at the soccer! This man's a tactical genius, clearly. If a guy does something special with a group who aren't laden down with expectations, you have to give it to him.

I'd love to sit down and chat away to him properly. He's a passionate guy about everything he does, and he completely transformed a county inside two years. I'd bet anything he'll do a Martin O'Neill and coach a top team.

Chapter 9

PREPARATION

One difference between when I started and when I finished is the level of preparation – specifically, just how time-consuming that has become.

Weights, food, back-up, meetings, analysis – all of that has come in more and more. When I started off in 1997 it was the tail-end of the old way, if you like. Páidí was starting off as manager, and, coming in after the Leaving Cert, I saw at first hand that he was totally and utterly professional, to my eyes.

If I look back now the preparation wasn't professional, of course. In general training there were just two concepts, really: ball work and running for fitness. There were no such things as drills, really, no tackling drills, one-on-one exercises, nothing like that. We wouldn't have analysed how we'd do on breaking balls, for instance, or in keeping possession. No stats. The analysis was what PO did.

Towards the end of my career with Kerry you didn't just prepare and analyse the man you were marking, or the other starters you might be marking: you prepared for every one of the players you might be marking, and there'd be files on all of them on computer.

After a game there would be a breakdown on possession, kick-outs, tackle counts, scoring chances, hand-passing and so on, both individually and as a team. Every clip of the opposition playing in the championship or league that had been televised could be pulled up, so there were no excuses for being caught by a player you'd never heard of.

When we were starting, the first time you might see or hear of the guy you were marking in the league was when you walked up and shook his hand before the anthem.

In Killarney in 1999 we played Wicklow, and I was marking a guy called Trevor Doyle, and he gave me a fair toasting: nowadays I'd have seen clips of him playing and would have known beforehand what he was capable of.

The physical training has changed hugely over the years. In 1997 Páidí did a lot of the training with us, but he brought in John O'Keeffe the following year. He was obviously a great player but is also a PE teacher, and he was in to do physical work with us too.

We did that in Killarney. Anyone who's been to Fitzgerald Stadium there will know there's a small pitch behind the terrace at the dressing-room end. A heavy pitch, no lights. As you're rounding that pitch out by the gate it slopes upwards, so you have to run up a hill, and there's a bar there. You cross at the top to another bar, go down the hill, and repeat. When we were training we'd do fourteen laps of that circuit, around, up, across and down the hill, usually into a huge puddle of water that'd pool at the bottom.

Éamonn Breen and Liam Flaherty would slag Ó Cinnéide off as he'd descend: they said he had a low centre of gravity and would be wobbling coming through the water and the soft ground. Ó Cinnéide wouldn't be a man for the long runs.

William Kirby, on the other hand, was a savage for those long runs. He was the man. If a new guy came onto the panel to put it up to him on one of those runs, he'd see it as a challenge – and ice them. Breen and Darragh were always up the front for the runs as well, and I had huge time for Breen's commitment. He'd be after plastering all day long – a demanding, physical job, and he'd come in with dust and plaster hanging off him – and then go out and train like an absolute dog for the two hours we were there.

After fourteen laps of that circuit you'd do ten laps. Then eight, six, and four. It was flat-out, full-out pace from start to finish.

Torturous, really, but at the same time I had the outlook that this is where you need to do the work. Darragh was the same: he always said that he loved those long runs, that they'd stand to you later in the year when you needed it.

If you had that work done, all you had to worry about was ball work, and you felt your skills would carry you if you didn't have to be concerned with fitness.

On top of that, the attitude was always good when it came to the slog. Everyone did it – goalkeepers, everybody. I always prided myself on being up the front, and if we were split into groups I always wanted to be in the first group. Even if the groups were all going at the same pace, I wanted to get it done first and out of the way.

There's the argument, of course, that maybe you shouldn't train twenty-five different players the same way. I met Paul O'Connell one time – a very nice guy – and asked him about how players in different positions in rugby are trained. Obviously it's different in Gaelic football, but I never really understood the logic of giving a specialist corner-back, say, the same training you'd give a midfielder, when the physical demands of their positions are so different.

There were fellas who weren't suited to the long runs, or who the long runs didn't suit. Maurice Fitz wouldn't have enjoyed those. Fitzmaurice and Ó Cinnéide the same. In fairness, it's not as if they weren't going hard or putting it in: it's just that the speed being set by the top fellas was ferocious altogether.

I noticed that when I came in as a teenager, the step up in speed, in physicality. I played Division 1 with An Ghaeltacht for a long time, but the step up when you went in training with Kerry – the hard tackling, the speed at which everything happened. If you weren't prepared for that mentally, for how you were going to be hit, you were in trouble.

Anyway, the session would be fitness and football: thirty minutes of fitness, forty minutes of football.

With the football, Páidí had a way of playing it, and if we weren't following that, he'd tell us. But there were no meetings about playing football, about where to stand, how to move. It was open, natural football. Declan O'Keeffe used to bomb the ball out; fellas won it. If you had the ball, you drove it into the full-forward, Johnny Crowley or Maurice Fitzgerald, but it was six backs against six forwards.

I've played in a lot of big games with club and county, and one thing people miss is that every training session with Kerry – every single one – was a test. That's how you had to treat it, and every training session with Kerry I treated as seriously as a championship match.

If a training session went badly for me I'd be sour about it for two days. Other fellas mightn't have been, but I was. I'd be thinking about what had gone wrong in the session, and why, all the way home in the car. It was the same if it went well: I'd analyse what had gone well; but if it went badly, on the drive from Cork for the next session I'd be thinking, 'I was beaten for three breaking balls the last time, so there's no way I'll be beaten for those tonight,' or 'I struggled in the last two runs the last night, so I'll drive that on this evening.'

I'd zone in on the way to training. As soon as I sat into the car to head down I was in that zone for those four or five hours when training was the focus, before you went back to your normal life.

I'd be there at least an hour beforehand. I hated getting to training late, or just late enough that you'd be in a rush onto the field. Having injured my ankle as a teenager, I was supposed to be undergoing a long strengthening rehab programme, but I hadn't the patience to go through with it. I'd have my ankles strapped before – heavy tape – by the physio. It was preventive, really: the ankle was fine. But in training I'd go over on it the odd time, and I'd think, If that wasn't strapped I'd be gone for a week or two. Tadhg Kennelly told me afterwards that the Aussie Rules players are all taught how to strap their own ankles when they're starting off.

There was always a process to the year, and to the season. You had a break from September – hopefully – to December, and then, because you had had that gap, you were looking forward to just going back training, even if that meant training in muck and shit. After that came the McGrath Cup, which meant games – great.

After that came the league – more games to break up the monotony of training in the muck – even better – and then you went into the stadium. Brilliant.

After that you were looking forward to the championship. Often after training in May or June, on a beautiful evening, you'd wonder how you'd managed to endure January to April, training in mud and rain; but it was a process, a sequence.

At the end of the season, then, after a couple of months off, you'd be looking forward to the laps on the back field in Fitzgerald Stadium all over again.

Which isn't to say that I'd take those couple of months off completely at the end of the year. Even in university, when I was sharing a house with Aodán, he, as a PE student, had the use of the Bowl at the University of Limerick, so we'd do a bit there even then. More would always stand to you, as we'd learnt watching Páidí all those years ago.

Once the ground started to harden, you knew it was getting close to the time when you'd be let into Fitzgerald Stadium itself, the main pitch. That was like a carpet after the winter on the back field, it was minded so well.

The physical element remained, but instead of laps of the back field you were doing wire-to-wire runs across the stadium. Sharpening and honing the body for championship – I loved that training. Or we'd run from the end line to the 21-metre line and back, then the end line to the 13-metre line and back, five times in a row.

At that stage, in the Páidí era, there were no weights, so the week was like this: training on a Tuesday for an hour and a half; the same on a Thursday – no meetings after training – and if there was a home league match at the weekend you met in the dressing-room, no meal together beforehand.

The week of a championship game, with Páidí you had a light session on a Tuesday night, and on the Thursday you'd tog out, stretch, have a tiny jog and then kick into one goal, then the other, and then stretch again, and home. Thirty-five minutes, maybe.

Nowadays the approach is very different. The Tuesday before a championship game you'd do ninety minutes on the field – thirty minutes of football at full pace, fellas driving into each other, a lot of tackling drills. That was unheard of when I started. On the Thursday night you'd still have a session of over an hour, conditioned games, and still pretty physical – plenty of contact.

That was always tricky enough for me, because, while I wouldn't dream of pulling out of challenges in a game, I would be of the old school the week of a championship game, keeping myself fresh for the clash at the weekend.

When Jack would say, 'We'll have a bit more' at those sessions, I didn't like it, and when Cian O'Neill came in, after Jack's time, those late sessions got longer still, which made me even crankier.

Then there were meetings. Before a championship game PO would have a meeting for us down in the Gleneagle Hotel in Killarney, but it wouldn't be nearly as long as the meetings we had when I was finishing up.

The ball work remained a constant, though. People remind me the odd time about the exchange I had with Des Cahill on *The Sunday Game*, when he asked me about the kicking skills in Kerry, and I said, 'Well, it's called football.'

I treated every part of training with Kerry seriously. That didn't just *include* the warm-up: it meant the warm-up specifically. If you saw us coming out to train and bombing the ball in on the goal, you might have thought we were messing or having some down time before the serious business got under way, but we weren't. You were kicking left, kicking right, with purpose, not ballooning the ball anywhere at all. As a half-back I'd be picking out a man and trying to land a ball into his chest forty yards away with the right leg. With the left leg. A different man. Another angle. Before training would even begin I'd have more than forty balls kicked.

When I see fellas coming out to train and running around in circles loosening themselves out … I'd do that in the dressing-room. Being out on the field is for kicking practice, and I wouldn't be alone in thinking that. Gooch would be out there, shooting with his left and his right. At various times over the years Maurice Fitzgerald, Dara Ó Cinnéide and Bryan Sheehan would be lining up frees – and all of them staying on afterwards to get some more practice in.

Everyone out on the field was working on skills, even though it wasn't organised. Looking at it, you might have thought it was just fellas booting a ball around the place, but it it wasn't. That was twenty minutes of skill work before the whistle went for training, and if you got twenty minutes of work done like that every few days, you'd be bound to improve, and that's what stood to us.

I'd have heard people saying we were training hard or getting up early in the morning for sessions. We weren't. Because of that warm-up work, and because I always had a ball when I was younger, we had the skills from a young age. I see kids now and they have Playstations, so spending that amount of time in the back garden kicking a ball around isn't the same.

Parents should realise that. They have a lot to answer for. The skills must be practised, whether that's football or hurling or whatever your sport. I love seeing kids in Cork and Kilkenny and these places walking around with the camán in the hand. I passed a shop one time in Kilkenny and there was a sign outside, *Hurleys must be left at the door.*

That's born into you. It's in Kilkenny for hurling, it's in Kerry for football, whereas in other counties, like Cork, it's diluted by other sports. Those skills count. I've never seen a midfielder who could deliver a ball like Darragh, for instance. He'd put the ball into your eye from forty yards, no problem.

Fellas are carrying the ball now, because they're not confident of delivering it accurately over distance. We had players who could find you 99 per cent of the time, and if you had to give a ball to someone like Johnny Crowley that was 60–40 against him, he'd turn his man upside-down to get it.

Throughout my career we had a golden era of players: the talent we had at our disposal was fantastic.

Weights were another huge change. PO always did his sit-ups and press-ups. It's a habit I carry on even now, and those weight-bearing exercises all stand to you. For all the science and progress, trainers still get players to do them.

John O'Keeffe tried to get us in to do weights, but there was no real system to it, no following it up. Nothing was monitored, and there were no collective sessions: if you wanted to do weights, fine, and if you didn't that was fine too, and when the championship came around we all forgot about them straight away.

Diet was the same. We'd eat in the Gleneagle when I started, but we moved on to the Brehon in time, and that all changed. Even getting fed regularly was a step forward: before Páidí's time the team would be fed after training in the run-up to championship games, but he made sure you were fed throughout the winter as well, which was great.

Now, you had the vegetables off to the side of the plate when you had a meal after training that time, but the meat might be covered in sauces. Diet wasn't as controlled as it is now.

On the other hand, you know well now what to eat and what not to eat. If you eat rubbish, you'll pay, so eat healthily. We had dietitians and nutritionists come in and talk to us, but you didn't need them to tell you that if you stuffed yourself with chocolates it would come against you.

I wouldn't kill myself either. I'd have a treat after my main meal every evening, no matter what, whether that was a bar of chocolate or two biscuits. I'd be fond of a pizza, and I might go to a chipper once in a while, but generally I wouldn't have a sweet tooth or too many bad habits. (I wouldn't be a wizard in the kitchen either, admittedly. In university, when Ó Cinnéide shared with me, I was spoiled a bit, because he was a great cook. His uncle John would give him fresh fish, so even when we were students, poor as church mice, we were having the best of fish, cooked very well by Dara. In return I did the washing-up. All of it.)

When Jack came in, one of the first things he insisted on was a trip abroad for training. Not a drinking holiday: a training camp, Club La Santa in Lanzarote.

And he brought in Pat Flanagan. John O'Keeffe had done great work with us, but that was the time when managers did a lot of the training themselves, and it had all ramped up.

When Pat came in he was questioned by the older players. Who is this guy? What's he doing? What does he know? Did he ever win an All-Ireland? Did he play for Kerry?

And a lot of the stuff he did with us was static: walking along, getting your knees up in the air, lifting your hands as you did it. Six times in a row. Then jogging, using the same technique, and eventually sprinting.

Fellas were laughing, but he was trying to get us quicker. In 2004 we won the All-Ireland, but he told us we wouldn't peak until 2006, and he was right. Against Mayo that year we peaked.

La Santa was the start of all that, and it was brilliant. If you were coming back in at the start of the year, it definitely gave you a great base to build on: train like a dog for a week, come back in great form and keep it tipping over then.

We'd train in the morning – a running session – then football in the afternoon and a weights session in the evening. Weights became a big deal with Pat. The programme was monitored – in fact, forget the monitoring: we actually got programmes that set out three sets of ten to do. In honesty, I found it hard to buy into the weights. I'd get tired, and eventually I just did sets of seven, and I stuck to that during my career.

I was afraid I'd get heavy, and slow, from the weights, and I said that to Pat. His answer was always that the fastest men in the world were sprinters; and, compared with long-distance runners, sprinters were the stronger, faster, bigger men.

In La Santa you were always left out for one night, though, and you'd drink so much you'd set yourself back and undo all the good work. You'd work Monday and Tuesday, and then someone would say, 'Look, you can go out Wednesday night,' and we'd dog it entirely. You'd have it in your head that you'd train hard on the Thursday, three times, but your body was destroyed. Flanagan couldn't understand that side of the GAA: 'What are ye doing to your bodies? The harm you're doing!'

One time myself and Séamus Moynihan slipped out on an afternoon for a few pints, and we came back for a weights session … We had a laugh and thought it was funny, but really you weren't treating your body properly at all.

We were as good a team for training as any, but we socialised as well. In Páidí's time we'd be gone after a championship game for three days solid. You wouldn't be expected back at all until the Thursday evening. When you did come back Johno would run the shit out of you, and our attitude was 'You do the crime, you do the time.' Madness, when you look back at it now.

Nowadays it's all about getting the body to recover. Players are let out the evening of a game for a few hours, but they're back fresh on a Monday – an easy session to get the body recovering. No punishing sessions.

In the back room Páidí had Aoife Ní Mhuirí as physio – the best, along with Neasa Long, I ever came across. First class. Dave Geaney was the team doctor, but that was it, and they wouldn't be there for every session.

When I left Kerry, Eddie Harnett (another top physio) was there as physio, with another physio alongside him. Ger Keane was the masseur – what that man can't do with his hands … He'd have you purring! And there'd usually be another with him, and maybe two doctors – and that was every session. Six there monitoring everything.

Because I was in Cork I went to Neasa Long, and she was fantastic. I never missed a championship game through injury for Kerry, and I put a lot of that down to her, even though it was dodgy enough at times whether I'd make it or not. It became a mental thing with me, that I'd have to go to her, because she always got me right. In fairness to Fitzmaurice, who wanted things done his way, if I rang him and said I wanted Neasa to look after me, he let me off. He was flexible enough.

Jack was the first to bring in analysis, and he put that to work. He allowed me to go forward, and he gave Paul Galvin the freedom to drift back. Rather than minding the house all the time, you had some freedom. Jack would shift the team around to suit our strengths: he did a lot of homework on other teams. Páidí did that, but not as much as Jack did. PO had a huge belief in Kerry's tradition, pride and history – 'Our football should be ahead of these,' that attitude. Jack tweaked things to make sure we were ahead of those teams.

The sessions got longer. I would have been a believer in tearing into the hard stuff, but Pat sometimes wanted us for a long time, and Jack would pull that back if he thought we were tiring.

Jack was also the first to bring in a head man. Páidí was our head man, and better than anyone I ever met, but Jack made that change. He also brought in diet as an issue. Pat Flanagan was the first to talk to us about the right food, but Jack brought in a dietitian to tell us not only what to eat but also when to eat.

Pat O'Shea brought another angle. Pat had no ego, which was fantastic. Jack had an attitude of 'This is the way it's going to be, and don't question it, or you can head off.' Pat listened to the older fellas in 2007. He took on board what the older fellas thought, and he was more inclined to work with the players. The only thing was that Pat Flanagan was a fully qualified fitness coach, and Pat O'Shea brought in John Sugrue, who would have been a minor with me. That meant Sugrue was younger than some of the players, and only the same age as others and Darragh, who'd be a good man for questioning things. Galvin would often have said, 'This is an actual science, and we should be able to guarantee peaking here or here.' Having said that, Sugrue had us lifting, and we won an All-Ireland with him.

You're asking fellas to peak in May, June, July, August and maybe September, though. Five games, maybe more. What are you going to do with players in between times?

We often had pow-wows, players and management, if results weren't going our way, and we'd ask why not. Fellas would be cranky, and nobody would be spared. I heard of these meetings in Munster rugby that cleared the air, but nothing beat the meetings we had. Physios would be lashed. Trainers. Players. If someone was throwing himself on the physio table for a rub and not coming out to train on time, he was lashed.

And you had to listen to fellas who'd been winning All-Irelands for seven or eight years. You couldn't dismiss their opinions, and everyone had to stand over their work.

After a meeting like that, though, you could be guaranteed a savage month's training. Everyone raised their game, from the manager and the selectors down to the players. They had to: there was too much at stake.

In my last year, this was my championship week:

Monday: Early morning: weight session, 45 minutes. That evening: a stretching programme, 30 minutes.

Tuesday: Leave Cork at half four for training, get strapped, loosen and stretch. Two hours' training and maybe a meeting afterwards, though generally the meetings were loaded for the week before the week of the game. Home in Cork, generally, at about eleven at night.

Wednesday: Weights in the morning.

Thursday: Same as Tuesday: gone from half four until eleven.

Friday: Stretching. Core session as well.

Saturday: Full football session.

Sunday: For the league we'd be in Killarney at 10 a.m. for a 2 p.m. throw-in. Breakfast together, hanging around.

As I got older that level of commitment took it out of me, obviously.

When Éamonn Fitzmaurice came in there were more changes, more improvements. Everyone had to wear the same gear, for instance. Cian O'Neill was very strong on that. The first night I came out I was only one of two or three who weren't in the right gear, and I was told to go back in and put on the right gear. I was like a spoiled brat going back in – 'What's this all about?' and so on – but, looking back, I see that it was good to be togged out in the same gear. In that first trip to La Santa, for instance, we all had different training gear on – every colour in the rainbow.

My retirement didn't have anything to do with the training regime, certainly. Fitzmaurice brought in Cian O'Neill, and I'd have questioned what he was at – 'How does a guy coming down from Kildare know what's best for us?' That kind of thinking. Páidí thinking, if you like. I didn't say it out loud, but I'd have been questioning it in my own mind all the time.

When I got to know him, I realised how wrong I had been. He was terrific, a great football man, and flexible, too. If I came to him and said, 'Look, Cian, I'm struggling with this weights programme,' he'd work around that. He'd come up with an alternative.

That's very important, for a trainer to acknowledge that everyone shouldn't do the same thing, and that everyone can't do the same thing. There'd be no point in me lifting the same weights as Anthony

Maher, particularly with my back and sitting in the car from Cork to Kerry three times a week.

That's an area where the GAA could be a little bit more professional: the weights programmes could be differentiated a little better. You hear all the time that players are doing different weights, but they're not: they're lifting lighter weights, that's what's different. Everyone is doing a bench press, but this guy is lifting a slightly lighter weight than another guy. The problem is that it's something that goes on in clubs as well, of course, where it may not be monitored as well.

One funny thing about Cian O'Neill as a trainer – funny the way it goes around – is that we did long runs, like we did years before with Johno. In those runs I'd try to be in the top three or four, always. I'd try to win every race. But in my last year we had a series of sprints: eight laps, six laps, four laps and two laps. I was well back in each of them.

I knew that wasn't me. Marc is only two years younger than me, and he won every race that night: the eight, the six, the four, the two. He was 31, and he fucked the younger fellas out of it afterwards: 'What am I doing winning these races? Why am I up the front? There's 22- and 23-year-olds in this dressing-room who should be pouring past me out on the field!'

He was right, but I had enough on my plate that night. I was very pissed off going home, thinking, Is this the writing on the wall here for me?

But I was mentally tough enough to drive on, and I also knew that the older you get, the harder it is to get up to the pace. In years past I'd have been at the pace of training in March; but by that stage I was getting to the pace of it only in May, and the last year it was taking me till July, nearly.

In 2015, when Marc came back late enough to Kerry, I asked him if he was still up the front, the top three or four, and he was.

Nowadays, David Moran and Anthony Maher are great athletes, outstanding at those long runs. Mikey Geaney and Jonathan Lyne can shift. Poor old Bryan Sheehan, you'd always beat him in the races – a great man for doing the work, but, as he said to me one time, if he even looked at a biscuit he'd put on weight.

The breed of footballer coming in now is generally different. If I look back at Darragh when he first played for Kerry, he was a slip of a young fella: he didn't see a weight until he was twenty-five, twenty-six. Now they're lifting weights at sixteen, so when they come into the senior set-up at twenty, they have the physique a 28-year-old would have had when I was starting.

Mark my words, with the pressure that's coming on players now to get stronger and stronger, it's only a matter of time before questions are asked whether some player is supping the wrong stuff. In my opinion it'll creep in: it's bound to. And it's a matter for the players, to be honest. We don't want our games going down this route. It won't make a better footballer out of you, so why bother doing it? Hopefully it won't creep into the game, but I have my doubts.

One interesting thing I noticed all through my career was the curiosity lads from other counties had about Kerry. If you were on a trip or at an All-Star do, or at some function where you'd meet other players, you soon noticed a pattern: they'd come over and ask what you were at in training, what runs you were doing, what you were lifting – *what you were lifting!* – or what drills you'd be doing.

I was often tempted to say, 'Lads, it's very easy: you do the basics right, and you do them over and over and over until you get quicker and quicker and more natural.' It sounds easy, right?

There was a time when Armagh and the northern teams brought in physical bulk, and that was great for a while, but it all comes back to football in the end. It has to. Now it's moving back to the basic skills being taught from the grass roots up, but that's always been the case in Kerry.

Through Páidí, Jack, Pat and Fitzmaurice, the greater proportion of time in training has been devoted to ball work. The weights can be done another time, and are, but it's all about the ball.

What good is lifting 100 kg if you can't put the ball where you want it?

Chapter 10

LIFE AS A PLAYER

I mentioned earlier that I got abused by a spectator after my first game against Cork, in 1998, and how that affected me – how I couldn't sleep for weeks properly after that game, how it scalded me.

That's one of the things spectators don't see. Supporters don't appreciate that side of things. Playing poorly or suffering a defeat never spilled into my place of work, luckily enough. The only slagging I'd get in the school would be from the teaching staff, say, rather than from the students, and it wouldn't be harsh.

I don't see Gaelic football as the huge, dominant topic in Fermoy, Cork, where I work, compared with back home, though my boss is from Kerry and the chat would be all football after a weekend, or before a weekend, when there are matches on.

It suited me in my career to be away from the intensity and pressure you'd face in Kerry. When I'd come back down to teach in Fermoy there'd be no huge interest in football from most of the kids. There'd always be one or two in the class who'd take an interest, probably because of the parents, but when we'd play Cork in a Munster final, for instance, everyone would be on holidays anyway.

It got funny when we played Cork in a couple of All-Ireland finals, because you'd be back teaching in September, and, with the county in the All-Ireland, flags and bunting would have to be put up. So, yes, I was putting up the red and white all over the school in Fermoy …

That helped me focus. And I'd always support Cork when they were playing. In fairness, I don't think any of the kids or parents would ever be able to say, 'Jaysus, he's black altogether against Cork.' That wouldn't be the case.

Some of the lads in Kerry would probably love that kind of low-pressure build-up. Kieran Donaghy told me one time that if he was on a lunch break in Tralee and saw a couple of likely lads coming against him who were obviously angling for a long football chat, he'd whip the phone out and jam it to the ear in order to put them off.

It's not that you're being rude, but if you were in the towns in Kerry there's nothing but football talk. You could get asked the same question twenty or thirty times if you're working in the bank or on the road. That would have to wear away at you. Obviously the older you get, the more experience teaches you: where you can go to lunch, a place where nobody bothers you about a game, where to avoid – all that.

I loved getting back to Cork, strolling around, with nobody asking how training was or how you'd do against Armagh or who-ever. Coming up to a game, I'd tune myself in and get myself ready, but there was a time for that: a few days before the game, not a full fortnight beforehand.

Everybody's different. Some lads liked talking football, morning, noon and night, but that wasn't for me. I'd throw out the party line – training's going well, the boys look very good, we've a big job on our hands – so much so that I could have predicted what I'd be saying for matches five years down the line. The names changed, but that was all.

That's why I didn't like talking to the media. My thinking was quite simple: what benefit would it be to me to reveal my real thoughts about a serious game, about serious opponents and their strengths and weaknesses?

In a team meeting it was different. I'd slate the opposition's weak points, but we weren't in the UFC: you weren't trying to drum up interest in a fight with Conor McGregor. I saw no benefit in being in the newspaper.

It's different now. I won't go so far as to say I love talking to journalists – that might be a stretch – but I like talking football. As a player I didn't.

For the last few years of my career I'd say to Jack or Fitzmaurice, if there was a media night, 'I'd love to hang on, but I've to get back to Cork.'

And if I had to go to the press event … We'd be told that the media night was down in the Brehon in Killarney, say, so I'd head home. The next night, then, at training, I'd say to Jack, 'The Brehon? I thought it was in the Malton. I was down there for half an hour waiting!'

He knew well. And towards the end I'd say his logic was 'If I tell him to go again, and he doesn't, I'll look bad,' so he just left me off.

The other two, Darragh and Marc, were the same – no interest in talking to the media.

But certain guys were very comfortable doing it. Donaghy was quite at home chatting away. So was Fitzmaurice, though he didn't enjoy it. The usual line-up of players assigned to the media night would be the captain (who had to go), the injured players and the suspended players.

There was always the argument that the supporters deserved a look inside the tent to see what was being done. My counter to that was that they'd enjoy us winning a match a lot more, and that we should be more concentrated on that than on giving out information.

For a while there were suggestions that there was a mole in the camp. There was an article written that contained stuff mentioned in a private meeting, and some of the players had their own ideas as to who was feeding this stuff.

It was frowned on. We were very tight, and this came out, and for a couple of years there were suspicions. People were very wary of the media as a result. I'm friendly with the sports editor of the *Examiner*.

He's a good Kerry supporter and has a tough job running a Cork newspaper: people see everything he writes as being pro-Kerry, while I'd say he's specifically not doing that at all.

We were out in Amendoeira in Portugal once at a training camp. Tony holidays there and wanted to come down to watch a session. It was pre-championship, April or May, but you'd get a fair idea of the shape of the team for summer if you were there. I knew well that he wouldn't be silly enough to write 'Tomás Ó Sé will be playing full-forward for Kerry in the championship' based on what he might see there. You need to be able to trust people in that game.

When Tony came down, though, some of the players wanted to know what he was at, and he was asked to leave a couple of times. That stemmed from the newspaper articles based on information being given out from the inner circle. You don't do that. There'd be certain stuff I wouldn't say, even now, that would cross boundaries. There's trust involved in a team, and when Jack wrote his book, as I've said before, I didn't trust him as much in his second stint, because I felt that trust had been broken. (Now, there's more he could have written – deeper stuff, in fairness – so it goes both ways.)

———

In my seventeen years with Kerry my buddies were the team: I went out with them, I socialised with them, I played golf with them. And now, when it's over … I stay in touch and I text them, but you wouldn't see them as much, obviously.

Throughout my career I always had the three or four buddies from home I'd be in touch with – the best buddies I had were Darragh and Marc, and obviously I'm still close to them – but when you're gone, you're gone. It's over. The players on the inside need to know that they can trust each other, that stuff that happens in-house stays in-house.

There were plenty of problems over the years – fights and bust-ups, fellas leaving panels and coming back – all of which never came out, and proper order. The time myself and Gooch went offside was an exception, though.

That year, 2009, we were working hard and training well, but it just wasn't clicking in games. There was just something about the games early on in the year: we were stuttering a bit, though we were super-sharp in training. Flying altogether.

I was cranky enough in myself. Even though I wasn't picking up red cards or getting suspended, I wasn't happy. In the back-door game against Sligo down in Tralee we were on the ropes, but it was one of my better games. Galvin had a good game as well the same evening.

We never liked playing championship in Tralee. The sod is different. The stand is different. The field itself seems narrower and shorter. The surroundings are different. All of which adds up to saying it's no Killarney, basically.

But we got over the line eventually against Sligo. I had buddies over from Birmingham. They were going to a wedding in Dingle, and, as I was driving back, I said I'd meet them for a pint in the Dingle Skellig.

We – by which I mean myself, Darragh and Marc, who were with me – went on and made a night of it inside in Dingle, hitting Dick Mack's and a few more places, and the following day the Birmingham lads were around as well, and we had a few pints that afternoon. Now, as a team we were good for socialising, but we also knew where and when to draw the line. We wouldn't have won what we did otherwise. But we transgressed that time, all right. Fair enough.

There were no contracts drawn up for the players, no agreements written in stone, but we knew we were wrong. There was a game the following weekend, and pints on the Sunday were wrong. We knew that.

Since Páidí had gone from Kerry, west of Dingle was a haven for us. Ard an Bhóthair is a long way from south Kerry, and we were having a few pints in Páidí's pub. But a neighbour of Jack's was inside there as well, and he carried the story back. It all came out.

I knew it was coming: a third party rang me to tip me off that there was trouble on the way.

A lot of people thought I was with the Gooch that time: not at all. To this day I don't know what he was doing, and I never asked him. After it all finished we'd have a great laugh about it – 'Where did we go on to after that?' 'What did we do then?' That kind of thing.

When Jack rang me and said, 'You were drinking,' I said, 'Yeah.' I'd say he was taken aback, but he said there'd have to be a sanction. He asked me to meet him and the selectors in the Park Hotel in Killarney before that night's training. At that point nobody really knew about Darragh or Marc, and I wasn't going to volunteer any information about them.

I met him and the selectors, and they said they were dropping me for the next game. I took it on the chin and said, 'Grand,' and off with us to training.

After training there was a players' meeting. Darragh just denied having pints, point blank. Marc hadn't had too many; he said he hadn't been drinking.

Darragh wasn't happy that we were dropped for the next game. We were playing Antrim, and it would have been interesting to see if we would have been dropped if we were playing Dublin, maybe.

I'd like to think that the players in the dressing-room would have known that I took nothing more seriously than Kerry. I wasn't right, and I went off and did it anyway; but it was wrong, and I knew it was wrong, and I certainly didn't make a habit of it. I took it on the chin.

Before the next game it came out on the front page of the *Examiner*. I rang Tony Leen and asked what was going on. Not only were we disciplined but we were disciplined for drinking – and this was on the front page of a national newspaper.

I thought it was completely and utterly wrong. If Páidí or Fitzmaurice had been in charge it wouldn't have come out like that. I didn't like the way it came out, and Jack could have handled that better; we could have organised releasing that information in a better way, and it wouldn't have mattered as long as we were strong-minded enough to keep focused. It pissed me off.

One thing I'll always be grateful for was the support of the Kerry crowd for that Antrim match. It was on in Tullamore, a hot, sunny day, and myself and Gooch were being watched by everyone when we came out and did our warm-up.

There was a big Kerry crowd there when we went out, and they gave us a huge welcome. It lifted us so much that it was mentioned in the dressing-room afterwards. We got the win, and Jack got to look strong out of it too – 'I'm not afraid to drop big names,' that kind of thing.

I had no beef with being dropped. I had no beef with the players' meeting either: Jack and the selectors stepped out of it, and we had as good a pow-wow as Munster rugby ever had. After that meeting we were able to go out and train hard together too.

I wouldn't have any grudges against anyone who said anything in that meeting. I admired the likes of Mícheál Quirke and Declan O'Sullivan, who stood up and said, 'What happened was wrong. It doesn't matter who did it or who didn't do it, but whoever did it should stand up and take their medicine.' They were two of the lads who'd back you the most and have the balls to say it. That's honesty, and I had no problem taking my medicine. There were others probably thinking the same, but those two said it out loud. Myself and the Gooch had no problem acknowledging it: we apologised to the team, and everything moved on. Sometimes players aren't happy, and the bitching carries on, but not in this case. You could tell that from the performance against Dublin and against Cork in the final that year.

We were just beginning to purr, and once we faced into Dublin, with the whole country saying we were gone, everything was in place.

———

Dealing with the media was easy when we started off, because, again, absolutely everything was run through Páidí. All the interview requests went to him.

It's gas now to think of the media nights we had back then. We'd be out on the field in Killarney, kicking balls into the goal, and then maybe a dozen or so journalists would come wandering out among us. Some guy would get caught, and they'd congregate around him, and of course all of us would rain balls down on top of them. Maybe that's how the kicking got so accurate, trying to pick out the odd journalist at the media nights.

Afterwards you weren't safe either: you might stroll out of the showers, balls naked, and there'd be a tape recorder shoved at you. But that's what it was like; that was the craic. You'd be chatting away and Darragh or someone might shove their backside into you, or into the journalist, for a laugh.

In general, though, as I've said, I didn't see the advantage in talking too much – particularly as I made a point myself of rooting through the papers the day or two before a big game to see the other side's interviews, to see if there was any chink in their armour that I could pick up on. And if there wasn't a chink I'd make one up. The last thing I wanted to do was to give them a way into our world.

I love talking football. Over a cup of tea, or dinner, I love a conversation about football – tactics, style, players. Always. I never got into Twitter before retiring, because I wanted to focus on football, pure and simple. If I hadn't it would have been thrown at me.

For instance, I know Paul Galvin well, and I'm well aware of the opportunities he's turned down over the years. Why? Because if he had a poor game it'd be the first thing thrown at him, that he was distracted by this or that, by whatever he was doing away from football.

Completely wrong. Everyone has a right to say and do what they want in private, away from football. There's an expectation when you're a Kerry footballer, a way to behave, but that's not written down anywhere. If as a Kerry player you're acting the clown on the field, or off it, a player will come up to you, or a manager or selector, and you'll be told how to behave.

———

Starting off, I got a lot of yellow cards, but I think you wouldn't find someone who'd say I was dirty or started a lot of fights, or fouled a lot. Bookies gave odds on me for the first yellow, or for me definitely getting a yellow. My friends would have been onto me, but that all settled down. I had a run of nine or ten years when I got no more yellow cards than the average player.

It's hard to pinpoint it when it happens, because you're in the middle of it. But if you're under pressure at work, or at home, or in university, it can get on top of you quickly enough. You're playing away, training away, but then you get a run when you're rising to it, and the cards are coming thick and fast.

That was 2012 for me. For a while there, if a guy hit me or got a rise from me I'd have no control over myself for a second or two. None at all. I was just back after two months' suspension, and I was back for a game against Laois in Killarney.

Jack rang me the night before: 'How are you now?'

'Good,' I said. 'I'm in a good place.'

'We can't afford to have this going on. You know that,' he said. And he was right.

I thought I was fine. I felt grand the morning of the game and drove away to Killarney in good form. I togged and went out – and within six or seven minutes I was sent off.

Brendan Quigley, a Laois midfielder, threw a dig at me, and I reacted by hitting him a box in the stomach. In fairness to him, most fellas would have thrown themselves down on the ground, but he stayed up. Unfortunately for me, the linesman had a good view of proceedings, and I got a straight red.

By the time the match was over I was at home in Cork. I was ashamed to face the players again, ashamed for them to be thinking, You can't trust him to stay on the field.

The one thing in my favour was that, when it came to the championship, I'd be zoned in.

Down the years if a fella wanted to get rough I was quite happy to dish it back to them. There were plenty of punches that nobody saw, and I could have been sent off a lot more if I'd been seen. Against Armagh in Tralee, for example, I was trying to get away from Ciarán McKeever in order to take a quick free, but he was holding onto me, and I lashed out.

The main point to make is that getting sent off doesn't make you a hard man: it shows that you're a stupid player, a clown. There's nothing hard about it. A hard man is someone who'll run thirty yards to go down on a ball at the risk of getting a boot in the head, or someone who'll make five runs in a row without getting a pass but who'll still make a sixth run even though he's knackered. Lashing out, losing your control – that's a cowardly way to act.

Those red cards came along in a short period of time. I wasn't on Twitter at that stage, but there were plenty of people to tell me about the reaction to all those red cards, the disgraceful behaviour and so on. I'd be tough enough to know that I was going to come out the other side of it, but it wasn't easy.

People need to remember that fact when they're commenting on players and their performances. That time my marriage had broken up, so there was a lot to deal with in matching the stress around that to preparing for an elite sport. There was a property boom in the country, and, like a lot of people, I took a punt. And, like a lot of other people, my punt didn't come in. I had a lot going on, and I dealt with it.

Jack, Fitzmaurice – all of them were very good to me, in fairness, and very accommodating; but a lot of people weren't aware of that in their commentary on games. There are players under similar stress on every team in Ireland.

I never got sick before games, ever. But it all came to a head going up on the train to play Meath in the 2009 All-Ireland semi-final. My vision blurred, and there were shadows in my vision. I was as weak as water, as though I had the flu, and I got a massive migraine. I wasn't right at all the night before the game, so the following morning I was going to pull out of the team. I couldn't eat on the Saturday night, and I barely had anything that morning either.

I got an injection before the game. It turned out to be one of the best games I played that year. I dropped two balls short, into the keeper, and if they'd gone over I'd probably have got the man of the match award.

I was marking Peadar Byrne, who'd won a certain number of breaks the previous day, and I never got onto as many breaks myself the same day, driving on with the ball every time.

I was shattered afterwards. Absolutely empty. It happened to me one other time, out on the golf course, but it hasn't happened to me since retiring.

It probably contributed to my retiring, in the end. It is what it is, and I'm not looking for sympathy: I'm just offering it as context. If people were to ask me why I was getting sent off so often, that would be the only reason I can come up with: the stress I was under away from the matches.

As an intercounty footballer it's not just a matter of being focused: it's a case of being selfish, and you have to be selfish about everything. For some players it's number two or three, but for me it was always number one, probably to my detriment, but it was always that way.

Certain fellas don't have that outlook, but, because I did, it made it hard for me when I retired. That's why I went back playing club football – for the enjoyment – but the day is coming when I won't be able to play club football, so I might as well enjoy it while I can.

People don't realise what an intercounty footballer faces on a Monday morning. I face a classroom. Other lads face different scenarios: they have customers and clients in front of them. Every one of them goes out to do their best, but in the case of the national league, for instance, Kerry might be training hard throughout the league, but if a guy doesn't go well in a league match, my God, it's like a tribunal of inquiry in the county. Why isn't he going well? What's wrong with him? Weeshie Fogarty on the radio asking questions …

We won a lot, and we lost a lot, but if someone came after me now with questions I'd be inclined to go for him. Darragh could laugh at lads and pay no attention, but my fuse would be shorter, and I'd react. Someone who has no notion of the effort being put in … I wouldn't take too kindly to their input at times, put it that way.

I didn't take too kindly to the input of some refs either, over the years, but I'm not blind to the challenges they face.

The first time I was ever put off I got a huge fright. I was a minor, and I mistimed a tackle on Denis Sayers from Stacks, which put him up in the air. The referee just flashed the red – gone. I thought I'd miss out on the Kerry minors, because it was about that time, and I started crying in the dressing-room.

The second time was against Dublin and Collie Moran in 2001. The same issue, mistiming a shoulder by half a second. I should have paid more attention to Séamus Moynihan, who was the best man I ever saw for timing a shoulder. (Peter Crowley is tasty enough at it now for Kerry.)

There are great referees around, or were, at any rate.

Pat McEnaney refereed on common sense, and he had a good, deep knowledge of footballers. He'd know if a fella was a scamp or not. If there was a situation so outrageous that a red card was warranted, fair enough, he'd flash it; but he was inclined to give players the benefit of the doubt. Another thing he'd do – something Maurice Deegan and David Coldrick would also do – is that he'd talk to you, rather than treat you like a child. Coldrick will admit to you that he's made a mistake out on the field, at least. That's not weakness; that's strength.

I've seen weak referees make a harsh call against you: the crowd reacts, you fuck the referee out of it – and then they give you the next dubious call.

That said, it's not all on the referees' side. They should get a lot more respect than they do, because who'd be a referee, with the abuse they get? A ref has a split second to make a decision, and on that basis they're doing a great job, though they're not helped by the fact that Congress change the rules every year on them. What might make their job easier would be for them to visit the dressing-rooms of both teams before championship games to explain what they were going to concentrate on, the way rugby referees do.

Would I be a referee? I would not indeed!

Chapter 11

MANAGERS: WEARING THE BIB

People imagine that I just didn't get on with Jack O'Connor as soon as he became Kerry senior football manager – that it was instant conflict, immediate and continuing. They forget that I knew Jack for a long time before that. Jack was the manager of the under-21 teams I played on, and PO worked with him then. I'd heard of him before that again, even, as an up-and-coming coach in south Kerry who was bound to go far.

Jack has a distinct personality. If you met him and didn't know him you might get the impression that he's a rude man. I know him, and I don't think so at all: he's a grand fella and a very good manager, as he's proved, over and over.

I go back with Jack, and he has a pile of good points. Absolutely. Coming in after Páidí, he probably thought we had an issue with him, given the way Páidí went. Now, we probably had an issue with the way Páidí went, but that didn't mean we had an issue with Jack. Those two thoughts didn't necessarily connect.

I'd won an under-21 All-Ireland medal with Jack and reached two finals and an All-Ireland semi-final. That's a lot of training sessions, a lot of games. I knew well that he had a different personality and a different approach from Páidí's long before he came in as manager.

His greatest strength was in setting out a way of playing tactically, and in analysing the opposition. He was the first manager we had, really, who broke down the opposition. For instance, a lot of the time people never copped it, including journalists, but I was always put on someone who suited me. The backs were always put on fellas specifically, particularly the corner-backs. Wherever Bernard Brogan went when we played Dublin, it didn't matter: Tom O'Sullivan always went with him. He was the man-marker, him or Mike McCarthy, or our Marc.

I was always put on a guy who would suit my game, which meant I was generally kept away from forwards who might cause us problems on the scoreboard. I would have marked them, and I could have, but it might take away from my attacking role. To be fair, Jack was the first manager at intercounty level who recognised what I could offer there.

If you break down the six forwards on any modern intercounty team, there'd always be one or two who'd range around the middle of the park, and they'd be the men I'd pick up, because it suited my game. I could cause trouble by ranging forward and forcing them to back-pedal in order to cover.

In fairness to Jack, he was the first fella to spot that. Páidí would have been more of a traditionalist, along the lines of his own playing days: 'You're the number 5. You wait there for your man to come into you at the start of the game, and you mark him. That's your job for the day.' Páidí's attitude was that, as a wing-back, you were a defender, there to defend. Anything you could manage after that, fine, but your first job was to stop your man. Páidí wouldn't always have welcomed me going upfield on the attack.

In 2004, when Jack came in, An Ghaeltacht had got to the All-Ireland club final. All that year I'd been bombing forward from centre-back, flying it, fit as a fiddle and well able to get up and down the field supporting the attack, as well as comfortably carrying out my defensive duties. And Jack allowed me to carry on like that with

Kerry. 'If you have the legs to go, go' was his attitude. I'd had six years, from 1998 to 2003, when I'd been playing for Kerry without having that freedom. Maybe if I'd had that run with the club earlier in those years Páidí might have given me that freedom, but I'm not sure.

I can remember playing for the club at sixteen in a senior game and nearly getting killed by older fellas. I'd solo up the field from the half-back line and present a fine target for more developed lads trying to break me in two with shoulder charges. Toots Mac Gearailt from back our way told me, 'You won't last two years if you keep going up the field like that.' Sorry, now, Toots, but I got a bit more out of it than that.

It was Jack who gave me that freedom. Certainly he had other areas where he was stronger than Páidí. For instance, he put more importance on the league. Páidí was all about the championship, always, but the first year Jack came in we won the league.

He'd always make sure we got as much as we could out of every game, and since those days Kerry have always treated the league with a lot more seriousness, getting something out of every game.

In breaking down the opposition, Jack would use video of the other team – their strengths, their weaknesses, how they attacked and defended. Páidí had done that – a little bit – but he used to do it all himself; he'd done everything, from organising the food to training us. But Jack brought it on.

When you look back at Páidí's work load in the cold light of day, or in the cold light of 2015, it was too much, but that was just the way it was. He had someone to do the work with the video. Fitzmaurice did it at first when he came in as a selector. And he didn't just do it for the opposition: he'd break us down in video sessions as well – lengthy meetings.

Those meetings could last an hour, an hour and a half, and I half dreaded them, they went on so long. But they were useful, and I recognised that. You learnt a lot: every time you came out of a meeting you had another nugget that would help. Every single player on the opposing team was analysed. What did they do with the ball? What way did they attack? What did they do when they were under pressure? There would have been ten or more different ways of analysing the opposition.

That has come on again in recent years. Practically every county now has access to a computer system in which their players can enter the name of an opponent from another county and – bang! – every instance of that opponent touching the ball in a league or championship game is brought up instantly.

Before Jack came in, the notion of doing that level of analysis was unheard of. If you were playing Tipperary you'd know of Declan Browne, but you wouldn't be hearing 'Their number 7 will play at number 5' or 'They like to bang the ball in long to their full-forward.'

A lot of the players from so-called weaker teams wouldn't be known at all to us. That was dangerous, and it was leaving yourself wide open to the unknown.

Jack would also ring you during the week to tell you who you were on. If one of the younger lads wasn't going well in training he'd zone in on them and spend a lot of time on getting them right. He paid attention to that kind of thing and was good at it.

His weak point for me was that, when a player wasn't going well in games, he didn't go the right way about helping them. You need to push certain buttons with certain guys. Take Declan O'Sullivan, when he was going through a rough patch and got booed off the field below in Páirc Uí Chaoimh. (That was a low point for those Kerry supporters who did so, by the way.) I don't know the full facts of it, but I'd know that Jack and Declan would have been travelling to training and games together, and I don't know if that was a huge help to Declan in that situation. Maybe it put pressure on him that was unnecessary.

There was pressure on Jack, obviously, because Declan was the captain he wanted – his own clubmate – and it wasn't working out for them. It was a very tough move for him to have to take Declan off in such a big game. That wasn't easy.

I suppose the media drove it on a bit too, by suggesting that there was a problem between us. But Jack wouldn't be able to say, really, that we had an issue with him.

One time Darragh was struggling with his game, and the management were trying everything they could to get him firing. Ger O'Keeffe actually met him one evening on a pitch in Tralee to fire balls out to him so that Darragh could fetch them and get his timing back. Did you ever hear the likes of that? In the end Darragh just picked up the phone to Jack and said to cut the bullshit: either pick him or drop him.

I'm a teacher myself, and maybe I recognised that we were treated like children in class at times. Sometimes that was good and sometimes it wasn't, but whichever it was you'd have to say that he was the most successful manager we had.

One thing about Jack was that, while he'd let on that he's thick-skinned enough, I think sometimes things got to him. Being Kerry manager is a tough job: you're in the public eye, and when the results aren't coming it's easy for fellas with six, seven, eight All-Ireland medals in their back pockets to be making comments.

And I'd say Jack took that personally: 'Oh, the lads think now that, because I didn't play at the level they played at, I can't do the job.' He needn't have felt like that. He was a far better coach than the lot of them put together, and he shouldn't have felt insecure about that. Maybe he'd disagree, but that was my impression.

He achieved more as a manager than every one of those guys, which was some feat, and I don't think he's finished yet. I think he's doing superbly with the minors, and management is like a drug for him: he gets a buzz off it. It's brilliant for Kerry under-age football that they have a guy like him there.

He knew the pressure the job could heap up on top of you before becoming manager, though. Remember, he was a selector of Páidí's when Páidí wasn't playing Maurice Fitzgerald, and I'd say that Jack, coming from south Kerry, heard plenty of complaints in his home place about Maurice being dropped from the team.

In my experience, though, the buck stops with the manager when it comes to picking a player, and Páidí must have had his reasons for not picking Maurice. He had a huge impact on games when we were bringing him on as a sub in 2000, but I don't know if he'd have had the same effect as a starter. Páidí won the All-Ireland that year, but it was still an issue, because Maurice is an icon not just in south Kerry but also in the rest of Kerry and in Ireland. And Jack is the kind of person who'd remember the comments made to him, or about him, at that time.

———

When Jack came back to manage us the second time it was different, though, because in the interim he'd written a book about Kerry, and it went into fair detail.

Now, as I've mentioned, there was a lot more he could have written in that book – stuff that would have rubbed us and others up the wrong way. We'd have stepped offside in our time: I'd have no problem admitting that. But, as I've said, trust is hugely important in a team set-up like that, and specifically the trust between management and players.

How did we keep winning together, you might ask? I got on well enough with Jack most of the time. We had a laugh together a lot of that time, in fact. I'd hate to fall out with him, because we won an awful lot together, and I have great time for him and for what he has achieved. We had great times, and some not so great ones, but the good far outweighed the bad.

But coming back after the book … It was spoken about among the players, and we – or I, at any rate – would have expected him to say something like 'Look, I wrote a book, and it might have pissed some of ye off,' or whatever. Maybe he did that on an individual basis, but it wasn't raised with the group as a whole.

In his book he referred to the game against Longford I was taken off in – and after which I shot off out the dressing-room door back to Cork before the game was over. That was wrong, and I knew it was wrong. When he rang me about it he said I'd have to apologise to the team.

So down I went to the bottom of the field in Fitzgerald Stadium before the next training session, and I had to stand up and say, 'I walked out the last day after being taken off, and I apologise for that. The next game is in Croke Park, so I won't be able to get a car outside the door for that, anyway.'

Jack mentioned in the book that I made a joke of it, but it was a harmless enough one. I don't agree with giving away secrets like that, though, particularly if you're going to come back and coach the team again.

Someone might point out that I'm discussing matters myself in this book, but most of it is related to myself and my experiences, and I wouldn't be giving away secrets about anyone either. That's important to me.

There were stories Jack used (such as O'Mahony considering retirement after going offside away on a training camp), and I thought that implicating fellas when you were going to be taking over the team again … I'd have been sceptical anyway, because of the trust issue I'd had with him in his first stint; but in the second stint he had I was dubious (though, to be fair, that's only my personal view).

We won the All-Ireland his first year back, but not afterwards. Did it make a difference? At that level, the very top, I think it does.

Every half per cent adds up, and I think it was an issue. Darragh was the same.

This isn't a witch-hunt, or a matter of settling scores with Jack: he has positives and negatives, as had Páidí and Pat O'Shea. So does Fitzmaurice. My abiding memories of the time with Jack are more positive than negative. He changed things up when he had to, and he was brave enough to make bold moves.

Moving Kieran Donaghy to full-forward for the Longford game back in 2006, for instance, was a master-stroke from Jack. It was the making of Donaghy, and it energised the team. We weren't going well at the time, and it can be unbelievably difficult to change things around for a team. Just saying that things are flat isn't enough to improve things, and, in fairness to Jack, it was a roll of the dice with Donaghy that worked out brilliantly: nobody could handle him. I'd joke with Donaghy in the dressing-room: 'That ball is going in, no matter what angle or height. If we're under pressure you're going to get it.'

And we'd laugh, but he'd field it. To be fair to him, we'd try to put it in to him at an angle, because if you put it on top of him you were giving the full-back the advantage. We weren't just bombing in the ball: Jack would bring up clips showing Donaghy winning the high ball – but winning it out beyond the 21. Jack would be saying, 'I don't want him to win the ball there: I want him winning it in on the edge of the square, so that, when he comes down, one tap and it's one on one.'

In Kerry the buck always stops with the manager, and Jack deserves the credit for it. He had to make tough decisions, and he made them. I'd have felt that Gooch, Declan and Moynihan were his men, that he didn't feel threatened by them the way he was by Darragh, say.

He lived and breathed the job, he took time off work for it, and he worked hard for his success. Bringing Mike McCarthy out to centre-back was another great move in 2009; so was the tactic of driving the ball into Johnny Crowley in 2004, who was the best man for dominating any ball to come into him.

I won four All-Stars under Jack, and I don't think I'd have won them if he hadn't allowed me to play my game. He's won at colleges, minor, under-21 and senior level, so you have to give him credit: he doesn't have to answer to anyone in relation to management.

I texted my best wishes to him before his minor team played their games in 2014, and, as I said, I wouldn't be wanting to fall out with him; but I have my views on his management style. I think the sanctuary of the dressing-room is sacred, and at times I don't think you have the right to breach that.

I had issues with his man-management; but nobody has all the virtues, have they?

Jack had stepped back after we won in 2006. The funny thing about him is that he has a knack for spotting winning teams, and he's always had that. When I saw him taking over the Kerry minors in 2014 I knew well that they had a great chance of winning the All-Ireland.

Did he think we were maybe going over the top? Possibly. He said he was mentally tired in 2006, and maybe he was, but a point worth making now is that we were certainly disappointed to see him go. People should know that. And he could well have been tired at that point.

———

If you asked any of the Kerry lads I played alongside what managers they'd be fascinated by, I'd say most would go for Mick O'Dwyer and Brian Cody. How Cody keeps a team hungry year after year, success after success, I don't know. He's obviously a psychologist of the highest order and would wipe the floor with any of these sports psychologists. O'Dwyer the same.

How else would you keep winning All-Irelands? Their ability to get inside fellas' heads … It's a mixture of things, but central to that has to be their own thinking: it's twisted. It has to be.

The likes of O'Dwyer and Cody would never give away their deepest, darkest secrets when it comes to tapping into different players, to getting the best out of them as individuals and as a team. Why should they? These are special men, once-off individuals.

Surprisingly enough, I know the Kilkenny man, Cody, better than I know the Kerryman. I've never sat down and had a decent one-to-one chat with O'Dwyer, but I've spoken to Cody numerous times – a deep, deep character. He knows how to get players going, he knows how to motivate them, and that's a gift.

I was at a promotion gig one time with Cody, and we were taking questions from the audience. One guy asked him a question – a normal enough question, seemingly, but there was obviously something to it, because straight away Cody asked if he had a background in psychology. He did, too. Cody knew that immediately. He's a step ahead all the time.

———

I went back a long way with Jack's replacement as Kerry manager, Pat O'Shea. I can remember being in primary school in west Kerry and him coming in to coach us. That was thirty years ago, and he's still doing it, still coaching kids, though now he's over all the coaches, with the Munster Council. To be doing that job for so long shows you how he feels about the game: he's fanatical about it, loves playing it, thinking about it, talking about it.

He loves his job, working on football all the time.

What I admired about him as a manager was that he came into us when we were a pretty seasoned bunch – plenty of All-Ireland medals in the group, a lot of experience of All-Ireland finals, Munster finals, all that. But Pat was immediately impressive, because there was no self-importance about him; there was no sense of him feeling that he had to put a big stamp on everything, or of him having to dominate the room all the time.

And that was a good change after Páidí and Jack. The two of them had egos, and I'm not saying that in a bad way. But in the first meeting we had with Pat after he became manager he said, 'There's more experience in this room about playing for Kerry and winning All-Irelands than I can give.' Now, he was still the boss, but he was trying to get across to us the importance of working together.

He made the point at the start himself that he hadn't played championship for Kerry, so he got that out of the way early. He planned the sessions meticulously. He often refereed the games himself, and he made it very enjoyable.

The great thing about having Pat as manager was that he'd always take your point of view on board. He'd come to you and bounce his ideas off you. One of his things was that he'd ask you, 'What are you going to take out of training tonight?' His attitude was that you always had to be learning, always developing, at training – that you had to make yourself better all the time.

To me that's the beauty of the GAA, because that's something you can say to a ten-year-old starting off or to a thirty-year-old with three All-Ireland medals won already.

Pat his own quirks too. Take the book …

Pat's a big basketball man. He follows it closely, and he played himself, to national level, under-age. A big hoops man: he loved Michael Jordan and Phil Jackson – their attitude as much as anything else. Anyway, after training one evening, he called me over as I was heading out the door and gave me a book, *How to Be Like Mike*, about Michael Jordan.

Fair enough, I thought. I took it and fired it into the boot before heading back to Cork, and I'd say it's there in the boot to this day. I never looked inside the cover of it. I'd recognise that Jordan was a great sportsman, but I just wasn't interested. I knew what Pat was trying to do, but I felt I had enough going on without trying to complicate things, so those were lessons I left unlearnt.

But a couple of years later I was having dinner with Tommy Griffin, who's a fair man with a one-liner, and I mentioned the book to him.

'Fuck me,' says Griffin. 'He gave me the same book.'

I thought I was special. Pat must have bought the book in a job lot of thirty and was slipping a copy to each of us on the sly.

More seriously, though, Pat brought in Seán and Dave Geaney as selectors, and John Sugrue as physical trainer. Good moves.

Pat still did things his own way. He was too cute to come in and make it plain that he was going to bump noses with us and have conflict. At times with Jack there was a sense of 'I'm a múinteoir here, like it or lump it.'

What we wanted to do in Kerry never really changed. How that was put across changed a bit, maybe, and there were some players who didn't rub along with Jack on that basis. But it was the same with Páidí in his time, the same with Pat. That's personality, though.

Pat certainly brought a freshness and a need to prove ourselves to the management team. Without that freshness, would we have won consecutive All-Irelands? I'm not sure. I think there was fair pressure on Pat coming in, so I was delighted for him on that score, to have won those finals.

The 2007 final against Cork, for instance, was a huge deal, and it brought huge pressure down on everybody. Only the players in Kerry – and Cork – would know how much pressure was on us that time. Before that final there were tears in our dressing-room, there was so much at stake.

The passion, the drive – what everybody was showing couldn't help but motivate you, and Pat was a great talker himself, very good for rising players.

Off the field, Pat knew he had a bunch that could go crazy, and he kept an eye on that too. There was a famous training camp in Spain that ended in a bit of controversy, for instance, though for once I couldn't be blamed, because I'd gone home a day or two early.

On the last night of the camp everyone was left out, and the following morning everyone was still seedy from the excursion. Pat was like a weasel over it, especially when he went onto the bus to go to the airport the morning afterwards. Fellas were still merry – laughing, being smart – from the previous night.

And one player was missing. A prominent character, we'll say.

Everybody was waiting to see how Pat would react. Would he lose the plot? What would he say when he realised he was a man short for the flight home?

Everyone waiting. He clocks that a player is gone – looks for the lost soul's friends.

'Where is he?'

'I saw him last at the back of the nightclub.'

Murder.

It was no big deal. The player missed the flight and was back home later. He was off work anyway, so there was no panic. If that had been me I'd have been down in myself for days, but he just came away home.

Pat was angry that day, but a few days afterwards it was seen for what it was: the kind of story that builds a bond. Managers – particularly club managers – have to realise that it can't all be drudgery. Players won't take that.

I wouldn't advocate drinking non-stop, but the benefits of letting a team out to socialise, to chat among themselves informally, to knock things around – the benefits of that are huge, and they stood to us for years.

I felt sorry for Pat that we didn't manage to beat Tyrone in 2008. It was a hard loss to take, and we'd feel it was probably our best chance to beat them, but it's no good crying over that now.

Tommy Walsh was a big addition to us that time, and, with Donaghy and the 'twin towers' approach that everyone was talking about, I felt we might have something different, that we could get the ball to stick. But it just didn't happen.

I really enjoyed my football with Pat. I had a bad year in 2006, but with him I started driving on again, and I picked up three All-Star awards in the next three seasons. He brought that freshness into my play, because I hadn't been enjoying football in 2006. He was positive, good to speak to, encouraging – all those things.

———

As a footballer Pat was a real townie, knacky forward with the Crokes: all tricks – the kind of guy you'd lift into the stands if you got a good shot at him with a shoulder. Only you'd never get near enough to get that good shot in, of course. Too cute to be caught.

When I say he's synonymous with Crokes, I mean that he'd epitomise that slick, clever passing game. An Ghaeltacht played them in the county final in 2000, when we were coming good as a team, but they were just that bit ahead of us, and they held onto the ball for about four minutes at the end. They talk now about teams hanging onto the ball and killing the game, but Crokes were able to do that all those years ago through pure cuteness. We were running around like rabbits in the headlights, and they were teaching us a lesson in retaining the ball.

The thing about Pat O'Shea is this: last year I had a gig down in Kerry, and it involved going into the Crokes field and doing a bit of coaching with kids. Pat was there coaching as well, under-6s. Here's a coach who's won All-Irelands, and his focus is the five- and six-year-olds in his club. I was getting a rise out of him, saying he'd want to make sure of them, but he shot back at me straight away. Legion in Killarney would be their big rivals, and they're coming strong at the moment. 'They won't be coming strong for too long with these kids,' he said.

What a lesson: the future is with the youth. While a lot of counties are strong on the youth now, he was at that for years before them.

There were times when Pat would have panicked in the dressing-room too. For one game in particular, against Monaghan, he obviously felt we needed a kick up the hole, because we weren't going well, and he was probably right, but Darragh stood up and said, 'Look, it's only half time, and we're well in it.'

But there were far more pluses to Pat, certainly, than minuses. Word went around through the players before it came out in the media that he was gone. And we still have a good relationship. Any time we meet, the craic is good.

———

Because of where we grew up, I always knew how intercounty management takes over someone's life. I saw the way it took over Páidí's life, and I know that it was the same for Jack and Pat, and now for Éamonn.

Have no doubt about it: everything has to be put on the back burner for Kerry when you're managing the county: family life, work life – forget about a social life – everything comes second. It's the same for county managers everywhere, but Kerry tend to go deep into the championship every year; the stress is there long into the summer. Year after year.

When Fitzmaurice came in as manager I took the initiative. I didn't want him to feel that I'd be expecting favours from him. We go back a long way. I'd shared a house with him and spent practically my entire Kerry senior career in the same dressing-room as him. We socialised together, played golf together …

But it began when we were minors. I was obsessed with making the Kerry minor team, but early on in that year – 1996 – the only man from west Kerry on the selection was Tommy Griffin.

The Kerry minors were training a lot that year in Kerins O'Rahilly's field, and John Dowling, a former Kerry star, used to go to all their training sessions there just to watch. He wasn't part of the management, but he knew what they were doing and who was in and out of favour. I hadn't been at any trials, and a month or so before they played in the Munster Championship there was still no phone call, no invitation. I didn't get a look-in.

At about that time myself and my father were in Tralee, and we went into Kerins O'Rahilly's for lunch, and Dowling joined us. My father was very cute and knew I was eager to get in, but he was subtle about it. He asked how the minors were going, and Dowling said they were going very well, training hard, all that. My father then asked if it was a closed shop, and Dowling said they'd settled on their squad, and that was it.

My heart sank when I heard that, of course. I was disgusted. It must have been the quietest trip we ever had back down to west Kerry, and my father knew well what was on my mind.

'Don't mind that,' he said. 'Those things are never closed. Don't worry about it.'

He was right. There was a trial game not long afterwards, and I was picked for the B team. Mike Frank Russell and Liam Brosnan were all there, having played on the previous year's team, and so was Fitzmaurice. I was wing-back on Liam Brosnan, who was a top minor. It was a week before they were to play Cork, so it couldn't have been more last-minute.

I grabbed the chance, and the game went well for me. The selection committee was Charlie Nelligan, Mikey Sheehy and Seán Walsh (who later became Kerry chairman), and at one stage Nelligan was going across the field and said to me, 'Keep it going. You're nearly there.' That drove me on: it was a good move from Nelligan. I realised that I had a chance of making the panel, and it worked out. I was called in to train with the panel the following Tuesday evening.

I knew Tommy Griffin but nobody else. It was crazy, when you think of it: these guys had been training together for six months, and there am I, parachuted into the middle of it. We jogged a lap to warm up, and I'll never forget Fitzmaurice coming over to me as we were stretching. 'Welcome,' he said to me. 'You were outstanding the last day. You're here on merit.'

I knew of him but I didn't know him, and it taught me a hell of a lesson in how to behave, particularly with young fellas. A youngster in that situation, brought onto a panel, might be so nervous and unsure that it could seriously affect his performance, but I'll always remember that for Fitzmaurice.

Afterwards I made the team for the Cork game, and I togged out at wing-back. I literally had to go through the programme in the dressing-room in Páirc Uí Chaoimh to get the names of the fellas I was playing with.

I got to know Fitzmaurice better when we played under-21 together, and I got to admire what he did as a player. In 1998 we won an All-Ireland under-21 championship, and he was our boss man. He played midfield – I was centre-back – and against Laois in the final that year, he dictated the game, really. He bullied the game and dominated the proceedings.

He went to UCC and I went to Mary Immaculate College in Limerick, but he came up to Limerick to do a one-year course there when he finished in Cork, so he lived with myself and Ó Cinnéide while he was going to UL.

Fitzmaurice is a solid guy. For instance, if I told my mother I was going off for a few jars with him she'd be quite happy, because he's such a steady guy. (Make what you will of what that says about other teammates.)

Of course, he comes from Finuge, in north Kerry, so he's hung around with some of the top messers in Ireland. You don't hang around with the likes of Éamonn Breen, Liam Flaherty and Paul Galvin without going wild every now and again.

We had great nights out. Fitzie is great craic when you're social-ising. He's in the public eye now and could come across as being by the book, very straight – and he is, certainly as a manager – but that doesn't mean he can't enjoy himself. We had a great year in the house, myself, himself, Ó Cinnéide and Rob Mac Gearailt from back home, who was also on the Kerry selection.

We had training one Tuesday evening with Kerry and went to our usual pick-up place, outside the George in Limerick, but Phil Sullivan couldn't come, so we said we'd have a pint instead, myself and Fitzie. After a while we thought the bags were a bit of a burden, so we were considering how we could get rid of them for the evening. We knew if we went back to the house, where Ó Cinnéide was studying, that, he being the rock of sense that he was, he'd talk us out of the evening.

We didn't want to pull back after the couple of pints we'd already had, so we hit on our idea: we went back to the house, tip-toed up as quietly as we could, opened the door and just left them inside the door. Then off for the night.

Phil Sullivan, who I've just mentioned, was very good to us in Limerick, and so was John Costello, who's originally from Lixnaw in north Kerry – Fitzie country. John served as a guard for years in Limerick, and he also had a pub there. He, along with his wife, Anne, and their three kids, looked after me very well while I was in Limerick – one of the greatest gentlemen and Kerry supporters I ever came across.

Because John had a pub, we'd roll out of a nightclub the odd time and feel that maybe the night wasn't quite over, so we'd check to see if there was a chance of a drink. The man we'd nominate to make the call would be the sensible one, Fitzmaurice: he'd be pushed into a phone box.

'Go on, Fitzie, and ring, will you? Sure he knows you're sensible. Go on.'

This would be at two in the morning. Fitzie would make the call and be looking out at us. 'Hello? Hello, Anne. Éamonn Fitzmaurice here ...' It was John's wife. Inside in the phone-box, Fitzmaurice would be making all manner of obscene gestures at us, in protest at having to make the call, but the Costellos were very good to us, and we'd go down for a late drink and a chat about football.

Student life, though, sometimes crossed over into real life. Rob Mac Gearailt was a teacher, so he was holding down a full-time job, the only one of us in the house who did, and sharing a house with three students wasn't always agreeable for him. The three of us went out after a match one night, and when we got back to the house there was savage noise made, and savage redecorating of the front room, to put it politely.

I decided to head to bed, with the entertainment going on well into the early hours of the morning; but as I was going up the stairs I met Rob, the working man, coming down against me with a big bag packed under his arm. His girlfriend lived somewhere else in Limerick, and he was off to her place for a night's rest. He grabbed me by the throat. I could only croak my innocence: 'It's not me at all. Sure I'm only heading up to bed ...' He stormed off into the night, and we didn't see him for two days.

The problem was that on the following Tuesday night he was supposed to bring us to training with Kerry, because he had a car, and the three impoverished students hadn't. We had a big argument before he even pulled up, over who was going to sit in the front seat and make the small talk with him.

On the way down, though, there were apologies, and everything was patched up. It wasn't long before the laughing crept back in too. It was even established that I was innocent of all charges, and Rob apologised over that too.

———

When Éamonn became manager he rang me. When we both made the Kerry senior team we'd have roomed together a lot before games and on team trips and holidays, so we'd know each other very well.

I was delighted that they won the All-Ireland on his watch, because I think a lot of it is due to him and his ability as a coach. People don't recognise what he's achieved with Pobalscoil Chorca Dhuibhne in colleges football, for instance – an incredible feat, given where they're situated.

An interesting comparison would be between Páidí's time and Éamon's in relation to resources, though you have to give credit there as well to the way the county board makes sure that all those resources are in place for the management team.

Fitzy is brilliant at organising all that, though. He's also very approachable. For instance, I was conscious that, because we go back a long way, he might think, 'Tomás, you're leaning on me here,' if I went to him with an issue about training or preparation. I didn't want to put him under that sort of pressure, but I didn't need to.

Éamonn has brought the whole thing to another level altogether, and that doesn't just mean high-tech stuff. For example, the gear is set out in the dressing-room, and the teams for a practice match are set out on the wall. That means you're not wasting ten minutes calling out who's on which team out on the field or issuing bibs during the session – 'You're in red, you're in red, you're in yellow …' – which streamlines the whole thing.

Before Éamonn took the job he rang me for a chat about it – not for my approval or anything: he's a strong-minded guy, and I'd say he had his mind made up anyway. But I told him that I thought it was a great idea, him taking over, and that there was no issue with our relationship. After all, he'd played with – and against – most of the players on the panel over the previous few years.

Because the two of us had been together on the journey for so long, there were probably some things I saw that maybe would have passed a few of the younger players by. For instance, nobody was better than Páidí at getting a reaction from a team: he'd say we weren't a team that were prepared to work hard enough, and he'd get his answer in a game after that.

Jack, on the other hand, was brilliant tactically. He always had something on the other team that he could use to our benefit, and he did.

Éamonn shows all those different traits, all those influences, in his management style. He obviously learnt from them, and, while he has different ideas and his own style, he didn't throw the baby out with the bathwater either. What worked from Jack's or Pat's or Páidí's time he hung onto, and what he wanted to improve he changed himself.

For example, he went bald-headed to get Cian O'Neill in as the physical trainer with Kerry. He went to huge lengths to bring on board a top video-analysis guy. He wanted to get fellas looking at the game differently, to analyse things differently themselves.

I know well that there might be a sense that I'm old-school, but I liked that stuff and I bought into it. I participated in everything new that was done. When it goes wrong though, it goes wrong.

In Jack's time there was one session where we were to go walking up around the mountains in Killarney. Now, I didn't see the point of this from the start, particularly after a hard week's training, when the body is tired before you even hit the slope. It was a bonding exercise: you're just told to rock up with your passport, and of course you've your hopes up about hitting Portugal or somewhere, but then you're brought off canoeing down a river in west Cork or somewhere.

Anyway, this time the bonding was going to happen up on a mountain overlooking Killarney. Jack's idea was that we'd hike around and get carried across the lake in boats at the end. I looked at Darragh as this was being explained, thinking, Is this a joke or what? All it was going to do for me was make me cranky: it was going to take hours tramping around the mountains.

Myself and Darragh, though, felt that Johnny Culloty, one of the selectors, would in no way be up for this long-haul hike, so we started to ask Johnny what his plans were. When we found out he wasn't going we stuck to him like glue, so we might – *might* – have told him we'd squared it with Jack about dropping out. Johnny's son had driven up to collect him, so we jumped into the car with them.

Jack copped it, and he didn't make a big issue out of it, which was no harm, because it wasn't a big issue. You pick your battles, and that showed a bit of experience on Jack's part, too.

Of course, when we found out that it irked Jack we'd hop it off him, and, fair dues to him, he'd hop it back off us in return. We didn't think of it as a big deal, and I think in the end they got carried back to Killarney from the mountain in jaunting cars, so it all worked out anyway.

———

Fitzmaurice is an ideal manager for Kerry, because he came onto the scene just as Kerry became a force again, in the late nineties. He was there with Páidí, with Jack, through the hurt of the Tyrone years … He's a bright guy, anyway, and I think the longer he's there, the better he'll be.

Take the letters: the morning of the All-Ireland final, letters were slipped under the players' doors in the hotel in order to motivate them. When I heard about that I was thinking, 'I'd love to have received one of those letters.' It would gee you up that much, a gesture like that.

I really enjoyed the year I had working with him, and one regret I have is that we didn't get that bit further.

———

All those men were serious managers: they all won All-Irelands, and you can't get any higher than that in GAA terms. All winners.

I got a taste of management recently with UCC's freshers team – a small taste – and it's a great buzz. I had a couple of guys with me from the university, and it was great; but I'd love to put a group of selectors together, that dynamic, surrounding yourself with people who can each bring something different to the table.

I'd enjoy challenging a team physically, as well as challenging them tactically, with taking on the blanket defence and all the other challenges the modern game throws at you.

Fitzmaurice offered people a great template in how he was able to change the way Kerry played in such a short space of time. Páidí was the man I learnt from in how to deal with fellas individually in order to get the best out of them – and where to draw the line. Jack taught me a lot about tactics, and tactical flexibility.

The big drawback for me at the moment is time: I'd have to have the time to commit myself to a team in order to do the job properly, and I just haven't got that at present. I'm happy to learn about management: I don't think I have all the answers at all.

I have huge admiration for what Ronan O'Gara has done in managing rugby, leaving his comfort zone entirely to go and learn about coaching in France. It's not all about winning: it's about learning.

I'd love to be involved with a club team, but to do anything like that you must be modern, you must be relevant, you must be up to date.

For a few years I thought that Kerry had the wrong men in charge of the county minors and that they were too old-school. I think you have to go with the times; you have to adapt. It would be great to play a traditional game that's easy on the eye, but that won't necessarily guarantee success.

That's one reason I disagree with Joe Brolly, for example, about Jim McGuinness. He worked within the rules with the Donegal team he had, and he created a team that could win an All-Ireland.

We all love open football, and Kerry's style was never defensive. But we never made a conscious decision to play open football: we played Kerry football. I'm fairly sick of this 'That team are playing a blanket defence: that's morally wrong' argument. That's nonsense. You can expect some defensive games, sure, but you can also expect some terrific open games as well. That's not to say we'll ever again have the open games we once had, but that's because our game and coaching and tactics have evolved hugely.

As a coach or manager it'd be great to pick your way through the blanket, but a lot of that comes back to basics, and to a command of the basic skills. When I fell back in with Nemo Rangers, what I found was that many of the drills in training have gone back to the basics of ball work: we do a lot of kicking, which is quite right. That's where the scores come from. There are great kickers in the game at the moment, the likes of Paul Flynn, Diarmuid Connolly, Johnny Buckley, David Moran, Paul Finlay, Michael Murphy and more. Those are the skills that break the blanket.

Preparing a team for taking on the challenges of the modern game appeals to me, but to do that you need 100 per cent commitment. That's the major lesson I took away from all the men who managed me with Kerry – and what a group of men to learn from, all different personalities with brilliant football minds.

Would I change much if I were a manager? I wouldn't compare the tiny taste I got of it with the UCC freshers to intercounty, in relation to pressure. The one thing that struck me was the time-consuming element of it. Whatever about the demands on the players, the management certainly haven't enough hours in the day to get everything done.

If I could manage that aspect of it, what would appeal to me would be the tactical approach before games. Breaking down the opposition you're facing would fascinate me, particularly having seen the way Jack brought that in so much in his time over Kerry, and the way Fitzmaurice brought that on again in his time.

To me, a manager has to be in charge of everything, but also has to be able to delegate: Fitzmaurice is very good at that, but that means you have to choose very wisely. When I started, Páidí did everything, but now you need people with you. A good liaison man with the county board is vital. So is the medical team, because if you haven't got a good back-up with you there's no way the team will buy into what you're doing. Players can be very touchy and selective about who they let at them. That has to be perfect.

Then there are the selectors. You need the right mix there as well.

And you have to have trust between everybody. I don't doubt that Fitzmaurice kicks everything into order every now and again, if things are slacking, but the manager's role is to keep that ticking over nicely – and to spot the slightest bit of rust in the machine. A manager has to know what's going on in the squad, what's happening with everyone … I don't know if you could improve that much on what Fitzmaurice is doing with Kerry now. He's setting the standards, because not everything looks after itself.

Something I don't understand, though, is why managers don't get more involved in the coaching. With some managers it's just a matter of refereeing the game after one of the selectors or the physical trainer has taken the rest of the session. But Fitzmaurice, who was a very good defender, would have done a lot of work on defending with us. Mikey Sheehy did similar work with the forwards. Some managers prefer to be much more hands-on, obviously.

Despite all that communal effort, if things go wrong it's always laid at the manager's feet. And that's wrong too. Sometimes the players have to man up and take the blame when things aren't going well. When Fitzmaurice came in first, for example, we had a horrendous start to the league, losing four or five games. He was tearing his hair out, because he was doing everything right, but it just wasn't going for us. In the dressing-room at the Donegal game he finally threw his hat at it. 'I'm sick of ye,' he said. 'There's no bit of life in ye at all. Ye won't do anything.' I was a big help that day: five minutes after half time I got the road for lashing out.

One aspect of the manager's job that many people wouldn't pick up on is his relationship with his county board. Any of them would tell you that if it's strong it's a huge plus, but if not … We'd have always been lucky in Kerry in that that relationship would have been strong, and officials were always focused on helping the team.

When I started off, Seán Kelly was the chairman of the county board, and he got on like a house on fire with Páidí. Later it was Seán Walsh. All I have to say about Walsh's tenure is that afterwards, whenever a player was getting married, he would have been invited to each and every one of those weddings, which tells you everything. He was one of the most popular county board officials we ever had with the players.

I'd be fussy enough about having boots, say, and if I wanted a pair the week of a championship game there was never an issue. Whatever gear you needed, it always appeared. Some of my best friends are the officials from those days, guys like John Joe Carroll and Patrick O'Sullivan (or 'The Bag', as he's known).

Ger O'Keeffe was another brilliant guy. He was a great secretary too, one who always looked after you. Peter Twiss has taken on that mantle now and, again, is an extremely approachable guy. All of them looked after us so well for so many years. There was no great secret to it: they were all singing from the same hymn sheet as us, in that they wanted Kerry to win All-Irelands, and they were happy to play their part in helping to achieve that. From what I've heard in Kilkenny, it's the same there.

That all helps, no doubt about that. There was never an issue with your expenses for travel and so on: those were always issued promptly, and that's appreciated by people. (There mightn't be the same situation in every county.) Because of that, we weren't as interested in the Gaelic Players' Association. Early on in the GPA's existence I was asked by Dessie Farrell why we weren't getting involved in it. At the time, Kerry were probably seen as a powerhouse, and it would have been good for the GPA to be backed by Kerry. I had nothing against the organisation, and I certainly had nothing against Dessie, but when they started they were looking for basic rights for teams: football boots, meals after training, that kind of stuff. In fairness, we were already being looked after fantastically well: for a match in Dublin we were being put up in five-star hotels, all that. We had no qualms with the GAA, or with our own county board.

We later joined the GPA, and I think they do fantastic work raising standards for county players. In recent years I've sought help and received it. They're help at the other end of the line no matter what difficulty a player is going through, whether it's legal advice or depression or a university course, or even looking into going back to education in the first place.

Great credit is due to Dessie Farrell, Seán Potts and Siobhán Earley for all the work they've done and keep on doing. They've ploughed through good times and bad, and they are there, genuinely, for players. I couldn't ring anyone in the GAA for help, but I can ring these guys any time. They think big and think outside the box, and they'll go from strength to strength, because they're genuinely working for the players.

But in Kerry we were being looked after to the highest standard already. For example, my cousin Neasa Long is a physiotherapist, and she was very good to look after me any time I needed help. If I called her at three I'd be seen by five, and I'd always ask her if she was looked after when she sent in a bill. 'No problem,' she'd answer. 'I send in the bill, and within a day, a day and a half, it's paid.' The county board does its business the right way, and, because of that, people want to do business with them.

And Kerry Group were a big part of that as well. The county board was lucky to have such a massive organisation on board as sponsor, and such a good sponsor. Frank Hayes was the liaison man and was outstanding. If we were on a team holiday Kerry Group would always dig deep and throw us a wad. As a company they have been synonymous with the green and gold; and with people like Denis Brosnan, and now Stan McCarthy, our future is safe and will be so for the future. The Kerry name is so big that it's fitting that we have one of the biggest food-ingredient companies in the world working with us.

That all left us with one job: simply playing. We were aware that in other counties lads had to struggle to get a pair of boots, while we were getting three pairs, as well as runners, leisure wear, anything you needed. Because I was living in Cork I couldn't go to a gym in Kerry for weights, so they sorted out membership of the Kingsley Hotel gym for me first, then the Maryborough Hotel gym, five-star hotel gyms. It's not as if they were throwing money into the fireplace, though: students were expected to use their university gyms, for instance.

Players didn't ride the system either, so there was mutual respect there. You'd hear the horror stories from other counties, and you'd be thinking, God, I wouldn't like to be part of that.

We didn't have a set of written rules or a code of conduct. We knew when to draw the line and when you could knock the craic out of it. These rules … What if your star man breaks the rules? What do you do then?

The amount of time that fellas now have to put into analysing opponents, the preparation that goes on even when you're supposedly not training – I don't think there's anything wrong with a pint or two here and there, within reason. In the GAA a lot – diet, conditioning, training – is taken from professional sport. As those pro sports learn what's good for players, it seeps into Gaelic football and hurling. You only need to look at the emphasis that's coming into the GAA now on recovery and rehabilitation. But the notion that players can't take a drink between January and September is ridiculous. If you carry a team away for a night somewhere, they should be let out – not to get drunk, but to have a drink or two – just enough to bring a shy player, or a new panellist, out of himself, so that he'll discuss things. That's not to say that players should be left to go off the wall, of course.

One of the best men in our dressing-room was always Mike Frank Russell, who never drank a drop but was a great guy for mixing it up with everybody. There was a notorious incident in a hotel when a fire extinguisher was set off, and Mike Frank was heavily implicated. His reputation as a teetotaller helped him beat the rap, though question marks remain in many minds about his innocence, I'm afraid.

If managers are dead against drinking, some other normal social outing – a meal together, say – would do to bring the players closer together. I think the whole thing's gone too serious now altogether.

The other side of that is that players go mad on the drink when they're not allowed outside the door for the length of their championship run. In our time, starting out, lads would be gone from the Sunday afternoon after a game, drinking, and would then fall in for training on the Wednesday evening again. There would be an unmerciful running session, and you'd be killed. The thinking then was 'You do the crime, you do the time,' which was wrong in itself.

When you think of it … that time you'd be in Killarney for a day, or maybe in Tralee or north Kerry, or Dingle. Wherever the craic was, or where the gang was going, if you were coming from Dublin after a game you'd have beer all the way down on the train, then maybe land into Tatler Jack's in Killarney off the train, where you wouldn't know if it was night or day, it was so dark. In Tralee the Bróg would be the place, Kirby's pub.

Páidí would have felt that players needed to let off steam, but Jack changed that. He wouldn't have been anti-drink, but he would have felt that there was a time and a place for it. And even at the end, with Fitzmaurice, there were no bans in place. You'd come in after a round of county championship games, after a few pints with the buddies at home, and when you'd roll back into Kerry there'd be one sentence: 'By the way, lads, the socialising is gone now.' And by socialising they meant drink, of course: you could go out for a meal or to the cinema, but not to the pub. (Though you could obviously have a pint of water in the pub.)

Jack started to change that, as did Pat O'Shea and Fitzmaurice. It became a case of three or four pints on the Sunday, an easy session on the Monday, and the body would be grand then for training on the Wednesday.

———

When you step away you drift away from the bubble a bit. We live in different counties now, so it's hard for me to meet up often with the lads I played with, though I'd text them a lot, particularly during the season, in order to talk about the matches. Fellas are so busy with work and family that it's hard to make arrangements, and it's harder to follow through on them.

It'd be good to meet up with someone like Fitzy for a pint or two, but if he's winning games with Kerry I'm happy to take that postponement.

PART III

Chapter 12

HEROES

It's not names I like: it's the way certain sportspeople behave, what they bring to their sport – their body language, their leadership on the field – guys who don't just wait for things to happen. They aren't guys who start playing well only when the team turns the corner. Those are the guys I admire. Their attitude. Guys who are a step ahead of everybody else.

For me it's not a question of them knowing it or showing off about it: it's about doing it on the field, doing it when it counts. Longevity is another factor: it has to count for more, to me, if a guy can do it over a number of years, for the duration of their career.

Roy Keane is an obvious example. I loved watching him play for United. I'd have read his first book and found it hugely interesting, and I know that a lot of GAA players would still read it in the run-up to big games – the way he was always tuned in, the way he was always a winner, the influence of Brian Clough and Alex Ferguson, the way he did whatever he wanted off the field early in his career and it didn't matter as long as he could do the job for the manager on a Saturday. That all seeps into fellas' heads.

Other things impressed me about Keane as well: he zoned in on a certain path for himself, and he seemed to trust only a few particular fellas along the way. He was his own man and wasn't afraid to speak his mind, even though it more often than not landed him in trouble. Every journalist hangs on to every word this man says, and he's box office to this day.

During the Saipan incident, when Keane came back from the World Cup and the whole country was split in two over it, for and against him, I backed him 100 per cent. Looking back now, I think he shouldn't have walked out, but if we read between the lines he didn't seem a man at ease with himself at all. There seemed to always be something that would set him raging. That was part of the draw, really, when it came to Keane. But at that time I was behind him all the way: he was right and that was that.

Sure I even wrote a letter to him, supporting what he'd done. The sister of a guy I know in Dingle was living near Keane in England, so I got the address and wrote him a letter, backing him. Madness!

I never got an answer, but I did meet him a few years ago.

There was a big function when Ronan O'Gara retired from rugby, a black-tie do in Cork City Hall, and Ger Fitzgerald, a Kerry businessman based in Cork, invited Orla and myself. Grand job – on with the monkey suit. I wasn't long retired myself, and I had a great evening.

Keane was at Dr Con's table, as Con is friendly with Olan Kelleher, who's been very close to Keane for years. I know Con, obviously, and I know Donal Lenihan (to say hello to, anyway), and he was at that table too. Allies in the search for Keane.

I said to Orla, 'Look over. Do you want to meet Keano?' I had an idea that I'd have a grand long chat with him, of course. Little did I know. So we headed over. Donal Lenihan stood up and said hello, shaking hands with me – and Orla stuck out the hand to Keane: 'Hello, Roy, nice to meet you.' Now, I found out later that Keane is either in the form to meet people and chat and sign things or he's not, but he has that decision made before he goes to a function – a kind of black-and-white attitude I'd admire myself. But when Orla just shook hands with him, no bother … I got a fit of laughing. So when Dr Con introduced me to him – 'Roy, this is Tomás' – I was laughing, and I couldn't even ask him a question. Sure I made a balls of the whole meeting.

The night wasn't a wash-out by any means, though. I bumped into Brian O'Driscoll and had a great chat with him – a great guy, down to earth, no bother at all, and genuinely interested in you and whatever you were at. When he came on the scene, Munster were top dogs in rugby in Ireland, and at some gig years before that I'd got the impression from him, and from a couple of comments, that he felt that people in Munster looked down on him.

Not at all. O'Driscoll was always a hero of mine. On the field and off. I always thought the real measure of his class was when Warren Gatland dropped him for the last Lions Test in 2013. For a guy with the career O'Driscoll had had, with his status in the game, it would have been very easy for him to throw the toys out of the pram, but he didn't. He stayed on side and helped the team. Top class.

I went up to Croke Park to watch him play for Ireland against England. The hits! He's not a huge man, but the bravery … I know that the running and the tries were how he made his name, but his guts and his defending were unbelievable.

Brian O'Driscoll, Paul O'Connell and Ronan O'Gara – Richie McCaw is another one, for the All Blacks – I don't know if it's the physicality of the sport or the hardness and competitiveness of these guys that draws me towards them. O'Driscoll, O'Connell and O'Gara are my three huge heroes outside the GAA.

I'd have met them, and they have no airs or graces. They're interested in the GAA themselves and knowledgeable about it, while being at the top of their own worldwide sport. They're icons of the game. Why? Because they did it at the top level over and over and over.

When Munster were going well in rugby I always felt that a big part of their appeal was that they were accessible. They were living among the people. Whether it's right or wrong, I always got the impression that the Leinster players were more remote, particularly years ago. (This has changed since, no doubt.) The Munster players seemed to realise earlier than other rugby teams that the supporters were the people who were driving the whole thing, and they were hugely accessible to those supporters as a result – more accessible, maybe, even than some GAA teams, if you like.

Generally, the GAA is at the core of the community everywhere in Ireland. Everybody acknowledges that. But it struck me, when the GAA season finished, just how many people in Kerry were rowing in behind Munster. Of course, we had Mick Doyle, Moss Keane and the great Mick Galwey too, in Kerry, which drew the rugby fan out of us.

O'Gara was a big part of that attraction for people. I watched Munster play these massive French teams in the Heineken Cup, and these huge French forwards always heading straight for O'Gara to take him out of it. You'd be thinking, Would he ever get bigger and stronger, or more aggressive?

But Mick Galwey would be a good buddy of ours, and he told us he'd never seen anyone to kick under pressure like O'Gara – unbelievable. He'd say that ROG would always land it when it's on the line, when the pressure really comes on.

———

I have a soft spot for the Kilkenny hurlers too. I'm a long time living in Cork, and maybe some of my pals in the county wouldn't like this, but you have to admire them. What they've achieved on the field of play is phenomenal.

What I've always noticed – and admired – is how they conduct themselves after the final whistle. In interviews there's no bull, no blowing themselves out of proportion: it's all about the next game, the next challenge. The likes of JJ, Tommy, Henry, Eddie Brennan, these guys – they're like machines, the way they kept the hunger, kept wanting to be there.

I've met them at All-Star functions, but I wouldn't pretend to know them well. Galvin was in university with Tommy Walsh in UCC, and he'd tell you that you wouldn't find sounder than Tommy. That said, I've never come across a GAA player, really, who you'd meet off the field and think, God, your man is a right pain. It's something the GAA shouldn't lose. That humility is part of the whole scene; you wouldn't like to hear guys shouting about how many medals they have. Henry Shefflin is the greatest hurler I've seen, but you don't hear him blowing his trumpet. Down to earth. The greatest footballer I've seen is Gooch, and he's the same. The two of them are basically the boys next door.

That's not to say I'd be sitting down with their autobiographies and combing through them for tips. More often than not you'd just hear something or see an interview and take away a gem or two.

In the GAA you probably don't see that kind of forthrightness, the kind of straight talking you'd get from the likes of Keane and O'Gara. For the most part GAA players aren't dissimilar to myself when I was still playing: they don't want to give anything away.

But those other guys are so straight that they can't help themselves, almost. You couldn't help but be engrossed in them. And, in fairness, they're professionals as well. It mightn't be fair to compare them to amateurs in the GAA in relation to what they feel they can or can't say.

People would often have asked me if I'd have liked a professional athlete's lifestyle. Of course I would have. When Tommy Walsh came back from Australian Rules I had a good chat with him about it, and he explained a lot of the work that goes on that you don't see.

One time in Dublin with Mick Galwey we were heading into a rugby international and we met O'Connell, and I had a great chat with him about training. For instance, I was asking if they all did the same training, every player in the rugby squad, and he said no, not at all, that the backs would do different work from the forwards.

And, of course, my argument then was why would someone like David Moran, a midfielder, be doing the same kind of work in training as someone like Gooch, a corner-forward?

———

I know a lot of GAA players are big into American football now, but I'd be more of a golf man. From the ages of twelve to twenty-two I worked every summer in Ceann Sibéal Golf Club back west – an odd job man, basically.

It was the kind of place where you'd start laughing when you went in in the morning, and you'd still be laughing when you finished work that night. A great crowd, no end of messing. One day I got into the car to drive home, and there was a rabbit in it – right in the driving-seat. I nearly sat on him, when the lads started shouting, 'Rat! Rat!' I looked down and saw the little ball of fur on the seat, and I exploded out of the car. I'd have a fairly low tolerance of rats and was sprinting down the road, the other lads rolling around laughing.

Your dinner could disappear at the club quick enough if it was dropped down for you. One day my mother baked an apple tart for myself and the lads. Cussy, one of the characters down there, was hovering around, and my father gave it to him to mind for me … schoolboy error.

It was a place where you could meet anyone. One day I was out around the thirteenth hole, doing whatever I was supposed to be doing, and I saw a guy there playing a round on his own. He looked familiar, but I couldn't place him there and then. It was only later I realised it was Bill Murray, from *Groundhog Day*. I'd have been as interested in looking for an autograph as he would have been in signing one, I'd say.

We had these Hiace vans we'd spin around the course on, and the brakes weren't working in one of them. One day I was spinning down the fairway in one of the vans, and of course it was the one with the faulty brakes. I drove straight down into the bunker. Panicked. If the boss saw it I'd be in some trouble, but I saw Cussy up the fairway leaning against a tractor, breaking his heart laughing at me, and he pulled the van out (after putting me through the wringer by waiting first, of course).

Another day myself and one of the lads were racing each other in little petrol buggies around the course. He was after winning one race, and I was sure I'd win the next one. We were getting ready to take off, and I was revving and revving without getting anywhere when I felt my seat getting warm … I hopped up, and there were flames everywhere. The buggy blew up, and there was a plume of black smoke going straight up into the sky, visible for twenty miles. I'd say the whole parish were wondering what they were burning at the golf club.

It was a great place to work, and it was a healthy job, because you were out in the fresh air all day … And, of course, it brought on your golf a ton. I played a lot, and by the time I was sixteen I was playing off 10 or 11. If I'd kept playing I'd have brought it down further, but about that time the football started getting more and more important.

Golf is great in that you can play it anywhere; it's a great social thing. The only drawback is that it possibly takes too much time. But I love sitting down to watch the Masters, all that. I really enjoyed Tiger's play when he was rolling well, and McIlroy and so on.

Shane Lowry is a big favourite of mine nowadays. He's a breath of fresh air – and a GAA man. When the Irish Open was in Fota I met him, and he's a fair reservoir of knowledge about Offaly and Kerry and 1982. That's the great thing about the GAA: no matter what the county is, chances are they've come across Kerry at some stage, so you've plenty to chat about. It doesn't matter if it's a rugby match, the Irish Open, anything – it'll all roll back to football eventually.

———

What sets a great player apart, for me, is being able to do things quicker with control. It's a mixture: a player with vision, who can see ahead of what's happening right now; a player with skill; a player who's unpredictable.

One day the Gooch said in a meeting that the first thing that came into his head when he got the ball was 'How can we make a goal out of this?', no matter where he was on the field when he got possession. That's a scary thing if you're playing against him.

I'd have seldom marked him, but one day he made some fool out of me. It was a simple dummy, but I looked some eejit when I bought it and went flying past him, flat out on my face. I let a roar out of me as the grass was rushing up to meet me, I was in such a temper, and of course a few of the others let out a snigger.

He and Marc had fantastic battles in training when the two of them were going very well. Gooch has a great attitude: he's a fantastic competitor. He has everything, really. He's got it rough in games, but he always came out on top.

He has such an array of skills … I'd say he was never without a ball as a kid, but he has that something extra: he can perform all the skills that small bit faster than everybody else.

We had good meetings after meals, maybe the Thursday night after training, or even the night before a big game in Dublin, if you were overnighting. Gooch is not a man for roaring and shouting inside in the dressing-room, but he's very good for speaking in those meetings, because he's clear, he's methodical. You'd listen to him, because everything he says has a point to it. He's a leader.

To be fair to Martin McHugh, I think that when he said Gooch was a 'one-trick pony' it was out before he knew it, and he probably regretted it as soon as it was said.

When Gooch retires it'll be akin to Shefflin retiring. They're not everyday players: they're consistent over years, like O'Connell, like O'Gara, like O'Driscoll, like Keane.

Those guys have dealt with huge levels of expectation, and so has the Gooch. You'd often hear in various counties that such and such is a great player, and he'd be as good as the Gooch, but he doesn't play intercounty, because he hasn't got the application. But that's part of it: the application might be nearly the biggest part of it, in fact, the drive to keep competing.

That can be affected by things people don't even consider. Dingle is a great place to be for the craic when the sun is shining and the tourists are around, and it's a great place too when they aren't. I never felt I was losing out because Marc and Darragh were staying out of there, and I'd say Gooch is the same in Killarney, which is another place with plenty of craic all year round. We always knew there would be plenty of craic once we'd looked after the football side of things, which always came first.

For me, heaven was walking off the field in Fitzgerald Stadium drenched in sweat after a good training session, everyone else the same. I miss those days still: off school, sun shining, fit as fiddles, and just ripping into matches. The football is what you miss, training matches and obviously championship. I'd love to do it all again tomorrow morning.

They're not all the same in personality, the sports heroes I've mentioned, but they're all winners. They don't talk nonsense: they go straight to the core. So many people look up to those sportspeople, and in each case the players have done it for a decade or more. If a fella can do it for two or three years, fair play; but can he do it for ten years? Longer?

To me that's a hero.

Chapter 13

KERRY TEAMMATES

You could pick ten players out of Kerry and, to me, they'd compete with any ten from any county. All counties have great players, and that's the beauty of it – arguing it out with lads about this guy being the best in this position, or better over here – all that.

Some of the players I've come across have been unreal: all those great Tyrone players (Canavan, O'Neill, Cavanagh). All of Galway (Joyce, Donnellan, the Meehans). Those Dubs (the Brogans, Michael Darragh MacAuley, Stephen Cluxton, Paul Flynn). The Cork lads (Canty, Lynch, Colm O'Neill). Declan Browne. Trevor Giles. Darren Fay. Graham Geraghty. John Galvin. Matty Forde. Those Donegal players. The McGeeneys and McGranes and McConvilles in Armagh. The Mayo players (Ciarán McDonald, Aidan O'Shea, the Mortimers and David Heaney.) That's some quality.

In our dressing-room … I'd sit here, Declan O'Sullivan would be on one side, Killian Young on the other. Kieran O'Leary beyond him. Marc in one corner, Donaghy and Galvin in the other. Gooch across from us, Darran O'Sullivan beyond him. Everyone has their spot.

Gooch is the best I've seen. The top. I've sat down to chat with Mikey Sheehy, who was part of that great, great team and is acknowledged as one of the greatest forwards ever to pull on a pair of boots. Even he wouldn't put himself in the same league as Gooch, and he's a man who's spent the last few years looking at Gooch in training and matches. (It's interesting that Páidí would look at things differently: he'd be keener, nearly, on grafters and workers who'd put in the hard yards for you. But then he was probably thinking most of the time as a manager, and about getting the best return from fellas in the team context.)

I base my rating of Gooch on unbelievable performances in big games and tight situations, literally winning All-Irelands. He got a goal against Mayo a few years ago in an All-Ireland that was a case in point: shimmy, dummy, shot. But he rarely powers in a goal. Watch for that. He'd often say that to me in training: 'Why are you blasting the ball? Why don't you just pick out your spot?' ('Because I can't pick it out like you, you little bollocks,' I'd think of answering).

His speed of thought, his vision, his kicking, his skills – they're all above anyone else's level. I often thought of him as the Terminator, the display on his screen working out angles and attacks long before we even considered them.

He's a leader, a great man for speaking in the dressing-room, good for mixing with the other players, even though basically he's a quiet enough lad unless you know him. He's close to his family, and a great Crokes man – and they mind him well – the whole package. He's bright, so he can talk to the media and give enough without giving anything away.

I haven't seen the likes of Canavan, from the Tyrone dressing-room, but I haven't seen better than the Gooch. If you were two points down with a minute left you'd be confident that, if you could get the ball to him, he'd make something happen.

Everyone thinks of him as a wisp of a thing, by the way. But Gooch is taller than me. He's six foot and might have been slight enough starting out, but he's over thirteen stone now, I'd say.

I'd laugh when people ask me if he lifts weights – I'd tell them he lifts a pound of sugar when he makes a cup of tea – but in fact he does his weights like everybody else.

What you don't want is him putting on a stone that would slow him down; you need him just hard enough to survive the challenges.

I'd compare him to Brian O'Driscoll – a guy who hit the heights early in his career and maintained those standards all the way through.

———

Ó Cinnéide is a very bright guy. He went to Mary I and did primary teaching with me, but before that he did four years of industrial chemistry in UL. Getting that far while balancing Kerry under-21 and senior commitments with such a difficult course is an achievement in itself, but he decided to switch over to Mary I. (He asked Darragh one time about Anthony Maher, with a view to finding out what kind of footballer he was, and Darragh's answer was 'You know that course you started in Limerick? Maher is top of the class in there.' Bad man.)

Ó Cinnéide's a sound guy, very popular, very capable. He's an obvious target RTÉ should hunt down for *The Sunday Game*, in time: he's very sharp on sport generally, and GAA in particular.

Anyway, he fell in with myself and Vincent Callaghan in Mary I, and people need to realise that Mary I isn't like UCD or UCC, a vast organisation where nobody knows you, and where you're just a number. It's almost like a continuation of secondary school: it's quite regimented, and the staff members know well who you are.

The parents put me into digs to ensure that I stayed on the straight and narrow, but Darragh was living in Limerick that time, so I spent all my time with him and Ó Cinnéide and a couple more instead. The first year didn't go well for me, what with Kerry winning the All-Ireland, so I failed everything. Winning the All-Ireland wasn't the only reason I failed, though.

Take the art classes. Those were on a Friday, which didn't suit us at all in relation to the timetable – our timetable – but we did our best. You kept a big portfolio of what you'd done all year, and you worked by weeks – a project in week 1, week 2 and so on – so when it came to week 13 you were getting near exams. Myself and Vincent Callaghan, who was also in the class, were all over the place with that subject, and with many others, but Ó Cinnéide was good: he was organised, he could pull everything together.

In week 13, anyway, I got pulled out of art class by a guy, and outside the door he said, 'Do you know who I am?' Now, there was never a conversation in the history of the world went well after that opening.

'You're vaguely familiar to me, all right,' I said, which probably wasn't an answer he wanted to hear.

'I'm your drama teacher,' he says. 'I haven't seen you for the year. What's been going on?' It went on like that for a while, and then he said, 'And where's the other fella?'

'Vincent, is it?'

'No, Ó Cinnéide.'

'Oh, he's back in there. That's him.'

If I was going down, he was going down with me.

But Ó Cinnéide was a great help as well. Take the philosophy: I decided to take it as one of my subjects in Mary I, and 20 per cent towards your final mark went on an essay you did during the year. Come the end of year, I was in an exam hall with hundreds of other students bombing away, when there was a tap on my shoulder: the philosophy lecturer.

'Tomás?'

'Yeah.'

'Did you write an essay for me during the year?'

Panic. Alarm bells. I knew straight away I hadn't. 'I did,' I said. 'I remember putting it under your door.'

'I don't have it.'

I started panicking inside in the exam hall. If the drama teacher had seen that he'd have been very impressed.

In fairness to to the philosophy lecturer, he said, 'Have you got it on disk?'

'I do.' More lies, but it'd buy me a few hours.

'Look, put that into my hand in the office at nine o'clock in the morning,' he said.

'I'll tell you what I'll do,' I said. 'I'll print it off and hand it to you first thing.'

When I went back to the house I told Ó Cinnéide about my predicament – the essay about Socrates or Plato I had to come up with – and he said he'd help. The thing about him that time was that he could work very late: he'd watch the television until half ten or eleven and then settle in with his books and his essay. He might stay up until three in the morning, working away.

So in the small hours we were sitting in his room, and he was consulting this book and that one, making notes. I was trying to help, but I was no help at all. Even if the world ended I'd have to have my sleep, so eventually I crawled under his duvet and conked out.

When I woke up at six in the morning he was writing away like a good thing, in fairness. He wrote it for me.

And all I could think of later was that if the philosophy man saw the essay I'd handed in for the exam the day before, and compared it with the essay I handed him the next day, he'd have seen a fair difference.

When Darragh and Ó Cinnéide were playing under-age, Darragh didn't prosper the way Ó Cinnéide did. Ó Cinnéide was earmarked for Kerry for a long time: he was sixteen when Gaeltacht won that first West Kerry Championship in years, back in 1991.

Ó Cinnéide's a huge club man – loves it, and loves home. I'd say he always had that plan in his head to get back home to live, and even though he got an A1 mark out of Mary I he never taught. But he fell in with Raidió na Gaeltachta. He loves the Irish and the culture back home.

As an analyst he's so sharp that he can read how a game is going in an instant and process what's happening. As a player he didn't enjoy the slog, mind you. If you were suffering and wanted a pick-up during the long runs early in the year with Kerry, you only had to look at Ó Cinnéide. Whatever you were feeling, he was ten times worse. You'd be so knackered yourself it was a struggle to laugh at him, but he'd be too bate even to laugh back.

He was the main man with the club for years: he drove it all on for us for years, particularly with his free-taking. (We were lucky to have three of the greatest exponents of the art of free-taking on hand: Maurice Fitzgerald, followed by Ó Cinnéide, followed by Bryan Sheehan. They all worked them off the ground, too, which I think is more reliable, and often they were the difference between us winning and losing.)

When Ó Cinnéide was captain of Kerry it was a huge, huge deal for the club, and the fact that he brought Sam back to the club was immense. *Immense.* He and Páidí were our two All-Ireland-winning captains, which is good going for a small, remote club. When Ó Cinnéide brought the cup back west it was a special night. You're in Dublin on the Sunday night, the cup goes to Tralee and Killarney on the Monday, but it goes to the captain's club on the Tuesday.

The night we came back Ó Cinnéide stopped in Dingle and then went on to his own place in Feothanach. There was a big marquee beside the Bóthar pub, and we had a great night, but he did everything right. He's that kind of fella.

For instance, an uncle of his, John, was in hospital in Dublin the time of the All-Ireland. He was a fisherman in Dingle, a very nice guy and very close to Dara, but he was dying that time. Ó Cinnéide brought the cup up to him in hospital that Sunday night and spent a good while with him, and I'd say John Kennedy was the proudest man in Ireland. It was a lovely touch.

Ó Cinnéide's a guy you could have a pint with at five o'clock in the afternoon and go at it for twenty-four hours, but he'd still be able for the same conversation at the end of it. Either that or a cup of tea, which is the main lubricant in his house back home.

One time his father dropped us back to Mary I after Christmas, and we were down enough about it: you'd always go back a bit earlier than other students, and the house we were going back to … If you lobbed a hand grenade into the front room it would only have made it tidier, put it that way. Anyway, Paddy, Dara's dad, came into the house, and I asked him if he wanted a cup of tea. He said he would, so I flicked on the kettle with the water still in it – water that had been standing there for three weeks at that stage. Paddy took one look and said, 'Ah, look, I'm in a bit of a rush. I'll see ye later.' And away with him.

There were other equally unproductive parental visits to Limerick. As I've said, I failed my first-year exams because of the small distraction of winning an All-Ireland with Kerry. When those results dropped in through the letterbox at home the parents weren't happy. My father wouldn't have pushed us, but he would have wanted us to do well in university.

'We're going up to meet the head of that college,' he said.

'Right,' I said.

Ventry to Limerick: a long spin. In the car park of the university he said, 'Look, we're heading in. What can I expect to hear?'

'Okay,' I said. 'I didn't show up for *that*, I didn't go *there*, I didn't show up for *that*, I had no interest in *this thing*, a lot of *that* I couldn't get a handle on …'

I was straight enough.

Up we went, and if I thought I'd given a full account it was nothing to what we heard in the office. It was about five times worse than what I'd said.

After a few minutes I saw my father shift in his seat. He stood up and said to the woman behind the desk, 'Sorry for wasting your time.'

We went out and started downstairs – a big, winding spiral stair-case. He was ahead of me, but after a few steps he stopped. I thought, Is he going to throw me down the stairwell here or what? But he didn't.

Without turning around he said, 'Well, that was fucking nice, wasn't it?'

We'd agreed that I'd repeat the year, and I did. And I passed, no problem.

That wasn't our only lengthy journey on that road. We celebrated one Gaeltacht win a little too much – myself, Rob, Tony O'Shea and Orla's dad, Morgan – and on the Monday I was in Keane's pub in Ballyferriter when I should have been in lectures. My father walked in looking for someone else – not me at all – but he saw me.

'What are you doing here?'

'I missed the bus.'

He dumped myself and Rob into the car and took us up to Limerick. In fairness, he fed us in McDonald's along the way.

We were on a team holiday another time in China, and we all visited the Great Wall except Aodán and Páidí, who were nowhere to be seen, until, suddenly, a taxi pulled up and the two of them tumbled out. Now, the Great Wall was just here, but there was a café next to it, and they went in for a beer, so I was saying, 'Would ye not go the last twenty yards and come up onto the Great Wall?'

Eventually they came up, and we got a picture taken of me, the camel and Páidí. I won't tell you who looked the roughest of the lot.

Another morning myself, Darragh, Marc, Aodán, Rob and Ó Cinnéide were chatting in a hotel before a game, and when Páidí saw us he lifted us out of it. 'Would ye spread out at least,' he said. 'Jesus Christ, ye'll get me in trouble' – and he was dead serious.

But it was a sign of how strong the club was then, and how important it was for Kerry.

———

Of all the guys I saw, Aodán was the one who minded himself more than anything – a really good example to me on how well you should eat and hydrate and rest. He was well ahead of the times and a player who really got the most out of himself: he took preparation absolutely seriously always, to the point where it'd nearly annoy you. But he's great craic. He spent a night duelling with songs with Moynihan one night, over in Cape Town. They were like two rappers making up songs.

Aodán got three goals against Cork one day but was taken off, and I thought he held that against Páidí. But if you look closely it was Jack who didn't seem to fancy him. He got plenty of runs under Páidí.

He was a great player for Kerry and for the club: he had a great temperament. And an eye for divilment, too. He was teaching in Cork, and we were sharing a house, so Páidí sorted out a sponsored car for him, so he could get to training in Kerry. It was a Pajero that was like the jeep Colt Seavers used to drive in *The Fall Guy*. It was like a bouncy castle going to training: you'd bob up and down on every dip and rise in the road. Sometimes Billy Sheehan would fall in with us for the spin. He'd sit in the back, and if Aodán saw a bump coming up he'd speed up and give it a rap, and Billy's head would bang off the roof in the back seat.

'Sorry, Billy, are you all right back there?'

Because Aodán was a secondary teacher he was often up later than me for work, and one morning I rolled downstairs and went for the milk in the fridge. Gone. I knew there'd been milk there the night before, and when I saw the hob I clocked the porridge, filled out and ready for the man upstairs. That's where the milk went.

Feck this, I thought, so I emptied a container of salt into the porridge.

That evening we were heading up to training, and in the car – out of the blue – he said it: 'Did you put salt in my porridge this morning?'

I denied it, but I'd say he saw through me.

We knocked great craic out of it, but when you leave that cocoon, where you're making plans and hanging around with each other a lot, you have to organise a different cocoon, different people. We wouldn't see each other that much now, and he has a young family himself.

Aodán would be very well organised, and coaching would suit him. Even when we were students we'd train away ourselves; he picked up drills English soccer players did in pre-season, and we'd do them to get us right before the season even started. It was the same when he was teaching in Carrigaline: he was training their football team, and we'd fall in and do the physical work with them before hitting back to Kerry.

His brother Rob was another fine footballer – a big man, and talented – but injuries cut across them both. Aodán was a handful for any defender and had a few unbelievable seasons in the Kerry jersey. His battle with Seán Óg de Paor in 2000 was a highlight, and now he's a respected pundit with TG4 and a school principal.

I always knew the boy would do well!

————

Tommy Griffin is stored in my phone as 'Two-Litre'. I'll get to that.

We played in school together and in minor, so we go back a long way. Another witty guy, and a great mimic. If we met in Dingle, say, he'd start taking guys off, and I'd do the same. Hopefully nobody has ever overheard us.

The nickname: years ago he was working for Finches, the soft drinks company. One time Páidí and I were heading to Fitzgerald Stadium in the west Kerry car for a Munster final, and the guards had the road off the bypass and down to the stadium blocked – nobody allowed down. Páidí was driving and pulled in to take the turn down, but there was a big white Finches van ahead of us, and these hands flying this way and that out of the driver's side window. The guard clearly didn't believe that anyone driving a soft-drinks van was going to play in a Munster final, but that was Tommy. Páidí baptised him 'Two-Litre' after the big white van, and he was known by that name ever after.

Tommy was a serious footballer. He won me an All-Ireland colleges medal with Dingle CBS when he gave a second-half display at midfield that was one of the best I've ever seen. He was so versatile as a player, so competitive, and great character in him. A tough man. Remember how he reacted after Colm O'Neill got that goal against us in 2009? Unbelievable.

————

Séamus Moynihan was a guy I'd heard whispers about a long time before he played senior. My brother Fergal was on the same Kerry minor team as him and brought back the stories about this guy from Glenflesk who was going to be the next big thing. Spotted early.

Séamo went to the Sem in Killarney, and that year so many of the guys in the school were on the Kerry minor team that they used to have their own bus for carrying them to minor training and matches. They had a practice game one evening early in the season over in Listowel, and myself and the father headed over to watch. We were waiting for Fergal afterwards, and I was looking around, saying, 'Where's Moynihan?' and my father said, 'Look, they're gone down the street, the fella who's as wide as a gate.'

He was right too. Séamo wasn't the tallest, but he was always very strong, a guy who always pushed himself physically. He was the ultimate team player, the ultimate leader on the Kerry teams he was part of: he'd do anything at all for a teammate. It didn't matter who you were, a big star or number 33, he'd give everyone the same time.

A steady guy, but great craic as well. Coming away on the bus in Dublin after we won in 1997, he stood up and sang the entirety of 'Bohemian Rhapsody'. Every voice that Freddie Mercury put on he replicated – up and down, high and low – and the whole bus was bopping along. Even when we were celebrating he was leading it.

I know there was a bit of talk when he was shifted back to full-back, but he put an end to that talk, as far as I'm concerned, when he got Footballer of the Year for his displays there. It was a problem area for us, because it was a time when you had three men in the full-back line, not like nowadays, when you have just two man-markers inside. He went in there and solved it.

It was Darragh who pointed out to me Séamo's unbelievable ability in breaking the ball down to himself in order to win possession. The other thing I always noticed is that he'd be bouncing the whole time, always ready to move, and I've often said I never saw better for timing a shoulder. When I came on the scene he was the number 5, but he played everywhere and could do the job in any slot.

He's the greatest defender I ever saw, with everything a great defender should have: speed, strength, good ability in the air; he's comfortable on the ball, tight as a limpet and never gave possession away. Fair, but hard as nails. An inspiration.

In 2000 Séamo was brilliant against Armagh and Galway, in the All-Ireland semi-final and final. His mantra was that, no matter what it took, we'd be mentally strong enough to get the job done: if it took extra time and replays we'd keep it going. He was one of the big talkers in the dressing-room at that time.

If we lost I'd be gutted, but I'd keep it to myself. I'd brood. He'd be gutted, but he'd be open about his disgust and his disappointment. He and Páidí are two of the greatest Kerrymen I can think of. To say they wore their hearts on their sleeves is an understatement.

The best midfielder I've ever seen is Darragh, and the best forward Gooch. The best defender I've ever seen is Séamo. Phenomenal.

Even now, retired, Séamo is mountain-climbing and cycling vast distances; he keeps himself in great shape. I know he was involved with Darragh and the under-21s, but he'd be a good guy for Kerry to get involved again at intercounty level. He commands so much respect from the people of Kerry, because of the way he wore the jersey and because of the commitment he gave. It would be foolish of the county board, in my eyes, not to tap into that energy.

———

Maurice Fitzgerald is another player up at Séamo's level. When Kerry were going badly he was always the man with 0-10 or 0-11 after his name, his free-taking was so good.

A few years ago myself and Ó Cinnéide were chatting about great players. While I went for Gooch, Ó Cinnéide made an interesting point: he felt that, although Gooch was more consistent over a longer time, Maurice could go higher than anyone on occasion, such as in the 1997 final.

Maurice is the best kicker of a ball I ever saw: in training, if he got the ball and you were a yard off your man, you'd grab his jersey, because Maurice was quite capable of bending the ball over your head and into your man's chest from anywhere on the field. Spectacular. Some of the things that guy did with a ball were nothing short of genius.

Towards the end, the body couldn't take the torture, though he tried. Páidí dropped him, but I wouldn't have done it. Maurice was a magician who could create something when there was nothing on; he was crucial for us in 2000: even coming off the bench he was still dictating games.

He was a quiet man, but a hard man. Mayo were naïve in that 1997 All-Ireland: I thought they might have put Trevor Mortimer on him that time, but they didn't. When Maurice drew on the ball and got Billy O'Shea's leg instead, breaking it, he was upset about it, but he was able to focus and give probably the greatest performance by a Kerry player in an All-Ireland final.

That night we were in the hotel, with the usual set-up, a big banquet outside and a smaller set-up for the team beyond, minded by security. I went out to the madness of the big outside area at one point, until the madness got too much, and when I came back to the team area, there was Maurice chatting away to the security lads, drinking a glass of water. After that performance he was probably the biggest sports star in the country, and not a bother on him.

There's an aura about him. Same as with O'Connell. The likes of Gooch and Moynihan and Darragh are in among the people with work and so on, but Maurice isn't like that. He wouldn't leave south Kerry that often, so people don't really know him; but if he landed into west Kerry he'd be treated as a god. It's the same anywhere else in Kerry, but being that bit remote just adds to the legend.

———

Then there's Galvin.

People have an image of him: he writes a piece about fashion, and there are plenty of amadáns having a cut off him. Why? Because he doesn't fit the stereotype of the Gaelic player: a farmer who likes his meat and spuds. Whatever kind of cliché you're having yourself. Galvin is very comfortable in himself, though. That's the key thing. He doesn't give a toss what people think about him.

He got some fairly close attention off the likes of Noel O'Leary in his time: the two of them just brought out the worst in each other. Some of the stuff that was done to him by different guys over the years – I wouldn't have taken it. Fellas pinching him – with their open hands, now, not the tips of two fingers. Pretending to pick you up off the ground but twisting your wrist instead. If someone did that to me I'd draw with the other hand as hard as I could.

He got very little protection from officials too. Take the famous time he was put off by Paddy Russell for slapping the notebook out of his hand. Now, Galvin was wrong: I'm not defending that. You can't put a finger on a ref or slap his book away. I was trying to drag him away, and we ended up fighting ourselves. 'Will you cop on or you'll get sent off!' I was roaring at him, and he turned around, saying, 'I fucking *am* sent off!' (We laughed at that after, but it would have been some sight if we'd started on each other.)

But, in all seriousness, he drew the linesman's attention four or five times that day to what the Clare defender was doing, but because of his reputation or whatever he wasn't getting a fair chance at that time. That's why he was remonstrating with the linesman as he was getting put off.

The popular image of him is all wrong. He has a huge love of Kerry and Kerry football; he's a family man. When people ask me about him, and they often do, I just tell them to sit down with him for five minutes and they'll learn what he's like. Can he be abrupt? If someone's rude or ignorant with him he can tell them to fuck off for themselves, the same as the rest of us.

There was a period when both of us were getting into scrapes on the field, and we were rooming together on trips that time as well. I'd be saying to him, 'I don't know about you, but when the flash goes I've no control,' and he'd be saying, 'I try to explain that to people, that when it goes, it goes, and I've no control.' The two of us the same, and both of us laughing our arses off at the fact that we were out-of-control footballers, not to be trusted to stay on the field. Seriously, though, his self-control has generally been excellent.

He dresses differently. Everyone knows that. The odd time he'd say to you, 'My God, what are you wearing?' I wouldn't even begin to describe what he'd have on, but I'd say, 'Look, you're comfortable wearing what you wear, I'm comfortable wearing what I wear, so would you just fuck off.'

Funny? We'd often have to pull the car over on the way to training from the laughing, with him blessing himself because of the jokes and comments being made. It may sound like nothing, but that's part of the scene I miss a lot, those journeys, and the time you would have with him and other teammates. You take it for granted while it's happening, but when it's gone you won't get it back.

He was on the scene when Páidí was manager, and I don't know if Páidí appreciated what it was that Galvin could offer the team. He had good time for him as a player but didn't see where he could slot in, what was in Galvin. Jack did, in fairness.

For instance, everyone said Brian Dooher had created this role, but I think Galvin brought it to another level, because he could do things Dooher couldn't. Galvin would run forty metres and, with no thought for his own safety, try to drive McGeeney into the ground, or Ciarán Whelan, or Graham Canty. He'd see that as a challenge, that they were the main men for the opposition, and he'd hop off them.

He's the best man I've ever seen under a dropping ball, and he explained his approach to me: he thought a lot of fellas just waited under the ball, waiting for it to drop, but he always felt you were far better off if you were on the move. So he'd take off from about twenty, twenty-five metres away, to where the ball was going to break, and when the ball was actually dropping in he'd still be ten metres away. Other players might be closer, but he'd be travelling fast, so he'd beat them to the ball.

He used to crack me up in training. There'd be desperate pulling and dragging and kicking by both of us under the breaking ball, but he had a canny knack not only of being able to drop back and help out but also of getting back up and supporting the full-forward line.

He had unreal energy levels, and to go as long as he did, and then go back again – you couldn't but have admiration for the guy.

That year he was sent off, 2009, was a tough one for him. I stood in as captain for him, but I was delighted for him getting Footballer of the Year. It was a just reward. When you're sent off you're no good to the management, and you're no good to your teammates while you're suspended. If it had been me I might have cleared out for a couple of weeks to clear the head, but he had a different outlook: he stuck around, because he was captain and felt he had to contribute still, and he did. He gave advice, he gave leadership – he was a captain.

When he was living in Cork we were members of the gym in the Kingsley Hotel, and so was Dr Con. We were often like three kids in the Jacuzzi, giving out about this fella and that fella. A story-fest, basically, laughing most of the time, with not a worry in the world.

One time Galvin was late, and myself and the Doc were sitting in the Jacuzzi. Galvin had had a new tattoo done, and the Doc was trying to work out what it was. 'I think it's mirror writing, Tomás. You have to read it back to front. Get him over to the mirror in the dressing-room.' Sure we were going left and right in there so that the Doc could get a good look at the writing. It looked like Latin to me, but I was keeping my trap shut.

He wrote his own book; he has a good command of the language. He'll do well. He gave up the teaching, and if it didn't suit him he was right to do so. He has other outlets, other businesses on the go, and those suit him. Teaching is brilliant, and there are a lot of rewards to it, but if there was something I could run alongside it I'd be very interested, because, as everyone says, when you're working for yourself you'll put the work in. I love teaching, but I'd also be very open to something new.

There's a streak to Galvin, times when you'd say, 'Well, if I try to control him there now I'd be wasting my time. I'll leave him off.'

Once himself and Declan O'Sullivan had a fair barney at training, two fine thick men when they wanted to be, and I thought it'd end in fisticuffs; but twenty minutes later they were laughing away together.

There were times when Galvin and I would be travelling back to Cork after training, and one of us might not be talking, because something happened in training. There wouldn't be an issue between the pair of us, but something about the session would have made him or me angry and broody. The competitiveness coming out, I suppose.

———

Declan, now that I mention him, was another huge asset – a massive competitor. The first time I saw him play was in the famous colleges game between Coláiste na Sceilge and St Jarlath's in Limerick, which was the curtain-raiser to a league final we were in. Michael Meehan was the star with Jarlath's, but even then you could see that Declan was special in that he was the man, well used to soloing the length of the field to bury it in the net, to carrying his team.

The skills he had were something else, but his toughness always stood out to me. He could absorb punishment, dirty strokes, and never respond, unlike myself or Galvin or Darragh. He'd soak it up and drive on again.

Within the team environment he was very good for talking to new players, for making them feel welcome. That sounds like nothing, but it's a huge help to a team if players settle in fast and feel part of it. We'd always work hard not to be cliquish, but some players are naturally quiet, particularly when they fall in with an intercounty team first, and getting them to relax into it is crucial. Declan was very important in doing that.

When we went out he could be as mad as the rest of us. I often thought that, when we got out, it must have been like a calf getting out into a field for the first time, lepping here and there, but we always kept it between us.

Declan was a captain when he was very young, and he was the main man for Dromid and for South Kerry when they were winning three county titles. He was always a central figure on the teams he played for, and no wonder: he was a mighty captain – someone you'd follow simply because he led by example in every way. He had a great soloing style, a great shimmy; he was desperate to mark, because he'd drive and drive at you all day long. It's funny how many intercounty players would pick him out as their favourite player, in regard to his style and skills. As I've mentioned, I was disgusted the time the Kerry supporters, so called, booed him down in Páirc Uí Chaoimh.

Our supporters were amazing during my career, from 1997 to my last match. I loved everything they brought to the table. But that was the one and, to be fair, the only time a small section of them let us down. You don't do that to one of our greats. You don't do that to a Kerry footballer. Let the opposition do it, not us. Declan was going through a tough time then, but none of the players doubted him for a second, and he bounced back in style.

He's a great speaker, a great thinker on the game, a guy who'll definitely go down the management route, I'd say, because he knows that you must be ruthless as well. There's a place for tactics, but there's also a place for being absolutely ruthless.

———

Inside, you had Donaghy, who's someone with a great attitude, and who's changed the way Gaelic football is played. How? Because of those unbelievable quick hands and that great vision. Catching and laying the ball off instantly to the man flying in from the wing: that was the trademark Donaghy move, and nobody did it better.

He's probably the best tackler around too, by the way, which nobody picks up on. If Donaghy gets those tentacles around you then you're in trouble. His arms are so long and strong that he's like a huge spider: he'll dispossess you in a split second.

His kicking isn't quite at that level, but Donaghy plays to his strengths, and he nearly always has two guys on him anyway. For him to perform like he did in 2014 after being in the wilderness for so long is the best example of his character I could give: he changed the course of the three biggest games we had that year.

He's a confident guy who will go down as one of the greats. A great guy, a sound guy and a loyal guy.

His ability to win the ball and distribute it so quickly makes up for any other weakness. The vision comes from basketball, of course – the little flick and he's gone, even though he might need a tidy acre to solo the ball.

He and Mike Quirke were great to talk to about the basketball – or to listen to, maybe. I'd annoy them, because I'd chime in from a position of total ignorance with something about basketball, to get a rise out of them. Donaghy would be bouncing around the dressing-room in a pair of tracksuit bottoms that four children could sleep in, they were so baggy – real American stuff – but he's another guy with huge confidence.

There's more to him than a smile, though. He put down two tough years with Kerry recently, because he wasn't on the team, which is torture. But his attitude was good, his outlook was positive. He helped out all along and then got his reward in 2014.

He's a golfer as well and, well, I think the handicap chairman in Tralee has a case to answer. I'll leave it at that.

Every player goes through a tough time sooner or later in their career. The people who get you through that time are your teammates, pure and simple. The banter. The support. That's true of the All-Ireland champions any year, and it's true of the team that's knocked out of the junior B championship at the first hurdle. A player does something stupid on a night out, and everyone brings it up at training some night when the bodies are hurting.

We had great camaraderie. Ruthless messing.

Eggs were the weapon of choice when I came on the scene, for instance. Darragh, Breen, Flaherty and William Kirby were the prime instigators, aided and abetted by Pa Laide, who was simultaneously a nice gentleman and a devious messer.

You'd come out after training in Fitzgerald Stadium and find that eight eggs had been hopped off your car. The whole panel would be laughing at you, all of them suspects.

Then you'd get into it yourself: I'd be in the car with Darragh, Breen and Flaherty, and we'd stop in Killarney and go to buy eggs in a shop and put an ambush together at the traffic lights. The first player down in his car to the lights would be battered with eggs at the red light, and he'd have to go off and have his car washed.

Children, that's what we were like.

There were counter-measures. Breen and Flaherty were on the way to the team hotel after training one night; for them that meant travelling through Killarney in Flaherty's Audi A4. Breen was standing up through the sunroof like one of Rommel's tank commanders, only he had eggs in his hand, ready to launch at anyone who egged the car.

They were rolling down the road when William Kirby, on the grassy knoll, launched an egg from forty yards and got Breen in the chest. It was only an egg, but the car was travelling, and the egg was travelling, and Breen slid down into the seat. We were laughing, but the mark on his chest was savage.

Retaliation was always expected. Marc, for instance, got done by

Bryan Sheehan and another couple of lads one time: they threw his underpants in the shower and soaked them, and that didn't sit well with Marc at all. He wouldn't like anyone laughing at him, and I knew he'd return the favour threefold.

When he was back in Dingle he got a sack of fish guts down the pier from one of the fishermen, and he took the keys of Sheehan's car at training the next night and hid the guts in it. Now, after the couple of hours' training, at the height of summer, the stink was horrific when the lads went out to the car. Negotiations began, and Marc eventually revealed where he'd hidden the guts.

As for me, my last year was marred by missing shoelaces. Every night I came in after training, there'd be laces missing from one of my shoes. I laughed away – you had to, because if you got thick it'd only escalate quickly – but for three weeks I was losing laces every night. I couldn't pick out a culprit, but Kieran O'Leary was on my shortlist. Children.

Sure another time we were in a pub in China and decided to have a high-fielding competition: we put a high stool next to a low one, and we decided we'd use those as the launch pads for fellas to get up to the ceiling. Now, we weren't completely reckless: a guy came into the bar with a motorbike helmet under his arm, so we asked to borrow that. Good thing we did, because the first player who tried to take off ran from the other side of the bar, slipped on the bigger stool and ended up going arse over tip and landing on his head, cracking the helmet.

The man with the helmet wanted compensation, and we gave him enough to buy half a dozen of them, but he still wasn't happy. We heard the sirens coming, though, and you never saw a crowd disappear as fast.

———

I fell in with Kerry as a minor in 1995 and retired after the 2013 championship. I played with some of the greatest players ever to play the game, and against some of the greatest players and teams the game has seen.

I feel privileged as a result. There are over a hundred men I played with in the Kerry set-up. Guys came and went, and the cycle of players kept turning, but I can honestly say they were all great men, in my eyes.

We never had issues with commitment. Everyone knew how lucky they were to be there and worked like a dog to stay there. Did I have run-ins with them? Plenty, as I did with a lot of guys in my playing career, but it stayed within the white lines of the field, and then it was forgotten and laughed about. That's the key thing.

I got on with all of them and had great times with them at training, while travelling to training and matches, at dinners, when staying overnight in hotels and on training trips and holidays. I see them all as friends. Some I'm still in contact with regularly, and others I haven't seen in a while, but I look forward to meeting them all again.

Winning and losing All-Irelands forges a bond that can't be broken by anything.

Chapter 14

THE GAA

The first I really saw of the GAA was back home in Gallarus, seeing how the club was run. You'd play a league game behind in the club, and afterwards you'd come in to hot tea and sandwiches. I never gave any thought to where that food was after materialising from, or to who was after providing it: volunteers.

Every aspect of the GAA, especially the clubs we have up and down every corner of this country, is backed and run by volunteers. These people have jobs and families to mind as well, but they give their time and expect nothing in return. It's hugely special when you take a step back to think about that.

That's the cornerstone, from the club up to Croke Park, and it's something we should be proud of – or prouder of, to be more accurate. In Ireland we have professional sports in soccer and rugby, yet the GAA runs its business better: it can throw up a stadium that's twice as good as the stadium that rugby and soccer combined can produce.

I've seen the world because of the GAA. I've been very lucky to have had opportunities for travelling abroad to other clubs, and when you see how proud the people of this country are of what they've achieved – in London or Birmingham, in New York or Dubai – it's amazing the way they have spread all over the world and brought the GAA with them.

Because of it I have contacts everywhere: there isn't a place I can't go. If I had to go to Donegal or Dunedin, where would I turn for advice about how to get there, who to meet, what to do? The GAA.

———

There's a brilliant set-up in Croke Park. Páraic Duffy is a sharp operator, as good as you'd get anywhere, and you'd hope that the GAA will always have men of his calibre in charge. The thinking at the top level is always razor-sharp, progressive, adventurous. Seán Kelly, for instance, pushing to open Croke Park, and the opposition to it – yet look at the good will it generated, the vast amount of money it brought in for the GAA.

As an organisation it's everywhere – from the tip of Antrim to the far corner of Wexford, and across to west Kerry and all points in between. No matter where you are, you're part of a vast, powerful organisation, and there's a lot of comfort in that.

My issue is that, while it's run fantastically well at the top, sometimes there are wrong decisions taken further down the chain of command. In any organisation the size of the GAA you're going to have mistakes – that's inevitable – but I believe we need to be clearer about what we're doing at times.

The rules – that's a bugbear of mine. A few years ago it was decided to change the handpass rule, for instance, and my conviction is that sometimes that kind of rule is brought in by people who aren't playing the game, or who haven't played the modern game. It's hard to avoid a mental image of old lads in a committee room somewhere saying, 'Look, this rule is just the way it is. The players will just have to take that on board.'

Sometimes journalists will push an issue regarding the rules, and the GAA may feel the need to react. Whether they're right or wrong, very often there's no consultation with present players, which in my eyes is crucial: they're the guys on the ground, and they'll have a better idea than most about whether something is going to work in the modern game.

You also have the fact that when GAA presidents are elected they seem determined to leave something after them, something they accomplish in their time in the role. I understand the job they do, representing the association and promoting the games. When Nickey Brennan was president I got talking to him one time in Croke Park, and I asked him to call to the school. No problem, he came away down, and it was a big deal for the school to have the president of the association visit. I always felt he understood things from the players' point of view.

Joe McDonagh was another brilliant president: he did it as a player, he did it as an official, and he's a great speaker in English and Irish. He came down to the Gaeltacht dinner dance one year, and people at home still talk about the speech he gave in Irish for an hour, talking about the history of our club, without a scrap of a note in front of him.

A lot of them go on to bigger jobs when they're finished: Joe McDonagh did, and Seán Kelly became an MEP. But before some of them leave office they might want to address some of the issues of the presidency. For instance, they always seem in a rush to appoint these Croke Park committees when they take office, and sometimes you'd wonder if they'd not be better off easing into the job first and only then creating those committees. Or maybe Páraic Duffy should appoint those committees, which might be better.

Above all, though, the fixture situation should be addressed. That's a nettle that has to be grasped.

I've seen it as an intercounty player: if your county is successful you'll be playing from January to December, because if the county goes deep into the championship the club scene will be more or less put on hold until you come back.

When we were winning county championships with An Ghaeltacht, we were winning those titles in October or November, say, and then having the Munster Club Championship in the run-up to Christmas. Early January and you were probably in with Kerry one night, back with the club two nights (an All-Ireland club semi-final and final), then back to the national league – and then the following year's club championship after that. A club that's produced an intercounty footballer or hurler often seems to be punished for that, with matches put back and postponed. It's wrong.

That wasn't ideal, hopping from club championship to county training and games. To me the ideal would be a game every two weeks. And that's where the provincial championship system complicates things, with twelve counties in Leinster and only six in Munster. But I'd simply start Leinster earlier to make up for that, and have everything zone in on one weekend in order to have a monster Sunday of provincial finals, say.

I know there are all sorts of ramifications with television rights, but it's something that needs to be dealt with. I'm playing with Nemo Rangers in club, and at the time of writing we have one championship game played, in May. The next game? That's in August. Now, I know Cork is a successful county with hurling and football, with a huge number of clubs, but that's crazy. There are two back-door chances in the Cork championships, one in Kerry, none in others. Then there are counties with league-based championships.

Back in west Kerry you have these competitions: the West Kerry League, the West Kerry Championship, the County League, the County Intermediate Championship and the County Senior Championship, with West Kerry. That makes five competitions, and four or five games in each means twenty to twenty-five weekends.

Now, Éamonn Fitzmaurice will be looking for his players three weeks before each game, and he's entitled to do that; but when the club championship kicks off he's dealing with players whose clubs have won, so they're in training with Kerry. But the players whose clubs have lost are back with those clubs, preparing for the back-door games.

What that means is that you have a county with a good chance of winning the All-Ireland, yet they can't get a full panel of guys in to train in Fitzgerald Stadium during the championship! Crazy stuff. Wouldn't it be great if we had a block of time specifically for running off club matches, and another block specifically for intercounty games, and no mixing? I'm not sure if it would be possible, but surely we can try. Have we too many competitions, and does one suffer because of another? Have no doubt but that they do.

Yet you have people giving out about small things, little infractions, playing styles – people moaning about Donegal and their style of play, for instance. They'd want to get over that. Donegal are playing within the rules, so either accept it or change the rules. Either way, they're doing nothing wrong, the way they're playing.

People would be far better off if they focused on a real problem, like the fixtures mess.

When you think about it, the extent of the problem caused by the poisoned chalice becomes obvious. Some counties are hurling-only, some are football-only and some are hurling and football together. So the notion that one size fits all, that there's one solution that will help every county, is wrong. But what's very obvious is that we have too many competitions.

Now, Seán Kelly brought in junior and intermediate competitions, which was a good innovation – and one that might seem to contradict my previous point – but the real problem in solving the fixtures issue is that there's too much politics in the organisation, and too many vested interests.

Croke Park can say to county chairmen and secretaries, 'Look, we want this to be done, and this championship to be run off this way,' and strong chairmen and secretaries will either tell them to get lost or just run rings around them in committees. What's needed is someone at the top to say, 'Look, lads, this can't go on.'

Because of the way things are interconnected in the GAA, then, the fixtures mess leads to unrealistic pressure on youngsters. Lads between minor and under-21 are being crippled by the demands being placed on them by their club teams, county under-age teams, college teams and county senior teams.

The greatest laugh of all is when you hear people saying, 'Well, we're helping Johnny here, because the coaches are all working together to make sure he's not burnt out.' They are in their eye! if Johnny comes in to county senior training on a Tuesday evening and seems tired, he won't play with the county senior team, because the senior team management aren't taking into account the fact that Johnny was training with both the club under-21s and the college team in the last three days and is knackered. Not to mention that Johnny might be playing both hurling and football.

Then, on top of all that, you hear, 'Well, we'll have no training from October to January,' which is when the Sigerson, Fitzgibbon and under-21 teams are training. They'd want to stop codding us about how much teams are pulling out of these young lads. It's no wonder they're breaking down with wear-and-tear injuries.

The encouraging thing with the GAA in the last few years is that every county board, it appears to me, has decided to focus hugely on youth and youth development. Without youth you have nothing. I think in ten or fifteen years you'll still see a lot of the same top counties, because tradition does count for something, but you'll have so-called weaker counties playing at a much higher level, because of that focus on youth.

But the issue of fixtures remains the elephant in the room. If the GAA accepts that whatever solution it comes up with is not going to please everyone, it can move forward on the question. Seán Kelly's proposal in the *Examiner* a few years ago was very good. It would allow us to keep the provincial championships, and then, based on the provincial finalists and league standings, the top sixteen teams would fight for Sam, and the other sixteen would fight for another cup, with the incentive of winning in order to gain promotion to the competition for Sam.

At least the weaker counties would have aspirations of winning something, which they haven't got now. It's a plan that deserves to get a run, and I believe that something very similar will be given a trial. Given how the GAA has worked so well in clearing the debt on Croke Park, if they concentrated on fixtures they'd surely be able to work out a solution.

They could start by looking at this idea of starting the championship in May and ending it in September; you could run the whole thing off in eight to ten weeks if you put your mind to it, possibly having a look at the back-door system. Seán Kelly's recommendations would solve that. That's the time it takes to run the Rugby World Cup off in, and that's a far more demanding sport physically.

As an intercounty player I hated playing a championship game against Tipperary in May but then having to wait five weeks for a crack off Cork. The lads in the North used to be slagging us about a handy five-week break, but that's wide of the mark: you're back with your club for two of those weeks, and the losers' round of club games takes up another week, so you really have only two good weeks.

By rights you should go into camp with your county in April and come out in August, with everything done at that level. As it is, you have the top teams and players in the club scene slogging through snow and mud in November and December. Think about the crowds you'd have if they were hopping off the ground in August and September!

I know there'd be casualties along the way. Hard decisions always involve some pain. The present situation can't go on, though. If you have a situation where there's a very strong manager – a Jim

McGuinness, say – he can have everything in club activity postponed if he demands it, and the Donegal County Board did that for him.

Should that be allowed? I don't know. But I feel that there should be a club season and an intercounty season, that this can be done, and that some competitions should be dropped. Someone in Croke Park should take the bull by the horns and, instead of appointing committees to deal with small issues, deal with this one.

I saw that there was a huge deal made at one point out of a recommendation to bring the All-Ireland finals forward by a week. A *week*? What difference is that going to make? Yet it was heralded as some huge breakthrough, as a massive innovation.

———

Players shouldn't be paid. I wouldn't agree with that. We'd all love to be paid athletes. That'd be great in an ideal world, and God knows the demands on amateur players have increased hugely in recent years. But the simplest question is the hardest one to answer: how would you pay for professional GAA players? Soccer and rugby are sports where the players earn vast amounts, but the difference is that those are on an international level. The English Premier League is broadcast to dozens of countries, which means dozens of broadcasting company rights, which generates money: everything is based on the TV deal in soccer – that's what generates the money. Where are those vast deals in the GAA?

That's the practical aspect of it. The emotional aspect is as important: the GAA club as we know it would die very quickly. Right now you have diehards and lifelong club people who'll line fields and hang nets, and train little kids – why would they do that in a professional set-up?

The GAA is a hugely powerful organisation, but it's hugely powerful because of the amateur ethos. The guys in Croke Park recognise that too. It's true that vast revenue flows through the GAA, and it's used well, though I'd like to see more of it dispersed around the counties. I've been abroad with Kerry, raising funds for facilities, and I think that's wrong: I know that the GAA has contributed to those projects from central funds as well, but more could be done for counties everywhere.

Even when I was finishing up with Kerry, early-season training could be tricky, because management would be trying to drum up a field with floodlights for doing a proper session on, and you'd often hear from a club, 'Look, we can't give ye the field tonight. We have a big game there this weekend, and we don't want the surface torn asunder.' And Kerry might have been All-Ireland champions at the time, so you can imagine how that works in other counties in a similar situation.

Depending on clubs to help out a county team: that's not a good system.

Players could be better looked after without being paid outright. The GPA went looking for something along those lines. I have no doubt that the day of the family man playing intercounty is gone or going – the same for lads who are living outside their home county (or living too far away from their home county, to be more accurate).

The notion of a tax break that was floated one time has merit to it and would be very welcome. The grant we got was grand – you'd rather have it than not – but it's only peanuts, at the end of the day. A lot of it comes down to the individual county board you're dealing with, and we were always looked after well in Kerry, without any backhanders being given out.

The GPA are doing good work in this area for players. I know that when they started off they were gung-ho on payment and so on, Dónal Óg and the lads. But I think they all recognise what the cornerstone of the entire GAA is, and that's amateurism. If we go away from that we're going down a dark road – one that nobody is familiar with and that would take us on a journey nobody can foresee.

———

What the GPA has done is that it's fought for players to be treated properly. It's also giving a huge amount of support to players that a lot of people don't know about, because of the sensitive nature of what they're dealing with.

They are a really helpful organisation, and they'll help any player in need of it. I've sought and received help many times from them, on a range of issues, mostly advice, and I'm grateful for it.

If a GAA player is invited to Dublin to help launch a product or to publicise something, they'll probably get a thousand euros and their expenses. But what do people want, for them to do that for nothing for maybe a multinational company? You often see a GAA player and a rugby player in photos for the launch of this or that. People surely don't expect a situation where the rugby player is getting maybe three grand, and the GAA player gets a sandwich and a train ticket home?

The GPA has done great work here, in that if you're approached by someone they'll handle it: they'll ring the company or the PR company and negotiate for you. I've been lucky enough to get some of those gigs, and I'm grateful to have got them, but only a few players do. The Dubs always get them, because Dublin is the centre of industry, of media. The team is successful, and a lot of the players are polished, presentable guys, and more luck to them.

It was thrown at the GPA early on that there were a lot of Dubs getting those gigs, but I see a lot of other counties represented at gigs now, in fairness. But, all in all, it's still only a tiny proportion of players, the guys at the very top. Companies want Henry Shefflin, the Gooch, the Brogans. They'll always want the top, top players – who else?

For instance, I've been very lucky with media opportunities, and I'm grateful for all the chances I've got. There are so many ex-players that you'd have to be grateful, because if you were ungrateful or awkward, or greedy, there are a couple of hundred retired guys who could do what you're doing.

I don't think that'll change. The top guys will always get their pick of the opportunities, and that applies in all sports, at all levels. Even at Man United the subs don't get offered the same opportunities as Wayne Rooney, after all. But I think we'd be losing track of ourselves altogether if that became the focus, rather than improving yourself and winning matches.

I know that Joe Brolly is fond of saying intercounty players don't enjoy themselves any more, but I doubt that. I'm well in touch with a lot of the Kerry lads, and they're enjoying it. Winning isn't as significant as you might think, either. We lost in plenty of years – All-Ireland finals, heartbreaking defeats – but even then you're knocking great craic out of it.

A lot of managers would want to take a good look at themselves about what they're doing with players. Many of them follow the letter, not the spirit, of the law in relation to seriousness. Players are adults and need to be treated as such, and if managers are going over the top the GAA should have the power to intervene, or, if not, it should empower itself to do so.

The GAA could benefit from being more proactive in other areas too. The Dubs have vast resources at their disposal, far more than any other county. Fair play to them, they have it, but having it won't guarantee that they win the All-Ireland every year. But you also have a situation where a county like Longford has to take them on, with less than a tenth of Dublin's population to draw from and with a fraction of the commercial and sponsorship opportunities. We in Kerry raised more than a million euros in the United States ourselves earlier this year, using good contacts there, and surfing on our success in the All-Ireland; but those aren't cards that every county can play. Some counties just haven't got the numbers or the support, simple as that.

The GAA should intervene there, though it would be difficult to work out who deserves what if it came to sharing out funds in a different way. What Croke Park could certainly do is assign a guy to each county to evaluate what a county needs, and then work out how to assign funding to them, and how much.

Take Monaghan, a county that's really punching above its weight at present, the result of good work at under-age level and of smart coaching. They're doing better than you'd expect, based on its population, but it's not like that in every county.

———

I know that Munster rugby was very popular in the south of the country and that other sports are strong in various areas, but I don't know if the GAA was ever as popular as it is now. I see hundreds of kids in Nemo every weekend when I drop my own off there: they're spread over every field in throngs.

The GAA learnt a few tricks from other sports that worked hard to keep kids as members, I think. When my lad is playing in the Nemo street leagues, there's a big deal made out of them in the club: there's a barbecue for them afterwards, parades – a great day out. They're carried on buses, they get the club tops and hoodies from the shop … When I remember my time with Gaeltacht, it was a thrill just to have a jersey with a number on it. There was no club shop, because there was no club merchandise for it to sell.

I can remember the first time I played on a field that had a net on the goals. Before that it was just the bare frame of a goal. When we finally had a net we wasted ten minutes kicking the ball into the goal just to see the net billow with a shot. A thrill.

The GAA has to provide those facilities, because other sports will provide them if it doesn't. The flip side is that the GAA is in every corner of the country, and it was there long before every other sport. Parents will bring kids back to the GAA, and that feeds into what I was saying earlier about amateurism, because they're bringing them to a superbly well-organised environment where they know the kids will have a good experience.

In my time back with An Ghaeltacht we had just the one man, Liam Ó Rócháin, looking after every team in the club; but now you have huge involvement – lots of people involved. Sometimes a parent will get involved now with the wrong motivation, just because little Johnny shows a bit of promise, and choosing the right people to have involved with a team is the kind of challenge that tests the GAA at every level. For a long time in Kerry, for instance, we didn't have the right people involved at minor and under-21.

The stronger the people at under-age level are, the stronger your club unit is going to be as a whole, and the better able it will be to withstand the wastage you get later on. It's a difficulty for clubs all around the country, lads at eighteen or so heading off to university and getting a taste of something a little different, an alternative experience. A lot of the time, they decide to give the bus home a miss for a few months, and in no time at all they're gone off the grid, lost to the club.

That's hard for clubs, particularly small rural ones. Lose two or three of those young lads and suddenly you're struggling for a team. When I was a student in Limerick I'd come down west for training, and Tony O'Shea, our cisteoir, understood the story with students. I hadn't two pence to rub together, but if you came home to train, the club would give you a tenner for the bus. Now, I was getting a lift up and down in a car, and Tony knew that well, but on the way back up he'd give me twenty quid, which, for a student, was a night out. The likes of him would be cute enough to give the few bob to genuine cases, and I don't know if that's done as much nowadays; though, on the other hand, many of the students I see now have cars of their own.

City clubs will always be okay, but rural clubs are suffering. Amalgamation is the only outlet for a lot of them, though it wouldn't work for us (amalgamate with Dingle?), and it mightn't be needed in any case. Even though we wouldn't have huge numbers in the schools, there are still four or five of them. One of those schools wouldn't sustain a club by itself, but all of them together can.

Even when we were playing the Corn Mhic Eoin between the schools you'd have girls on teams to make up the numbers, but there are enough for one club, all right. The fact that we have young officers there now – a young chairman, a young secretary – who are well versed in Twitter and so on is also encouraging. An Ghaeltacht will be fine. We'll be safe enough, and we'll have what we want (something I base on the numbers at the club and, more important, on the good structure we have in place).

South Kerry is different – decimated. Huge areas of land with no people there, because they've cleared out to the United States and elsewhere. The GAA could be more proactive in that case. Kerry wouldn't be the worst case, in that there's always tourism, there's always some money coming into the county. But the west coast generally has problems of this kind.

Numbers aren't an issue in Dublin, obviously, where population is always constant. But I see some similarities with the very old days, when people moved from all over the country to the capital city.

A man from the parish of Ventry, Joe Fitzgerald, captained Dublin to an All-Ireland final in the forties, because when you moved to another county you threw in your lot with that county. That seems to be coming in more and more now, a lot of people moving clubs to Dublin. I know that people could say I did the same, moving county, but that was at the tail end of my playing days.

For remote clubs in general there's a dependence on lads travelling from the capital city – or further afield – and maybe losing a day's work. Those guys need to be looked after, and that has nothing to do with professionalism.

The GAA has a good record of drawing up its plans and executing them properly. I'd like to see Páraic Duffy's influence become stronger, as he's a very able person, very sharp.

I think the GAA is the best organisation in the world. Absolutely. You look at Croke Park and think, *This* is the home of an amateur organisation? Peter McKenna, the stadium manager, has done exceptionally well for the GAA as well: he's increased revenue significantly, and that money does trickle back down to the clubs. Let's hope One Direction and the like keep coming back …

———

Technology is another area that's changed things hugely in the GAA, as it has in every other aspect of modern life. I can remember the letter telling Darragh he was playing for Kerry in the league falling on the mat at home – that doesn't happen now, obviously.

Not all the changes are positive. You only have to see the trolling and abuse that players have to take from anonymous heroes on social media to appreciate that. How do you control that? I don't think you can. Legally there's nothing you can do.

The traditional media are something I'm involved in now myself. And now that I am I can say it's not as easy as it might appear!

I've gone through a lot in football, and if I have a column in the paper and someone disagrees with me I often find myself thinking, 'I'd love to sit down and thrash this out with that guy. He's all wrong, and I'll pick his brains about that.' I love that – I love arguing football with people, making my own points, and if someone comes back strong against me I love that too, having it out with them, and I respect people who do the same.

I think a lot of the coverage of the GAA is terrific. There's obviously far more coverage, on all platforms, than when I started, and the competition drives the quality. Take *Seó Spóirt* on TG4, which for me is an outstanding programme, even if I might be biased, because it's a buddy of mine, Dara Ó Cinnéide, who's driving it. He's as good an analyst as you'd get.

Páidí never trusted journalists who'd never been there or done that, but what I'm finding is that a lot of the journalists who've never been there or done that can read the game a lot better than those who were and who did!

The one thing journalists have to do is stay relevant. What I find difficult is that everyone who watches a game sees something different: they look for certain patterns you may not be watching for, so everyone has a different angle on events. There are journalists I read and journalists I don't, but I definitely pay a lot of attention to certain analysts and pick out what they focus on.

One thing that surprised me about writing a column was that beforehand I'd be thinking, How is such-and-such firing out a column every week for years and years? But once I got into it I realised that there's always something going on in the GAA. Even at quiet times there's something going on in a club game, or a rule changes, or a fella retires, which is a godsend.

When I'm on *The Sunday Game* I try to give something to the viewer that they mightn't notice at first. They don't need me to tell them, 'Oh, Gooch got 2-2 there. He was very good.' I'd say most of the audience can work that out for themselves – easy stuff. It's far more rewarding to be picking out why this happened, why this space opened up, why he went this way and not that way. I enjoy that a lot more. I enjoy the column as well.

As a player it didn't suit me, and I didn't like the media, but that was just me. It's one of the few areas where there might be an opportunity for a player. Being at a live game, sifting through what's going on – that's something that gives you a great buzz.

Sure even Joe Brolly is able to make a good point the odd time, once you get through the crazy stuff. He's the one person people always ask me about. I'm a teacher, and he's one guy I'd hate to have in my class – clever, funny and no point in arguing with him, because he'll beat you even if he's wrong starting off. Loves his football.

I was in Thurles for a game with him one time, and I got there early, so I was waiting for him up on the terrace near the studio. Down below me there were about thirty maors, lads in high-vis bibs massing around before going to the gates and stiles and so on. I saw Brolly roll through into them in his suit, and within seconds you could see all their heads flung back in the air, roaring with laughter at whatever he was saying to them. That's him.

If you meet Brolly you'll enjoy him, but he and I are different. Controversy and argument come naturally to him, that's the main thing. If I started trying to be controversial just for the sake of it, people would see through me straight away: they'd know it was all put on. For me the challenge is to be relevant and to stay up to date, but I love staying in touch with what's going on in football, so I'd be doing that anyway.

———

The GAA is founded on ordinary people in the community – people working, living and interacting within that community. Somebody who slates a player without thinking of the ramifications, of the hurt that that causes to people's families … There's an element in every county's support that you could do without.

Clearly you're talking about a tiny percentage there. The vast majority of GAA supporters are ordinary people who wouldn't dream of abusing anyone. The power of the GAA has always been the ordinary people, all of us, who are its members.

I've got so much out of the GAA: through it I've met people all over Ireland – and all over the world – simply by playing for Kerry. I go down on one knee and thank God I was born in Kerry at roughly the same time as the Gooch, Declan, Darragh, Moynihan and Maurice Fitz, not to mention having the likes of Páidí, Jack, Pat O'Shea and Éamonn to manage us.

Those were the guys who carried me on a journey that very few people take in life. I was grateful for that experience. I always will be.

Chapter 15

LIFE NOW

Life now is work and family. I thought that when the football went I wouldn't know what to do with my time, which shows you what I know.

My medals were all in a Tesco bag in the cupboard, but I lent them to Croke Park for an exhibition. The jerseys I gave to Mícheál. I used to swap them a lot of the time, but I decided to hang on to the Kerry jerseys. They're his now. The same with those tracksuits and tops and so on: I'd give those away. You'd only have to see the pleasure you'd give some kid if you gave him your top or jersey.

I never wore a gumshield. I still don't, in club football, but hopefully the refs won't cop it. I could never get used to breathing with one. I always had the same bag, an old Adidas one, and I never got a county one. I never used new socks: it was the same pair all the time. I'd use the first pair of togs we got, early in the season, and use those for the year.

Underarmour and that stuff? I get fair use of it now for golf, all right.

———

The kids, Mícheál and Ailidh, are nine and six. They're good kids, growing fast. People ask me what I'd do if Mícheál wanted to play for Cork. That's an easy one: nothing. I don't mind what he does, as long as he's happy. As long as they're both healthy and active, everything else is irrelevant. They go back to Kerry often. I think it's important that they become familiar with their roots. They follow Kerry football and love to see the lads doing well.

Things change in your life when kids are around, and the change is for the better. They grow so fast you're afraid you'll miss things. The pair of them are good craic, and I enjoy watching them grow and get cleverer.

—

I teach out in Fermoy, in Gaelscoil de hÍde. Seán Mac Gearailt is the principal and is very good to me; he was fantastic when I was playing for Kerry. He's a GAA man and a Gaeltacht man, and, as I've often said, the GAA needs people like him, people who are willing to facilitate fellas' intercounty careers.

We're trying to sort out new facilities there, and hopefully that'll work out. They're badly needed, and the kids deserve them.

I've been there since 2001, and though I've had offers from other schools I'm very happy there: I have no interest in going anywhere else. The kids are great, and they were never that interested in my football career, which was great. The staff there are excellent, and I have great banter with all of them. It's a great school.

—

Orla and I live together in Cork, and her daughter, Éabha, lives with us. My two are around a lot, and they all get on well. We're in an area with plenty of open spaces for them to enjoy themselves in – and to tire themselves out in, which any parent reading will understand.

Orla is from back in the Gaeltacht too, and we're happy in Cork. She's a huge part of my life, and we really enjoy each other's company, having a lot in common and sharing a dark sense of humour, in particular. She makes me laugh like no one else, and, in fairness, I laugh a good bit. She works in a school as well, so we have the same time off.

I'm enjoying life at the moment, and a lot of that is due to Orla. It was hard juggling all the commitments I had after football, and she was the one who suffered most there, so there is a lot to be thankful for in her patience.

When I retired from football I thought I wouldn't fill the gap at all, but I love the time it's freed up for spending with Orla and the kids. I'm happy and she's happy – hopefully we'll grow old together!